METAPHYSICS . COSMOLOGY . TRADITION . SYMBOLISM

# STUDIES IN COMPARATIVE RELIGION

**The First English Journal on Traditional Studies — established 1963**

*Studies in Comparative Religion* is devoted to the exposition of the teachings, spiritual methods, symbolism, and other facets of the religious traditions of the world, together with the traditional arts and sciences which have sprung from those religions. It is not sectarian and, inasmuch as it is not tied to the interests of any particular religion, it is free to lay stress on the common spirit underlying the various religious forms.

One of our primary aims is to meet the need for accurate information created by the now world-wide interest in the question of "ecumenical relations" between the great religions, by providing a forum where writers of proven authority can exchange views on various aspects of religious life, doctrinal, historical, artistic and mystical, not forgetting the element of personal experience and reminiscence.

By collecting accurate information about the great religions under their many aspects and rendering them available to interested readers we feel we are fulfilling a very pressing need of our time and also contributing in a practical manner to the cause of inter-religious understanding. If there is to be an effective measure of this understanding at any level this can only be on the basis of accurate presentation both of teachings and facts. An ill-informed benevolence is no substitute for genuine insight, based on information that is neither willfully distorted nor confined to the surface of things.

In this manner we think that we are best serving the interest of our readers in their search for truth.

(*Excerpt from the Introduction to our first publication, almost fifty years ago*)

World Wisdom

# Universal Dimensions of Islam

*Studies in Comparative Religion*

*Edited by*
Patrick Laude

World Wisdom

Publisher's Note:
*Studies in Comparative Religion* has published articles from over 400 different authors. The original editors of *Studies* did not insist upon a common convention for the transliteration of foreign terms; consequently a variety of different systems of diacritical mark usage can be found in any given issue of *Studies*. The current publisher has chosen to continue this policy and will thus remain faithful to the original transliteration convention used by each of its contributors.

Library of Congress Cataloging-in-Publication Data

Universal dimensions of Islam : studies in comparative religion / edited
by Patrick Laude.
p. cm. -- (Studies in comparative religion)
Includes bibliographical references.
ISBN 978-1-935493-57-0 (pbk. : alk. paper)
1. Islam--Universality. 2. Islam--Relations. 3. God (Islam)--Attributes. I. Laude, Patrick, 1958-
BP170.8.U545 2011
297.2'8--dc22

2010039310

Printed on acid-free paper in USA.

For information address World Wisdom, Inc.
P.O. Box 2682, Bloomington, Indiana 47402-2682
www.worldwisdom.com

# CONTENTS

# Universal Dimensions of Islam

## *Editorial*

One of the fundamental problems of our contemporary world has been judiciously referred to as a "clash of the uncivilized."[1] This conflict has been particularly acute in the encounter between certain mainstream elements of the secular West—with which one must aggregate, at least outwardly, a few zones of resilient Christian identity and emerging neo-Christian cultures—and some of the most visible contemporary expressions of people and societies for whom Islam is the predominant principle of collective identity. In the West, one of the praiseworthy responses to such tensions and oppositions has come from those who have called for a better "understanding" of Islam. Here, understanding is not meant to refer to a full acceptance, but to a sufficient grasp of the inner and outer "logic" of Islam, as well as to a degree of recognition of its spiritual and moral values. Perhaps paradoxically to some, such a capacity to understand others presupposes an inner attitude which has everything to do with the degree to which one has assimilated the core principles of one's own civilization. This holds true, needless to say, on any side of the civilizational "divide." There is no civilization formed by the sacred that does not ultimately lead its most discerning representatives to perceive in some measure the relativity of its own exclusiveness, at least *in petto*. To this extent, to be "civilized" amounts almost as much to recognizing the intelligence and beauty of other civilizations as it is to fathom the foundations of one's own; the latter being, in fact, the precondition, if not the guarantee, for the former.

The writings collected in this volume make the case for a vision of Islam as a religion and civilization intrinsically equipped to address universal human predicaments, and converging thereby with the highest spiritual expressions of all authentic religious heritages. They point to fundamental "universals" of Islam, such as the doctrine of Unity and "unification" (*tawhīd*), the essentialness of Divine Mercy, the inclusive and integrative nature of the Muslim concept of prophecy, the Islamic ability to assimilate various cultural and ethnic languages, and the capacity of Islamic mysticism to serve as a spiritual bridge between diverse religions. They include now classic essays by "founding fathers" of the Perennial Philosophy, testimonies from spiritual figures of Sufism, and contemporary studies of Islam and Sufism by experts and younger scholars of religion. Finally, as the universal language par excellence, poetry could not but be included in this volume.

*  *  *

The universal dimensions of Islam refer to the dimension of breadth as well as depth. They pertain to both form and essence.

On the level of form, there is to our mind no better way of pointing out this universality than by quoting Schuon's assertions that "Islam . . . has given a religious form to that which

[1] The expression was coined by Zaid Shakir in the context of recent inter-cultural polemics, especially relating to Samuel Huntington's claim of a so-called "clash of civilizations."

constitutes the essence ["substance" in the original French] of all religion"[2] and that "Islam . . . aims to teach only what every religion essentially teaches; it is like a diagram of every possible religion."[3] The simplicity of the form renders it accessible to any man or woman, and therefore potentially to all of mankind. It speaks to all capacities and levels of understanding. It also allows for its manifestation through diverse cultural contexts, from Sub-Saharan Africa and the Balkans to India and China.

From another point of view—notwithstanding the expansive potentiality of Islam's schema-like form—other aspects of its form have placed limits on Islamic expansion. This is particularly true when referring to the Bedouin and Arab cladding, as it were, of the message. Such a cladding is not the best means of "exporting" Islam, as it enters into conflict with psychological and cultural traits predetermined by other civilizational "logics". Be that as it may, this twofold aspect of the Islamic form may correspond to the distinction, on the one hand, between form as an expression of divine essence, or "archetypal form," and, on the other hand, form as a providential but necessarily exclusive clothing of human culture.

On the level of the essence of the message, the principal element of Islam's universality undoubtedly lies in its doctrine of Unity, understood either from an exoteric or esoteric perspective. From an exoteric standpoint, the universality of Islam is to be found, in a sense, in the aforementioned "schematic" aspect of its affirmation of one supreme God as opposed to many divine manifestations. The Qur'ān and the traditional teachings and interpretations of its message have shown the way of universality through the affirmation of a metaphysics of the Unity of Divine Reality and through the corresponding affirmation of a divine recognition of other traditional faiths. They have done so to the extent that it is possible within the context of a religion, that is to say, within an exclusive belief system. Esoterically, *tawhīd* opens onto the metaphysics of essential Unity, which the various spiritual and traditional languages couch in so many "syntaxes," either affirmatively or apophatically, objectively or subjectively, doctrinally or methodically.

Thus, Islam arrives at the religious paradox of founding the providential legitimacy of its own exclusiveness on the very principle of its overall inclusiveness; a paradox that lies at the core of the unity of Islam, while being the source of its diversity throughout all times and places.

*Patrick Laude*

2 Frithjof Schuon, *Roots of the Human Condition*, "Outline of the Islamic Message" (Bloomington, IN: World Wisdom, 2002), p. 81.

3 Frithjof Schuon, *Spiritual Perspectives and Human Facts*, "Contours of the Spirit" (Bloomington, IN: World Wisdom, 2007), p. 68.

# ESSAYS

# Outline of the Islamic Message

## *Frithjof Schuon*

The enigma of the lightning-like expansion of Islam and its adamantine stability lies in the fact that it has given a religious form to what constitutes the essence of all religion. It is in this sense that some Sufis have said that, being the terminal religion, Islam is *ipso facto* the synthesis of the preceding religions—the synthesis and thereby the archetype; terminality and primordiality rejoin.

On the surface of Islam, we find some features of the Bedouin mentality, which quite obviously have nothing universal about them; in the fundamental elements, however, we encounter as it were religion as such, which by its essentiality opens quite naturally onto metaphysics and *gnosis*.

All metaphysics is in fact contained in the Testimony of Faith (*Shahādah*), which is the pivot of Islam.[1] Exoterically, this Testimony means that the creative Being alone is the Supreme Principle that determines everything; esoterically, it means in addition—or rather *a priori*—that only Beyond-Being is the intrinsic Absolute, since Being is the Absolute only in relation to Existence: this is the distinction between *Ātmā* and *Māyā*, which is the very substance of esoterism. "Neither I (the individual) nor Thou (the Divine Person), but He (the Essence)": it is from this Sufi saying that the pronoun "He" has often been interpreted as meaning the impersonal Essence; and the same meaning has been attributed to the final breath of the Name *Allāh*.

After the Testimony of Faith comes Prayer (*Salāt*), in the order of the "Pillars of the Religion" (*Arqān ad-Dīn*): the human discourse addressed to the Divinity, which is of primary importance since we are beings endowed with intelligence,[2] hence with speech; not to speak to God, yet to speak to men, amounts to denying God and His Lordship. The intention of primordiality, in Islam, is manifested by the fact that every man is his own priest; primordial man—or man in conformity with his profound nature—is a priest by definition; without priesthood, there is no human dignity. The meaning of prayer is to become aware—always anew—of total Reality, then of our situation in the face of this reality; hence to affirm the necessary relationships between man and God. Prayer is necessary, not because we do or do not possess a given spiritual quality, but because we are men.

The Testimony and Prayer are unconditional; Almsgiving (*Zakāt*) is conditional in the sense that it presupposes the presence of a human collectivity. On the one hand it is socially useful and even necessary; on the other hand it conveys the virtues of detachment and generosity, lacking which we are not "valid interlocutors" before God.

As for the Fast (*Siyām*)—practiced during Ramadan—it is necessary because asceticism, like sacrifice in general, is a fundamental possibility of human behavior in the face of the cosmic *māyā*; every man must resign himself to it to one degree or another. Indeed, every man, whether he likes it or not, experiences pleasure, and thus must also experience renunciation,

1 "There is no divinity if not the (sole) Divinity (*Allāh*)." This may be compared with the Vedantic formulation: "*Brahmā* is real, the world is an appearance."

2 We could say "endowed with reason", but it is not reason as such which counts, it is integral intelligence of which reason is only the discursive mode.

since he chooses Heaven; to be man is to be capable of transcending oneself. At the same time, Islam is well aware of the rights of nature: all that is natural and normal, and lived without avidity and without excess, is compatible with the spiritual life and can even assume in it a positive function.[3] Nobility is here the awareness of the archetypes, and above all the sense of the sacred; only he who knows how to renounce can enjoy nobly, and this is one of the meanings of the Fast.

* * *

Unlike the Testimony of Faith, the Prayer, the Fast, and to a certain extent Almsgiving, the Pilgrimage, and the Holy War are conditional: the Pilgrimage depends on our capacity to accomplish it, and the Holy War is obligatory only under certain circumstances. We need not take into consideration here the fact that every obligation of the religion—except for the Testimony—is conditional in the sense that there may always be insuperable obstacles; the Law never demands anything impossible or unreasonable.

The meaning of the Pilgrimage (*Hajj*) is the return to the origin, thus what is involved is a living affirmation of primordiality, of restoring contact with the original Benediction—Abrahamic in the case of Islam. But there is also, according to the Sufis, the Pilgrimage towards the heart: towards the immanent sanctuary, the divine kernel of the immortal soul.

In an analogous fashion, there is, along with the outer Holy War (*Jihād*), the "Greater Holy War" (*al-Jihād al-akbar*), that which man wages against his fallen and concupiscent soul; its weapon is fundamentally the "Remembrance of God" (*Dhikru 'Llāh*), but this combat presupposes nonetheless our moral effort. The all-embracing virtue of "poverty" (*faqr*) is conformity to the demands of the Divine Nature: namely effacement, patience, gratitude, generosity; and also, and even above all, resignation to the Will of God and trust in His Mercy. Be that as it may, the goal of the inner Holy War is perfect self-knowledge, beyond the veilings of passion; for "whoso knoweth his soul, knoweth his Lord".

To return to the Testimony of Faith: to believe in God is to believe also in that which God has done and will do: it is to believe in the Creation, in the Prophets, in the Revelations, in the Afterlife, in the Angels, in the Last Judgment. And to believe is to acknowledge sincerely, drawing the consequences from what one believes; "belief obligates", we could say. Whence the crucial importance, in the thought and sensibility of Islam, of the virtue of sincerity (*sidq*), which coincides with "right doing" (*ihsān*), whether it be a question of religious zeal or esoteric deepening.[4] Theologically, one distinguishes faith (*īmān*), practice (*islām*), and their quality (*ihsān*), the "right doing", precisely; and this right-doing, according to a Muhammadan saying, consists in "worshipping God as if thou seest Him; and if thou dost not see Him, He nonetheless seeth thee".

*Translated by Mark Perry*

[3] This is what is expressed and in principle realized in every religion by the formulas of consecration such as the *benedicite* or the *basmalah*.

[4] Echoing the parable of the talents, Saint James in his Epistle says that "to him that knoweth to do good, and doeth it not, to him it is sin"; which is to say that God requires even wisdom of him who possesses it potentially; whence the inclusion of esoteric spirituality (*tasawwuf*) in *ihsān*.

# Sufism and Mysticism

## *Titus Burckhardt*

Scientific works commonly define Sufism as "Muslim mysticism" and we too would readily adopt the epithet "mystical" to designate that which distinguishes Sufism from the simply religious aspect of Islam if that word still bore the meaning given it by the Greek Fathers of the early Christian Church and those who followed their spiritual line: they used it to designate what is related to knowledge of "the mysteries". Unfortunately the word "mysticism"—and also the word "mystical"—has been abused and extended to cover religious manifestations which are strongly marked with individualistic subjectivity and governed by a mentality which does not look beyond the horizons of exotericism.

It is true that there are in the East, as in the West, borderline cases such as that of the *majdhūb* in whom the Divine attraction (*al-jadhb*) strongly predominates so as to invalidate the working of the mental faculties with the result that the *majdhūb* cannot give doctrinal formulation to his contemplative state. It may also be that a state of spiritual realization comes about in exceptional cases almost without the support of a regular method, for "the Spirit bloweth whither It listeth". None the less the term *Taṣawwuf* is applied in the Islamic world only to regular contemplative ways which include both an esoteric doctrine and transmission from one master to another. So *Taṣawwuf* could only be translated as "mysticism" on condition that the latter term was explicitly given its strict meaning, which is also its original meaning. If the word were understood in that sense it would clearly be legitimate to compare Sufis to true Christian mystics. All the same a shade of meaning enters here which, while it does not touch the meaning of the word "mysticism" taken by itself, explains why it does not seem satisfactory in all its contexts to transpose it into Sufism. Christian contemplatives, and especially those who came after the Middle Ages, are indeed related to those Muslim contemplatives who followed the way of spiritual love (*al-maḥabbah*), the *bhakti mārga* of Hinduism, but only very rarely are they related to those Eastern contemplatives who were of a purely intellectual order, such as Ibn 'Arabī or, in the Hindu world, Śrī Śaṅkarāchārya.[1]

Now spiritual love is in a sense intermediate between glowing devotion and knowledge; moreover, the language of the *bhakta* projects, even into the realm of final union, the polarity from which love springs. This is no doubt one reason why, in the Christian world, the distinction between true mysticism and individualistic "mysticism" is not always clearly marked, whereas in the world of Islam esotericism always involves a metaphysical view of things—even in its bhaktic forms—and is thus clearly separated from exotericism, which can in this case be much more readily defined as the common "Law".[2]

[1] There is in this fact nothing implying any superiority of one tradition over another; it shows only tendencies which are conditioned by the genius and temperament of the peoples concerned. Because of this bhaktic character of Christian mysticism some orientalists have found it possible to assert that Ibn 'Arabī was "not a real mystic".

[2] The structure of Islam does not admit of stages in some sense intermediate between exotericism and esotericism such as the Christian monastic state, the original role of which was to constitute a direct framework for the Christian way of contemplation.

Every complete way of contemplation, such as the Sufi way or Christian mysticism (in the original meaning of that word), is distinct from a way of devotion, such as is wrongly called "mystical", in that it implies an active intellectual attitude. Such an attitude is by no means to be understood in the sense of a sort of individualism with an intellectual air to it: on the contrary it implies a disposition to open oneself to the essential Reality (*al-ḥaqīqah*), which transcends discursive thought and so also a possibility of placing oneself intellectually beyond all individual subjectivity.

That there may be no misunderstanding about what has just been said it must be clearly stated that the Sufi also realizes an attitude of perpetual adoration molded by the religious form. Like every believer he must pray and, in general, conform to the revealed Law since his individual human nature will always remain passive in relation to Divine Reality or Truth whatever the degree of his spiritual identification with it. "The servant (i.e. the individual) always remains the servant" (*al-'abd yabqā-l-'abd*), as a Moroccan master said to the author. In this relationship the Divine Presence will therefore manifest Itself as Grace. But the intelligence of the Sufi, inasmuch as it is directly identified with the "Divine Ray", is in a certain manner withdrawn, in its spiritual actuality and its own modes of expression, from the framework imposed on the individual by religion and also by reason, and in this sense the inner nature of the Sufi is not receptivity but pure act.

It goes without saying that not every contemplative who follows the Sufi way comes to realize a state of knowledge which is beyond form, for clearly that does not depend on his will alone. None the less the end in view not only determines the intellectual horizon but also brings into play spiritual means which, being as it were a prefiguring of that end, permit the contemplative to take up an active position in relation to his own psychic form.

Instead of identifying himself with his empirical "I" he fashions that "I" by virtue of an element which is symbolically and implicitly non-individual. The Qur'ān says: "We shall strike vanity with truth and it will bring it to naught" (21:18). The Sufi 'Abd as-Salām ibn Mashīsh prayed: "Strike with me on vanity that I may bring it to naught." To the extent that he is effectively emancipated the contemplative ceases to be such-and-such a person and "becomes" the Truth on which he has meditated and the Divine Name which he invokes.

The intellectual essence of Sufism makes imprints even on the purely human aspects of the way which may in practice coincide with the religious virtues. In the Sufi perspective the virtues are nothing other than human images or "subjective traces" of universal Truth;[3] hence the incompatibility between the spirit of Sufism and the "moralistic" conception of virtue, which is quantitative and individualistic.[4]

Since the doctrine is both the very foundation of the way and the fruit of the contemplation which is its goal,[5] the difference between Sufism and religious mysticism can be reduced to a

[3] It will be recalled that for Plotinus virtue is intermediate between the soul and intelligence.

[4] A quantitative conception of virtue results from the religious consideration of merit or even from a purely social point of view. The qualitative conception on the other hand has in view the analogical relation between a cosmic or Divine quality and a human virtue. Of necessity the religious conception of virtue remains individualistic since it values virtue only from the point of view of individual salvation.

[5] Some orientalists would like artificially to separate doctrine from "spiritual experience". They see doctrine as a "conceptualizing" anticipating a purely subjective "experience". They forget two things: first, that the doctrine ensues from a state of knowledge which is the goal of the way and secondly, that God does not lie.

question of doctrine. This can be clearly expressed by saying that the believer whose doctrinal outlook is limited to that of exotericism always maintains a fundamental and irreducible separation between the Divinity and himself whereas the Sufi recognizes, at least in principle, the essential unity of all beings, or—to put the same thing in negative terms—the unreality of all that appears separate from God.

It is necessary to keep in view this double aspect of esoteric orientation because it may happen that an exotericist—and particularly a religious mystic—will also affirm that in the sight of God he is nothing. If, however, this affirmation carried with it for him all its metaphysical implications, he would logically be forced to admit at the same time the positive aspect of the same truth, which is that the essence of his own reality, in virtue of which he is *not* "nothing", is mysteriously identical with God. As Meister Eckhart wrote: "There is somewhat in the soul which is uncreate and uncreatable; if all the soul were such it would be uncreate and uncreatable; and this somewhat is Intellect." This is a truth which all esotericism admits *a priori*, whatever the manner in which it is expressed.

A purely religious teaching on the other hand either does not take it into account or even explicitly denies it, because of the danger that the great majority of believers would confuse the Divine Intellect with its human, "created" reflection and would not be able to conceive of their transcendent unity except in the likeness of a substance the quasi-material coherence of which would be contrary to the essential uniqueness of every being. It is true that the Intellect has a "created" aspect both in the human and in the cosmic order, but the whole scope of the meaning that can be given to the word "Intellect"[6] is not what concerns us here since, independently of this question, esotericism is characterized by its affirmation of the essentially divine nature of knowledge.

Exotericism stands on the level of formal intelligence which is conditioned by its objects, which are partial and mutually exclusive truths. As for esotericism, it realizes that intelligence which is beyond forms and it alone moves freely in its limitless space and sees how relative truths are delimited.[7]

This brings us to a further point which must be made clear, a point, moreover, indirectly connected with the distinction drawn above between true mysticism and individualistic "mysticism". Those who stand "outside" often attribute to Sufis the pretension of being able to attain to God by the sole means of their own will. In truth it is precisely the man whose orientation is towards action and merit—that is, exoteric—who most often tends to look on everything from the point of an effort of will, and from this arises his lack of understanding of the purely contemplative point of view which envisages the way first of all in relation to knowledge.

[6] The doctrine of the Christian contemplatives of the Orthodox Church, though clearly esoteric, maintains an apparently irreducible distinction between the "Uncreated Light" and the *nous* or intellect, which is a human, and so created faculty, created to know that Light. Here the "identity of essence" is expressed by the immanence of the "Uncreated Light" and its presence in the heart. From the point of view of method the distinction between the intellect and Light is a safeguard against a "luciferian" confusion of the intellectual organ with the Divine Intellect. The Divine Intellect immanent in the world may even be conceived as the "void", for the Intellect which "grasps" all cannot itself be "grasped". The intrinsic orthodoxy of this point of view—which is also the Buddhist point of view—is seen in the identification of the essential reality of everything with this "void" (*śūnya*).

[7] The Qur'ān says: "God created the Heavens and the earth by the Truth (*al-Ḥaqq*)" (64:3).

In the principial order will does in fact depend on knowledge and not vice versa, knowledge being by its nature "impersonal". Although its development, starting from the symbolism transmitted by the traditional teaching, does include a certain logical process, knowledge is none the less a divine gift which man could not take to himself by his own initiative. If this is taken into account it is easier to understand what was said above about the nature of those spiritual means which are strictly "initiatic" and are as it were a prefiguring of the non-human goal of the Way. While every human effort, every effort of the will to get beyond the limitations of individuality is doomed to fall back on itself, those means which are, so to say, of the same nature as the supra-individual Truth (*al-Ḥaqīqah*) which they evoke and prefigure can, and alone can, loosen the knot of microcosmic individuation—the egocentric illusion, as the Vedāntists would say—since only the Truth in its universal and supra-mental reality can consume its opposite without leaving of it any residue.

By comparison with this radical negation of the "I" (*nafs*) any means which spring from the will alone, such as asceticism (*az-zuhd*) can play only a preparatory and ancillary part.[8] It may be added that it is for this reason that such means never acquired in Sufism the almost absolute importance they had, for instance, for certain Christian monks; and this is true even in cases where they were in fact strictly practiced in one or another *ṭarīqah*.

A Sufi symbolism which has the advantage of lying outside the realm of any psychological analysis will serve to sum up what has just been said. The picture it gives is this: The Spirit (*ar-Rūḥ*) and the soul (*an-nafs*) engage in battle for the possession of their common son the heart (*al-qalb*). By *ar-Rūḥ* is here to be understood the intellectual principle which transcends the individual nature[9] and by *an-nafs* the psyche, the centrifugal tendencies of which determine the diffuse and inconstant domain of the "I". As for *al-qalb*, the heart, this represents the central organ of the soul, corresponding to the vital center of the physical organism. *Al-qalb* is in a sense the point of intersection of the "vertical" ray, which is *ar-Rūḥ*, with the "horizontal" plane, which is *an-nafs*.

Now it is said that the heart takes on the nature of that one of the two elements generating it which gains the victory in this battle. Inasmuch as the *nafs* has the upper hand the heart is "veiled" by her, for the soul, which takes herself to be an autonomous whole, in a way envelops it in her "veil" (*ḥijāb*). At the same time the *nafs* is an accomplice of the "world" in its multiple and changing aspect because she passively espouses the cosmic condition of form. Now form divides and binds whereas the Spirit, which is above form, unites and at the same time distinguishes reality from appearance. If, on the contrary, the Spirit gains the victory over the soul, then the heart will be transformed into Spirit and will at the same time transmute the soul suffusing her with spiritual light. Then too the heart reveals itself as what it really is, that is as the tabernacle (*mishkāt*) of the Divine Mystery (*sirr*) in man.

In this picture the Spirit appears with a masculine function in relation to the soul, which is feminine. But the Spirit is receptive and so feminine in its turn in relation to the Supreme

[8] Sufis see in the body not only the soil which nourishes the passions but also its spiritually positive aspect which is that of a picture or résumé of the cosmos. In Sufi writings the expression the "temple" (*haykal*) will be found to designate the body. Muḥyi-d-Dīn ibn 'Arabī in the chapter on Moses in his *Fuṣūṣ al-Ḥikam* compares it to "the ark where dwells the Peace (*Sakīnah*) of the Lord".

[9] The word *rūḥ* can also have a more particular meaning, that of "vital spirit". This is the sense in which it is most frequently used in cosmology.

Being, from which it is, however, distinguished only by its cosmic character inasmuch as it is polarized with respect to created beings. In essence *ar-Rūḥ* is identified with the Divine Act or Order (*al-Amr*) which is symbolized in the Qur'ān by the creating Word "Be" (*kun*) and is the immediate and eternal "enunciation" of the Supreme Being: ". . . and they will question you about the Spirit: say: The Spirit is of the Order of my Lord, but you have received but little knowledge" (Qur'ān, 17:84).

In the process of his spiritual liberation the contemplative is reintegrated into the Spirit and by It into the primordial enunciation of God by which "all things were made . . . and nothing that was made was made without it" (St. John's Gospel).[10] Moreover, the name "Sufi" means, strictly speaking, one who is essentially identified with the Divine Act; hence the saying that the "Sufi is not created" (*aṣ-ṣufi lam yukhlaq*), which can also be understood as meaning that the being who is thus reintegrated into the Divine Reality recognizes himself in it "such as he was" from all eternity according to his "principial possibility, immutable in its state of non-manifestation"—to quote Muḥyi-d-Dīn ibn 'Arabī. Then all his created modalities are revealed, whether they are temporal or nontemporal, as mere inconsistent reflections of this principial possibility.[11]

*Translated by D. M. Matheson*

My heart has become capable of every form: it is a pasture for gazelles and a
convent for Christian monks,
And a temple for idols, and the pilgrim's Ka'ba and the tables of the Torah and
the book of the Koran.
I follow the religion of Love (*adīnu bi-d-dīni al-hubb*): whatever way Love's
camel take, that is my religion and my faith."

*Muhyīddīn Ibn al-'Arabī*

[10] For the Alexandrines too liberation is brought about in three stages which respectively correspond to the Holy Spirit, the Word, and God the Father.

[11] If it is legitimate to speak of the principial, or divine, possibility of every being, this possibility being the very reason for his "personal uniqueness", it does not follow from this that there is any multiplicity whatever in the divine order, for there cannot be any uniqueness outside the Divine Unity. This truth is a paradox only on the level of discursive reason. It is hard to conceive only because we almost inevitably forge for ourselves a "substantial" picture of the Divine Unity.

# The Universality of Sufism

*Martin Lings*

Those who insist that Sufism is "free from the shackles of religion"[1] do so partly because they imagine that its universality is at stake. But however sympathetic we may feel towards their preoccupation with this undoubted aspect of Sufism, it must not be forgotten that particularity is perfectly compatible with universality, and in order to perceive this truth in an instant we have only to consider sacred art, which is both unsurpassably particular and unsurpassably universal.[2] To take the example nearest our theme, Islamic art is immediately recognizable as such in virtue of its distinctness from any other sacred art: "Nobody will deny the unity of Islamic art, either in time or in space; it is far too evident: whether one contemplates the mosque of Cordova or the great madrasah of Samarkand, whether it be the tomb of a saint in the Maghreb or one in Chinese Turkestan, it is as if one and the same light shone forth from all these works of art."[3] At the same time, such is the universality of the great monuments of Islam that in the presence of any one of them we have the impression of being at the center of the world.[4]

Far from being a digression, the question of sacred art brings us back to our central theme, for in response to the question "What is Sufism?",[5] a possible answer—on condition that other answers were also forthcoming—would be simply to point to the Taj Mahal or to some other masterpiece of Islamic architecture. Nor would a potential Sufi fail to understand this answer, for the aim and end of Sufism is sainthood, and all sacred art in the true and full sense of the term is as a crystallization of sanctity, just as a Saint is as an incarnation of some holy monument, both being manifestations of the Divine Perfection.

According to Islamic doctrine, Perfection is a synthesis of the Qualities of Majesty and Beauty; and Sufism, as many Sufis have expressed it, is a putting on of these Divine Qualities, which means divesting the soul of the limitations of fallen man, the habits and prejudices which have become "second nature", and investing it with the characteristics of man's primordial nature, made in the image of God. Thus it is that the rite of initiation into some Sufi orders actually takes the form of an investiture: a mantle (*khirqah*) is placed by the Shaykh over the shoulders of the initiate.

The novice takes on the way of life of the adept, for part of the method of all mysticisms—and of none more than Islamic mysticism—is to anticipate the end; the adept continues the

[1] So it is in a way, but not in the way that they have in mind.

[2] This emerges with clarity from Titus Burckhardt's *Sacred Art in East and West: Its Principles and Methods* (Bloomington, IN: World Wisdom; Louisville, KY: Fons Vitae, 2001), as does also the close relationship between sacred art and mysticism.

[3] Titus Burckhardt, "Perennial Values in Islamic Art" in *Studies in Comparative Religion*, Vol. 1, No. 3, Summer, 1967 and in *Mirror of the Intellect* (Albany, NY: SUNY, 1987), p. 219.

[4] This idea has been borrowed from Frithjof Schuon's masterly demonstration of the difference between sacred art and art which is religious without being sacred. I have also taken the liberty of transposing it from its Christian setting. The original is as follows: "When standing before a [Romanesque or Gothic] cathedral, a person really feels he is placed at the center of the world; standing before a church of the Renaissance, Baroque, or Rococo periods, he merely feels himself to be in Europe" (*The Transcendent Unity of Religions* [Wheaton, IL: Quest, 1984], p. 84).

[5] Editor's Note: The present article is a chapter from Lings' book *What is Sufism?*

way of life he took on as novice. The difference between the two is that in the case of the adept the way, that is, Sufism, has become altogether spontaneous, for sainthood has triumphed over "second nature". In the case of the novice the way is, to begin with, mainly a discipline. But sacred art is as a Divine Grace which can make easy what is difficult. Its function—and this is the supreme function of art—is to precipitate in the soul a victory for sainthood, of which the masterpiece in question is an image. As a complement to discipline—we might even say as a respite—it presents the path as one's natural vocation in the literal sense, summoning together all the souls' elements for an act of unanimous assent to the Perfection which it manifests.

If it be asked: Could we not equally well point to the Temple of Hampi or to the Cathedral of Chartres as to the Taj Mahal as a crystallization of Sufism? the answer will be a "yes" outweighed by a "no". Both the Hindu temple and the Christian cathedral are supreme manifestations of Majesty and Beauty, and a would-be Sufi who failed to recognize them and rejoice in them as such would be falling short of his qualification inasmuch as he would be failing to give the signs of God their due. But it must be remembered that sacred art is for every member of the community in which it flowers, and that it represents not only the end but also the means and the perspective or, in other words, the way opening onto the end; and neither the temple nor the cathedral was destined to display the ideals of Islam and to reveal it as a means to the end as were the great mosques and, on another plane, the great Sufis. It would certainly not be impossible to point out the affinity between the particular modes of Majesty and Beauty which are manifested in both these Islamic exemplars, that is, in the static stone perfections and in their dynamic living counterparts. But such an analysis of what might be called the perfume of Islamic spirituality could be beyond the scope of a book of this nature. Suffice it to say that the Oneness of the Truth is reflected in all its Revelations not only by the quality of uniqueness but also by that of homogeneity. Thus each of the great theocratic civilizations is a unique and homogeneous whole, differing from all the others as one fruit differs from another and "tasting" the same all through, in all its different aspects. The Muslim mystic can thus give himself totally, without any reserve,[6] to a great work of Islamic art; and if it be a shrine he can, by entering it, put it on as the raiment of sanctity and wear it as an almost organic prolongation of the Sufism which it has helped to triumph in his soul. The same triumph could be furthered by the temple or the cathedral; but he could not "wear" either of these—at least, not until he had actually transcended all forms by spiritual realization which is very different from a merely theoretic understanding.

Sacred art was mentioned in that it provides an immediately obvious example of the compatibility between the universal and the particular. The same compatibility is shown by the symbolism of the circle with its center, its radii, and its circumference. The word "symbolism" is used here to show that the circle is being considered not as an arbitrary image but as a form which is rooted in the reality it illustrates, in the sense that it owes its existence to that reality, of which it is in fact an existential prolongation. If the Truth were not Radiant there could be

[6] That is, without fear of receiving any alien vibration, for two spiritual perspectives can be, for doctrinal or methodic reasons, mutually exclusive in some of their aspects while converging on the same end. But sacred art is an auxiliary and does not normally constitute a central means of spiritual realization. Any danger that might come from the sacred art of a traditional line other than one's own is thus incomparably less than the dangers inherent in practicing the rites of another religion. Such a violation of spiritual homogeneity could cause a shock powerful enough to unbalance the soul.

no such thing as a radius, not even a geometric one, let alone a spiritual path which is the highest example. All radii would vanish from existence; and with this vanishing the universe itself would vanish, for the radius is one of the greatest of all symbols inasmuch as it symbolizes that on which everything depends, namely the connection between the Divine Principle and its manifestations or creations.

Everyone is conscious of "being at a point" or of "having reached a point", even if this be no more than consciousness of having reached a certain age. Mysticism begins with the consciousness that this point is on a radius. It then proceeds by what might be described as an exploitation of this fact, the radius being a Ray of Divine Mercy which emanates from the Supreme Center and leads back to it. The point must now become a point of Mercy. In other words, there must be a deliberate realization or actualization of the Mercy inherent in the point which is the only part of the radius which one can as yet command. This means taking advantage of those possibilities of Mercy which are immediately available, namely the outer formal aspects of religion which, though always within reach, may have been lying entirely neglected or else only made use of exoterically, that is, considering the point in isolation without reference to the radius as a whole.

The radius itself is the religion's dimension of mysticism; thus, in the case of Islam, it is Sufism, which is seen in the light of this symbol to be both particular and universal—particular in that it is distinct from each of the other radii which represent other mysticisms and universal because, like them, it leads to the One Center. Our image as a whole reveals clearly the truth that as each mystical path approaches its End it is nearer to the other mysticisms than it was at the beginning.[7] But there is a complementary and almost paradoxical truth which it cannot reveal,[8] but which it implies by the idea of concentration which it evokes: increase of nearness does not mean decrease of distinctness, for the nearer the center, the greater the concentration, and the greater the concentration, the stronger the "dose". The concentrated essence of Islam is only to be found in the Sufi Saint who, by reaching the End of the Path, has carried the particular ideals of his religion to their highest and fullest development, just as the concentrated essence of Christianity is only to be found in a St. Francis or a St. Bernard or a St. Dominic. In other words, not only the universality but also the originality of each particular mysticism increases in intensity as the End is approached. Nor could it be otherwise inasmuch as originality is inseparable from uniqueness, and this, as well as universality, is necessarily increased by nearness to the Oneness which confers it.

While we are on this theme, it should be mentioned that there is a lesser universality as well as the greater one which we have been considering. All mysticisms are equally universal

[7] It reveals also, incidentally, the ineffectuality of dilettantism, which corresponds to a meandering line that sometimes moves towards the, center and sometimes away from it, crossing and recrossing various radii but following none with any constancy while claiming to follow a synthesis of all. The self-deceivers in question are, to quote a Sufi of the last century (the Shaykh ad-Darqāwī) "like a man who tries to find water by digging a little here and a little there and who will die of thirst; whereas a man who digs deep in one spot, trusting in the Lord and relying on Him, will find water; he will drink and give others to drink" (*Letters of a Sufi Master*, translated by Titus Burckhardt [Louisville, KY: Fons Vitae, 1998], pp. 61-62).

[8] A symbol is by definition fragmentary in that it can never capture all the aspects of its archetype. What escapes it in this instance is the truth that the Center is infinitely greater than the circumference. It therefore needs to be complemented at the back of our minds by another circle whose center stands for this world and whose circumference symbolizes the All-Surrounding Infinite.

in the greater sense in that they all lead to the One Truth. But one feature of the originality of Islam, and therefore of Sufism, is what might be called a secondary universality, which is to be explained above all by the fact that as the last Revelation of this cycle of time it is necessarily something of a summing up. The Islamic *credo* is expressed by the Qur'ān as belief *in God and His Angels and His Books and His Messengers.*[9] The following passage is also significant in this context. Nothing comparable to it could be found in either Judaism or Christianity, for example: *For each We have appointed a law and a path, and if God*[10] *had wished He would have made you one people. But He hath made you as ye are that He may put you to the test in what He hath given you. So vie with one another in good works. Unto God ye will all be brought back and He will then tell you about those things wherein ye differed.*[11] Moreover—and this is why one speaks of a "cycle" of time—there is a certain coincidence between the last and the first. With Islam "the wheel has come full circle", or almost; and that is why it claims to be a return to the primordial religion, which gives it yet another aspect of universality. One of the characteristics of the Qur'ān as the last Revelation is that at times it becomes as it were transparent in order that the first Revelation may shine through its verses; and this first Revelation, namely the Book of Nature, belongs to everyone. Out of deference to this Book the miracles of Muhammad, unlike those of Moses and Jesus, are never allowed to hold the center of the stage. That, in the Islamic perspective, must be reserved for the great miracle of creation which, with the passage of time, is taken more and more for granted and which needs to be restored to its original status. In this connection it is not irrelevant to mention that one of the sayings of the Prophet that is most often quoted by the Sufis is the following "Holy Tradition", (*ḥadīth qudusī*), so called because in it God speaks directly: "I was a Hidden Treasure and I wished to be known, and so I created the world."

It is no doubt in virtue of these and other aspects of universality that the Qur'ān says, addressing the whole community of Muslims: *We have made you a middle people;*[12] and it will perhaps be seen from the following chapters, though without there being any aim to demonstrate this, that Sufism is in fact something of a bridge between East and West.

[9] 2:285

[10] The Qur'ān speaks with the voice of the Divinity not only in the first person (both singular and plural) but also in the third person, sometimes changing from one to the other in two consecutive sentences as here.

[11] 5:48.

[12] 2:143.

# The Mysteries of the Letter *Nūn*

## *René Guénon*

*Nūn* is the fourteenth letter of both the Arabic and the Hebrew alphabets, its numerical value being 50; it occupies, however, a more especially significant place in the Arabic alphabet, of which it ends the first half, the total number of letters being 28 as against the 22 of the Hebrew alphabet. As for its symbolic correspondences, this letter, in the Islamic tradition, is considered principally as representing *al-Ḥūt*, the whale; and this accords with the original meaning of the word *nūn* itself, from which the letter takes its name and which also signifies "fish"; it is by reason of this meaning that *Sayyidnā Yūnūs* (the prophet Jonah) is called *Dhūn-Nūn*. This naturally refers to the traditional symbolism of the fish and more especially to certain aspects of this symbolism that we have mentioned in a previous essay, notably that of the "Fish-Savior," represented by the *Matsya-Avatāra* of the Hindu tradition and the *Ichthus* of the early Christians. Moreover, in this respect, the whale fulfils a similar role to that allotted by other traditions to the dolphin, and like the latter corresponds to the zodiacal sign of Capricorn in so far as it represents the solstitial gateway giving access to the "ascending way"; but the similarity to the *Matsya-Avatāra* is perhaps the most striking, as is shown by certain considerations deriving from the geometrical form of the letter *nūn* itself, particularly if they are related to the Biblical story of the prophet Jonah.

To understand the question properly it should be remembered that *Vishnu*, manifesting himself in the form of a fish (*matsya*), commands *Satyavrāta*, the future *Manu Vaivasvata*, to construct the Ark in which the germs of the future world are to be enclosed, and that, in this same form, he then guides the Ark over the waters during the cataclysm which marks the separation of two successive *Manvantaras*. The role of *Satyavrāta* is here similar to that of *Sayyidnā Nūḥ* (Noah), whose Ark also contains all those elements which are destined to survive until the restoration of the world after the deluge; it makes no matter that the application may be different, owing to the fact that the Biblical deluge, in its more immediate significance, appears to mark the beginning of a more limited cycle than the *Manvantara*; if not the same event, they are at least analogous to one another, since in each case the former state of the world is destroyed in order to make place for a new state.[1] If we now compare what has just been said with the story of Jonah, we shall see that the whale, instead of simply playing the part of the fish which conducts the Ark, is in reality identified with the Ark itself; thus Jonah remains enclosed in the body of the whale, like *Satyavrāta* and Noah in the Ark, during a period which is for him also, if not for the exterior world, a period of "obscuration", corresponding to the interval between two states or two modalities of existence; here again the difference is only secondary, as the same symbolic figures are always susceptible of a double application, macrocosmic and microcosmic. Moreover, the emergence of Jonah from the belly of the whale has always been regarded as a symbol of resurrection, and thus of the passage of the being to a new state; and this in turn may be related to the idea of "birth" attaching to the letter *nūn*, particularly in the Hebrew *Kabbalah*, to be understood spiritually as a "new birth", that is to say as a regeneration of the being, individual or cosmic.

[1] See *The King of the World*, chap. 11.

The same thing is moreover clearly indicated by the actual form of the Arabic letter *nūn*, which is made up of the lower half of a circumference and a point representing the center of this circumference. Now the lower half of a circumference is also a figure of the Ark floating on the waters, and the point at its center represents the germ enclosed within the Ark; the central position of this point shows in addition that this germ is the "germ of immortality", the indestructible "core" which escapes all exterior dissolutions. It may also be remarked that the half-circumference in question is a schematic equivalent of the cup; thus, like the latter, it has in some respects the signification of a "matrix" in which the as yet undeveloped germ is contained, and which, as we shall see later on, is identical with the inferior or "terrestrial" half of the "World Egg".[2] Considered in this aspect, as the "passive" element of spiritual transmutation, *al-Ḥūt* also represents in a certain sense every individuality in so far as it contains the "germ of immortality" at its center, represented symbolically as the heart; and in this connection we will recall the strict relationship which exists between the symbolism of the heart and that of the cup and the "World Egg". The development of the spiritual germ implies that the being emerges from his individual state and from the cosmic environment to which it belongs, just as Jonah's restoration to life coincides with his emergence from the belly of the whale; and we may mention in passing that this emergence is equivalent to the issuing forth of the being from the initiatic cavern, the concavity of which is similarly represented by the half-circumference of the letter *nūn*.

The new birth necessarily implies a death in relation to the former state, whether in the case of an individual or a world; death and birth or resurrection are in reality inseparable from one another, being simply the two opposite faces of the same change of state. In the alphabet the letter *nūn* immediately follows the letter *mīm*, one of the principal significations of which is death (*al-mawt*). The form of this letter depicts the being in a completely contracted or merely virtual state, to which the attitude of prostration corresponds ritually; but this virtuality, which in appearance is an extinction, becomes at the same time, by virtue of the concentration of all the being's possibilities in one unique and indestructible point, the germ from which all development in the higher states will proceed.

It should be added that the symbolism of the whale possesses not only a beneficent but also a "malefic" aspect, which, apart from general considerations relating to the double meaning of symbols, is justified in a more special way by its connection with the two forms of death and resurrection under which every change of state appears, according to whether it is regarded in relation to the earlier or the subsequent state. The cavern is a place of burial at the same time that it is a place of "rebirth", and the whale fulfils precisely this double role in the story of Jonah; furthermore, might it not be said that the *Matsya-Avatāra* itself is first presented in the sinister guise of announcer of the cataclysm, before assuming the role of Savior? In its malefic aspect the whale is clearly allied to the Hebrew Leviathan;[3] but in the Arab tradition this aspect is represented primarily by the "daughters of the whale" (*banāt al-Ḥūt*), who are equivalent from the astrological standpoint to *Rāhn* and *Ketu* in the Hindu tradition, notably in their rela-

[2] By a curious concordance the sense of "matrix" (in Sanskrit *yoni*) is also contained in the Greek word *delphus*, which is at the same time the name of the dolphin.

[3] The Hindu *Makara* (which is also a sea monster), although above all possessing the "beneficent" meaning attached to the sign of Capricorn, whose place it occupies in the Zodiac, has none the less, in many of its representations certain characteristics which recall the "typhonian" symbolism of the crocodile.

tion to the eclipses, and who, it is said, "will drink the ocean" on the last day of the cycle, on that day when "the stars will rise in the west and set in the east". We cannot pursue this subject further without digressing from our main theme; but we may remark in passing that here once again we find a direct allusion to the end of the cycle and the change of state which follows; this in itself is significant and brings added confirmation to what we have been saying.

Returning to the form of the letter *nūn*, a further observation may be made which is of considerable interest from the point of view of the relations existing between the alphabets of the different traditional languages: in the Sanskrit alphabet, the corresponding letter *na*, reduced to its fundamental geometrical elements, is likewise composed of a half-circumference and a point; but here, the convexity being turned upwards, it is formed by the upper half of the circumference, and not by the lower half as in the Arabic *nūn*. We thus have the same figure placed the other way up, or more exactly two figures that are strictly complementary to each other. If they are joined together, the two central points naturally merge into one another, and this gives a circle with a point at its center, a figure which represents the complete cycle and which is also the sign of the Sun in astrology and of gold in alchemy.[4] Just as the lower half-circumference is a figure of the Ark, so the upper half-circumference represents the rainbow, which is analogous to the Ark in the strictest meaning of the word, all true analogy being "inverse". These two half-circumferences are also the two halves of the "World Egg", the one "terrestrial", in the "Lower Waters", the other "celestial", in the "Upper Waters"; and the circular figure, which was complete at the beginning of the cycle before the separation of the two halves, must be reconstituted at the end of the cycle.[5] We may say, therefore, that the reunion of the two figures in question represents the accomplishment of the cycle, by the junction of its beginning and its end; and this appears particularly clearly if we refer to the "solar" symbolism, since the figure of the Sanskrit *na* corresponds to the sun rising and that of the Arabic *nūn* to the sun setting. On the other hand the complete circular figure is commonly the symbol of the number 10, the center being 1 and the circumference 9; but here, being obtained by the union of the two *nūn*, it has the value of $2 \times 50 = 100 = 10^2$, which indicates that it is in the "intermediary world" that the junction must be brought about; this junction is in fact impossible in the "inferior world", which is the domain of division and "separativity", and on the other hand it is always accomplished in the "superior" world, where it is realized principially in a permanent and unchangeable manner in the "eternal present".

To these already lengthy remarks we will make just one addition so as to connect them with a question which was recently alluded to in this very journal:[6] it follows from what we have just been saying that the accomplishment of the cycle, as we have envisaged it, should have a certain correlation, in the historical order, with the meeting of the two traditional forms

[4] One will recall here the symbolism of the "Spiritual Sun" and the "Embryo of gold" (*Hiranyagarbha*) in the Hindu tradition; moreover, according to certain correspondences, *nūn* is the planetary letter of the Sun.

[5] See *The King of the World*, chap. 11.

[6] Frithjof Schuon, "Le Sacrifice", in *Études Traditionnelles*, April 1938, p. 137, n. 2. [Editor's Note: The passage in question is: "To return to the question of India, one is within one's rights to say that the expansion of an orthodox foreign tradition, Islam, seems to indicate that Hinduism itself no longer possesses the full vitality or actuality of a tradition in integral conformity with the conditions of a given cyclic period. This meeting of Islam, which is the last possibility issuing from the Primordial Tradition, and of Hinduism which is doubtless the most direct branch of that Tradition, is moreover very significant and leads to very complex considerations."]

which correspond to its beginning and its end, and which have Sanskrit and Arabic respectively for their sacred languages: the Hindu tradition, on the one hand, inasmuch as it represents the most direct heritage of the Primordial Tradition, and, on the other hand, the Islamic tradition which, as the "Seal of Prophecy", represents the ultimate form of traditional orthodoxy for the present cycle.

*Translated by Alvin Moore Jr.*

What shall I do, O Muslims?
I do not recognize myself. . . .
I am neither Christian nor Jew,
nor Magian, nor Muslim.
I am not of the East, nor the West,
not of the land, nor the sea. . . .
I have put duality away
and seen the two worlds as one.
One I seek, One I know.
One I see, One I call.
He is the First, He is the Last.
He is the Outward, He is the Inward.
I know of nothing but *Hu*, none but Him.

*Jalāl ad-Dīn Rūmī*

# Universal Foundations of Islam

## *Michael Oren Fitzgerald*

Can we gain a deeper insight into the universal dimensions of Islam through a focused examination of what Islam says about other religions? This article attempts to answer this question by presenting passages from the earliest and incontestable sources of Islamic scripture—the Koran and Hadith[1]—that demonstrate how Islam views other religions, thus providing an unbiased picture before centuries of political conflicts and theological embellishments confused the issue. We hope these excerpts provide a deeper insight into the universal foundations of Islam.

For each of the world's 1.2 billion Muslims the Koran is the compilation of the Word of God exactly as It was revealed to the Prophet Muhammad over the course of many years. The collection called Hadith is made up of thousands of recorded sayings of Muhammad speaking under various levels of inspiration from God. In this article we only use quotations from the most widely used translations of the Koran[2] and the most widely accepted traditional compilations of Hadith.[3] It is generally accepted that these sources present traditional Islam in its most authentic form available in the English language.

These selections illuminate the universal foundations of Islam because the Koran names twenty-four different messengers from God who came before Muhammad, and it makes numerous references to additional messengers. For example:

> Verily We have sent messengers before thee (Muhammad); of them there are some whose story We have related to thee, and some whose story We have not related to thee (Koran 40:78).

This hadith is more specific:

> God's Messenger was asked the number which made up the full complement of the prophets, and he replied, "There have been one hundred and twenty-four

[1] The word *hadith* in Arabic refers to a single utterance or saying of the Prophet. The plural is *ahadith.* We will use the singular "hadith" in all cases, which is now an accepted term in the English language, because the plural will undoubtedly confuse too many readers. When used with the uppercase "H" (i.e. "Hadith"), we are referring to the formal collection of the many individual prophetic utterances.

[2] Our two most frequently used translations are by Marmaduke Pickthall and Yusuf Ali. We have also consulted the translations by Shakir and A.J. Arberry and occasionally substituted one of their formulations or added a parenthesis with an alternative formulation to add clarity. Even with this process it is impossible to convey the multiple levels of meaning that are inherent in the revealed Arabic text.

[3] The death of the Prophet Muhammad in 632 A.D. started a three-hundred year process of collecting and archiving all of his sayings and actions. Great care was taken to authenticate each saying by tracing it back to Muhammad through an unbroken chain of valid interlocutors (*isnad*). The chain of transmission is usually recounted together with the text (*matn*) of each hadith to allow the reader to judge its degree of authenticity. A fourteenth century collection entitled the *Mishkat Al-Masabih* contains the six compilations of hadith that are almost universally considered as canonical. To insure authenticity, all of our selections come from the 5,945 hadith contained in the *Mishkat Al-Masabih*, but for easy readability we have chosen not to present the corresponding list of interlocutors and compilers that always begins each hadith.

thousand prophets, among whom were three hundred and fifteen messengers."[4]

Not every revelation is as explicit in stating that other prophets have brought the same message to other peoples in other times, as is evidenced in these quotations:

> And verily We (God) have raised among every nation a messenger, (with the command), "Serve God and shun false gods" (Koran 16:36).
>
> Say ye (O believers): "We believe in God, and in the revelation given to us and that which was revealed to Abraham, Ishmael, Isaac, Jacob, and the Tribes, and that (revelation) given to Moses and Jesus and in that (revelation) given to (all) prophets from their Lord. We make no distinction between one and another of them, and unto Him we have surrendered" (Koran 2:136).[5]

To organize these diverse citations we have created six major sections based upon how each quotation refers to the revelations of non-Islamic religious traditions. The major sections start with "References to Multiple Religions." The other major sections are: "Ancient Messengers from God," "The Abrahamic Tradition," "Judaism," "Christianity," and "'People of the Book.'"[6] Within each major section we have identified sub-sections, most of which identify specific messengers or prophets. We first present quotations from the Koran and then we present the Hadith.

Space limitations oblige us to limit the excerpts that can be presented; thus, our focus is on passages that refer to multiple religions and on the Abrahamic traditions, including Judaism and Christianity. An appendix lists the names of prophets that space did not allow us to include, together with the relevant Koranic citations.[7] Many Koranic verses address the same subject from different points of view, reinforcing the overall message by repetition. To avoid a disproportionate repetition of similar verses, the appendix also contains relevant Koranic verses that we did not utilize.[8] However, this repetition demonstrates that the message contained in these selections is the rule, not the exception. A person with a narrow religious perspective can attempt to disregard the apparent meaning of one or another of these quotations, but we

[4] In the Arabic language, a prophet (*nabi*) is a person inspired by God to bring a warning. A divine messenger (*rasul*) promulgates a new sacred law, which often results in a new religion. Not every prophet is a messenger, but every messenger is by implication a prophet. The Koran also addresses "those who are sent" (*mursaleen*), which refers to both the prophets and the messengers sent by God.

[5] This verse, 2:136, is virtually identical to verse 3:84. The first verse is addressed to all believers and the second verse is addressed to Muhammad. The Arabic is slightly different in use of prepositions, but it is almost impossible to convey that fine a difference in English.

[6] The phrase "People of the Book" refers to the common spiritual ancestry of Islam, Judaism, and Christianity, which are all traced back to the Abrahamic tradition, and highlights the fact that each of these religions possesses a revealed scripture: the Torah, the Gospels, and the Koran.

[7] The award-winning book, *The Universal Spirit of Islam,* edited by Judith and Michael Fitzgerald (Bloomington, IN: World Wisdom, 2006), contains a much larger selection of quotations about each of these topics, together with additional materials and illustrations. All of the passages presented here are included in that book.

[8] This Appendix is only a partial list of the most analogous passages and is not a comprehensive concordance that lists all references to religions other than Islam. It provides a starting point to locate additional primary references.

believe that the cumulative weight of this authority presents a clear picture of the universal spirit of Islam that is difficult to dismiss.

As Christianity and Islam are the two largest religions in the world, it is worth noting the many fundamental tenets of Christianity that are shared and accepted by the Koran and Hadith:

- The Virgin Birth of Jesus, conceived by the Holy Spirit;
- Jesus and Mary are the only two people in all creation not touched by Satan at birth;
- The Virgin Mary was chaste, a perfect woman, and chosen above all other women;
- Numerous miracles and inspired teachings by Jesus;
- The resurrection of Jesus after his crucifixion;[9]
- The descent of Jesus to fight the anti-Christ in Armageddon.

Despite various distinctions, the shared beliefs about Christianity greatly outweigh the differences.[10]

The Koran and Hadith are not without their criticism of Christians and Jews, primarily that many so-called Christians or Jews have strayed from their original faith; however, the Prophet Muhammad also predicted that in time Muslims would lose knowledge of their true faith, as have all preceding civilizations. This saying of Muhammad is one of many such examples:

> The Prophet said, "There will come a time when knowledge will depart." A man asked him, "How can knowledge depart when we recite the Koran and teach it to our children and they will teach it to their children up until the day of resurrection?" The Prophet replied, "I am astonished at you. I thought you were a man of great learning. Do not these Jews and Christians read the Torah and the *Injil* (the Gospel) without knowing a thing about their contents?"

There are many other hadith that describe how Muslims would fall away from their religion in later days, including a lengthy section of hadith on the trials of the last days (*fitan*) when all men will fall away from religion.[11] These hadith help us recognize that every form of religious faith is under pressure from today's secular, technological society to compromise its fundamental beliefs and turn away from prayer, which eventually leads to an abandonment of

[9] This is the most evident meaning of the Koran 4:156-159: "But [the Jews] killed not [the Messiah Jesus], nor crucified him, but so it was made to appear to them; . . . for of a surety they killed him not. Nay, God raised him up unto Himself." The resurrection of the Messiah Jesus is also confirmed in this Koranic passage: "(And remember) when God said, 'O Jesus! Verily I am gathering thee and causing thee to ascend unto Me'" (Koran 3:55). Many Muslim theologians do not accept the most straightforward interpretation of these passages and postulate alternative interpretations. The entire verses are presented in the text, together with explanatory footnotes.

[10] The Koran and Hadith put forward two specific exaggerations by Christians from the Islamic point of view: the requirement of celibacy in the priesthood and the idea that God is one of three equal partners in the "Trinity" of the Father, Son, and Holy Spirit. These criticisms are presented in the text and discussed at more length in the subsequent notes.

[11] The great majority of such hadith do not make references to other religions, so they have not been included in this article.

faith in God.[12] Perhaps the greatest common ground among the religions is the need to come together to withstand this attack of secularism on every form of spirituality.

We believe true interfaith understanding must be based upon recognizing the existence of one, all-powerful God, who is so merciful that He has manifested Himself in many forms for different collectivities at different times. Thus, there is one timeless Truth underlying the diverse religions—demonstrating what Frithjof Schuon termed the "transcendent unity of religions." This timeless Truth, often referred to as the *Sophia Perennis* or perennial Wisdom, finds its expression in the revealed Scriptures, as well as in the oral and written words of the great spiritual masters, and in the artistic creations of the traditional worlds. A comparative study of the canonical writings of the different religions, especially revealed Scripture, is therefore an indispensable key to interfaith understanding. Several principles can provide important context for a comparative study.

First, it is evident that every revelation is addressed to a specific people in a specific historical circumstance. For example, the Prophet of Islam was charged with leading a pagan people of the Arabian Peninsula, who were in a state of spiritual and moral decadence, back to the pristine monotheism of Adam and Abraham. However, if there is a transcendent unity of religions, then there must also be shared universal truths within each religion that are addressed to all humanity.[13] For example, the Koran and Hadith sometimes limit their messages to the Arabs of Muhammad's time and culture; yet, in other instances, they address the "children of Adam"—humankind as such—and appeal to that which is common to all people. We can also think of these as the historical and the supra-historical teachings of the Scriptures. These selections demonstrate that Islam has a deep appreciation of supra-historical manifestations of the Divine outside of the world of seventh century Arabia.

In addition to these identifiable universal truths, the sacred Scriptures and writings of the great sages of each of the major religions have different levels of meaning that may not be apparent to each and every believer. Islam refers to an outward or revealed aspect (*zahir*), and an inner, hidden one (*batin*). The following hadith reinforce this principle and provide practical advice to believers when the meaning of Scripture is not clear:

> The Koran came down showing five aspects: what is permissible, what is prohibited, what is firmly fixed, what is obscure, and parables. So treat what is permissible as permissible and what is prohibited as prohibited, act upon what is firmly fixed, believe in what is obscure, and take a lesson from the parables.

> Things are of three categories: a matter whose right guidance is clear, which you must follow; a matter whose error is clear, which you must avoid; and a matter about which there is a difference of opinion, which you must entrust to God.

[12] There are 30 million people in the United States who openly acknowledge they have no religious faith, a number which has grown at more than 5% per year over the past fourteen years, which is twice as fast as our population growth.

[13] Space does not allow us to provide canonical quotations to illuminate the universal truths in Islam. *The Universal Spirit of Islam* contains a section, entitled, "Islam—Universal Truths from the Koran," that clearly demonstrates the inner unanimity of Islam.

By analogy, we should not be troubled if the reasons for the apparently irreconcilable differences in the forms of the religions appear ambiguous. This happens because the differences involve various levels of meaning at varying levels of essential universality. If we consider that the identifiable shared universal truths represent essential Truth, then the conflicting forms of the religions are based upon certain principles that have a more relative importance. A principle of relative importance may not be necessary for all people, but it may be of compelling importance for a particular people based upon their collective temperament. Muhammad has two sayings that support the idea that different people have different tendencies and each religion has a different character or signature:

> Every people has a temptation, and my people's temptation is property.
>
> Every religion has a signature, and the signature of Islam is modesty.

The idea of universality does not mean that the outward laws of religion may be disregarded—quite the contrary. Every religion states that it is not possible to create a new religion by combining elements from different forms of spirituality—religion and spirituality must be on God's terms, not on man's terms. Rather, the integral foundation for interfaith dialogue is based upon the realization that:

- The universal truths within the diverse religions are identical;
- Outward differences in the forms of the religions do not alter their inner unanimity;
- Each religion is providential for the people and time in which it has been revealed;
- No revealed religion or messenger of God can be fundamentally superior to another;
- There are different levels and signatures to each revelation that collectively describe the Divine plan;
- Each person's primary responsibility is to his or her personal relationship to God, trusting that He will judge our differences.

The following selection of Koranic passages and hadith support these propositions:

> Verily those who disbelieve in God and His messengers, and seek to make distinction between God and His messengers, and say, "We believe in some and disbelieve in others, and seek to choose a way in between," such are disbelievers in truth; and for disbelievers We prepare a shameful doom. To those who believe in God and His messengers and make no distinction between any of the messengers, we shall soon give their (due) rewards, for God is oft-forgiving, most merciful (4:150-52).
>
> And unto thee have We revealed the Book (Koran) with the Truth, confirming whatever Scripture was before it. . . . For each (people) We have appointed a divine law and a traced-out way. Had God willed He could have made you one community (5:48).
>
> We did send messengers before thee. . . . For each period is a Scripture (re

> vealed) (13:38).
>
> We never sent a messenger except (to teach) in the language of his (own) people, in order to make (the message) clear to them (14:4).
>
> To every people have We appointed (different) rites and ceremonies which they must follow, so let them not then dispute with thee on the matter; but do thou invite (them) to thy Lord, for thou art assuredly on the right way. And if they wrangle with thee, say, "God is best aware of what ye do." God will judge between you on the Day of Resurrection concerning that wherein ye used to differ (22:67-69).
>
> Nothing is said to thee [Muhammad] that was not said to the messengers before thee (41:43).
>
> When the prophet Muhammad heard someone say that he was superior to the prophet Jonah, he said, "Do not say that I am better than Jonah. Do not treat some of the prophets of God as superior to others."
>
> Then sent We our messengers in succession; every time there came to a people their messenger, they accused him of falsehood, so We made them follow each other (in punishment). We made them as a tale (that is told)—so away with a people that will not believe! [The stories of Moses, and Jesus and the Virgin Mary are briefly told.] O ye messengers! Enjoy (all) things good and pure, and work righteousness, for I am well acquainted with (all) that ye do. And verily this your religion is one religion and I am your Lord, so keep your duty unto Me. But they (mankind) have broken their religion among them into sects, each group rejoicing in its tenets. But leave them in their confused ignorance for a time (23:44-54).

This last quotation contains an important declaration for every believer, regardless of faith—focus on your individual duty to God, not upon outward differences in the forms of worship.

These quotations allow Muslims and non-Muslims to set aside all preconceptions and examine what authentic Islam actually says about Christianity and Judaism, indeed all other religions. These teachings also allow non-Muslims to realize that their fundamental religious beliefs are not in opposition with Islam, but rather share the same universal truths. They also reinforce the fact that all people throughout history are equally susceptible to the danger of losing their real knowledge of their religion. And they demonstrate that God will be the ultimate judge of the outward differences in the religions.

## REFERENCES TO MULTIPLE RELIGIONS

### General

Verily We inspire thee as We inspired Noah and the prophets after him, as We inspired Abraham and Ishmael and Isaac and Jacob and the Tribes, and Jesus and Job and Jonah and Aaron and Solomon, and as We imparted unto David the Psalms; and messengers We have mentioned unto thee before and messengers We have not mentioned unto thee; and God spoke directly unto Moses; messengers who gave good news as well as warning, that mankind, after (the coming) of the messengers, should have no plea against God—for God is exalted in power, wise (4:163-165).

We gave it (Our message) unto Abraham against his folk. We raise unto degrees of wisdom whom We will, for verily thy Lord is wise, aware. And We bestowed upon him Isaac and Jacob, each of them We guided; and Noah did We guide aforetime; and of his seed (We guided) David and Solomon and Job and Joseph and Moses and Aaron—thus do We reward the good. And Zachariah[14] and John and Jesus and Elias, each one (of them) was of the righteous; and Ishmael and Elisha and Jonah and Lot, each one (of them) did We prefer above (Our) creatures, with some of their forefathers and their offspring and their brethren; and We chose them and guided them unto a straight path. Such is the guidance of God. He giveth that guidance to whom He pleaseth of His worshippers. But if they had set up (for worship) aught beside Him, (all) that they did would have been vain. Those are they unto whom We gave the Scripture and command and prophethood. But if these disbelieve therein, then indeed We shall entrust it to a people who will not be disbelievers therein. Those were the (prophets) who received God's guidance—copy the guidance they received (6:84-91).

To every people (was sent) a messenger; when their messenger comes (before them on the Day of Judgment), the matter will be judged between them with justice, and they will not be wronged (10:47).

Who receiveth guidance, receiveth it for his own benefit, and who goeth astray doth so to his own loss. No bearer of burdens can bear the burden of another, nor would We visit them with Our wrath until We had sent a messenger (to give warning). When We decide to destroy a population, We (first) send commandments to those among them who are given the good things of this life and yet transgress; and then the Word (of warning) is proved true against them and We destroy them utterly. How many generations have We destroyed after Noah? It suffices for thy Lord to note and see the sins of His servants. If any do wish for the transitory things (of this life), We readily grant them—such things as We will to such person as We will. In the end have We provided hell for them—they will burn therein, disgraced and rejected. Those who do wish for the (things of) the hereafter, and strive therefore with all due striving, and have faith—they are the ones whose striving is acceptable (to God) (17:15-19).

We bestowed on Abraham of old his rectitude of conduct, and well were We acquainted with him. . . . Abraham said, "Your Lord is the Lord of the heavens and the earth, He who created them (from nothing), and I am a witness to this (Truth).". . . And We rescued Abraham and (his nephew) Lot (and brought them) to the land which We have blessed for (all) peoples. And We bestowed upon him Isaac, and Jacob as a grandson. Each of them We made righteous. And

[14] Zachariah is the father of John the Baptist and the uncle of the Virgin Mary, who looked after Mary in the Temple of Solomon when she was a temple virgin; in Arabic, Zakariah.

We made them leaders, guiding (men) by Our command; and We sent them inspiration to do good deeds, to establish regular prayers, and to practice regular charity; and they constantly served Us (alone). And unto Lot we gave judgment and knowledge, and We delivered him from the community that did abominations—verily they were folk of evil, lewd. And We admitted him to Our mercy, for he was one of the righteous. (Remember) Noah, when he cried (to Us) aforetime; We listened to his (prayer) and delivered him and his family from great affliction. And delivered him from the people who denied Our revelations—verily they were folk of evil, therefore did We drown them all. And remember David and Solomon, when they gave judgment in the matter of the field into which the sheep of certain people had strayed by night, and We did witness their judgment. To Solomon We inspired the (right) understanding of the matter, and unto each of them We gave judgment and knowledge. It was Our power that made the hills and the birds celebrate Our praises along with David—it was We who did (all these things) (21:51-79).

Nothing is said to thee that was not said to the messengers before thee, that thy Lord has at His command (all) forgiveness as well as a most grievous penalty (41:43).

The same religion has He established for you as that which He enjoined on Noah—which We have sent by inspiration to thee—and that which We enjoined on Abraham, Moses, and Jesus: namely, that ye should remain steadfast in religion, and make no divisions therein. To those who worship other things than God, hard is the (way) to which thou callest them. God chooses to Himself those whom He pleases, and guides to Himself those who turn (to Him) (42:13).

We verily sent Our messengers with clear proofs, and revealed with them the Scripture and the balance, that mankind may observe right measure; and He revealed iron, wherein is mighty power and (many) uses for mankind, and that God may know him who helpeth Him and His messengers, though unseen. Verily God is strong, almighty. And We verily sent Noah and Abraham and placed the prophethood and the Scripture among their seed, and among them there is he who goeth right, but many of them are evil livers. Then We caused Our messengers to follow in their footsteps; and We caused Jesus, son of Mary, to follow, and gave him the Gospel and placed compassion and mercy in the hearts of those who followed him. But monasticism they invented—We ordained it not for them. . . . So We give those of them who believe their reward, but many of them are evil livers[15] (57:25-27).

God's messenger came out to a group of Muslims who were arguing about God's decree. He was angry and his face became so red that it looked as if pomegranate seeds had been burst open on his cheeks. He then said, "Is this what you were commanded to do, or was it for this purpose

[15] The Koran identifies monasticism in the priesthood as an exaggeration in Christianity. It is important to note that this injunction does not forbid monasticism, but states that God did not ordain or command monasticism for the Christian priesthood. Islam does not separate the sacred and the secular domains, as does monasticism; rather, Islam seeks to bring the essence of monasticism (humility, charity, veracity) into the world (see Frithjof Schuon, "The Universality and Timeliness of Monasticism" in *Light on the Ancient Worlds* [Bloomington, IN: World Wisdom, 2006] and *Crossing Religious Frontiers: Studies in Comparative Religion*, edited by Harry Oldmeadow [Bloomington, IN: World Wisdom, 2010]).

that I was sent to you? Your predecessors perished only when they argued about this matter. I adjure you, I adjure you, not to argue about it" (hadith).

No people have gone astray after following right guidance unless they have been led into disputation (hadith).

At the beginning of every century God will send one who will renew its religion for this people. In every successive century those who are reliable authorities will preserve this knowledge, rejecting the changes made by extremists, the plagiarisms of those who make false claims for themselves, and the interpretations of the ignorant (hadith).

When the Prophet was asked which people suffered the greatest affliction he replied, "The prophets, then those who come next to them, then those who come next to them. A man is afflicted in keeping with his religion; if he is firm in his religion his trial is severe, but if there is weakness in his religion it is made light for him, and it continues like that until he walks on the earth firm in his religion" (hadith).

God's messenger was asked who was the first of the prophets, and he replied that it was Adam. He was asked if he (Adam) was really a prophet and he replied, "Yes, he was a prophet to whom a message was given." God's messenger was then asked how many messengers there had been, and he replied, "There have been three hundred and between ten and twenty in all" (hadith).

**The Last Days**

Among the signs of the last hour will be the removal of knowledge, the abundance of ignorance, the prevalence of fornication, the prevalence of wine-drinking, civil strife will appear, niggardliness will be cast into people's hearts, and slaughter will be prevalent (hadith).

The last hour will not come before the anti-Christ (*al-dajjal*) will come forth. While the best people on earth are preparing for battle and arranging their ranks the time for prayer will come and Jesus, son of Mary, will descend and lead them in prayer. When God's enemy sees him he (the anti-Christ) will dissolve like salt in water, and if he were to leave him he would dissolve completely; but God will kill him by his (Jesus, son of Mary's) hand and he will show them his blood on his spear (hadith).

Let me tell you something about the anti-Christ (*al-dajjal*) which no prophet has told his people. He is one-eyed, and will bring with him something like Paradise and hell, but what he calls Paradise will be hell. I warn you as Noah warned his people about him (hadith).

When the anti-Christ (*al-dajjal*) comes he will summon people and they will believe him. He will [produce miracles and turn people away from their religion. When his actions are the worst] God will send the Messiah, son of Mary, who will descend at the white minaret in the East of Damascus wearing two garments dyed with saffron and placing his hands on the wings of two angels. When he lowers his head it will drip and when he raises it beads like pearls will scatter from it. Every infidel who feels the odor of his breath will die, and his breath will reach as far as he can see. He will then seek anti-Christ until he catches up with him and kills him. People whom God has protected from the anti-Christ will then come to Jesus who will wipe their faces and tell them of the ranks they will have in Paradise. While this is happening God will reveal to Jesus that He has brought forth servants of His with whom no one will be able to fight and tell him to collect His servants. God will then release Gog and Magog[16] "and they will swarm down from every slope" [to create destruction]. God's prophet Jesus and his companions will then beseech God [to send various punishments to evildoers. After various punishments have occurred], God will send a pleasant wind which will take the righteous under their armpits and the spirit of every believer and every Muslim will be taken, but the wicked people will remain in the earth and will be disorderly like asses. Then the last hour will come to them[17] (hadith).

## ANCIENT MESSENGERS FROM GOD

### Adam

(God said) "O Adam! Dwell thou and thy wife in the Garden (of Eden) and eat from whence ye will, but come not nigh this tree lest ye become wrongdoers." Then Satan whispered to them that he might manifest unto them that which was hidden from them of their shame, and he said, "Your Lord forbade you from this tree only lest ye should become angels or become of the immortals." And he swore unto them (saying), "Verily I am a sincere adviser unto you." Thus did he lead them on with guile. And when they tasted of the tree their shame was manifest to them and they began to hide (by heaping) on themselves some of the leaves of the Garden. And their Lord called them, (saying), "Did I not forbid you from that tree and tell you, 'Verily Satan is an open enemy to you'?" They said, "Our Lord! We have wronged ourselves. If thou forgive us not and have not mercy on us, surely we are of the lost!" He said, "Go down (from hence), one of you a foe unto the other. There will be for you on earth a habitation and provision for a while. There shall ye live, and there shall ye die, and thence shall ye be brought forth. O Children of Adam! We have revealed unto you raiment to conceal your shame, and splendid vesture, but the raiment of righteousness, that is best." This is of the signs [*ayat*] of God, that they may remember. O Children of Adam! Let not Satan seduce you as he caused your (first) parents to go forth from the Garden and tore off from them their robe (of innocence) that he might manifest their shame to them. Verily he seeth you, he and his tribe, from whence ye see him not. Verily We made the evil ones friends (only) to those without faith. . . . O Children of Adam! Wear your beautiful apparel at every time and place of prayer, eat and drink, but waste not by excess, for God loveth not the wasters. . . . O Children of Adam when messengers of your own come unto you who narrate unto you My signs [*ayat*], then whosoever refraineth from evil and amendeth—there shall no fear come upon them neither shall they grieve. . . . Verily your Lord is God who created the heavens and the earth in six days, then mounted He the Throne. He covereth the night with the day, which is in haste to follow it, and hath made the sun and the moon and the stars subservient by His command. His verily is all creation and

16 Gog and Magog are two nations led by Satan in a climactic battle at Armageddon. Cf. Revelations 20:8 and numerous hadith.

17 Cf. Koran 21:96.

commandment. Blessed be God, the Lord of the worlds! (O mankind!) Call upon your Lord humbly and in secret. Verily He loveth not aggressors. Do no mischief on the earth, after it hath been set in order, but call on Him with fear and longing (in your hearts), for the mercy of God is (always) near to those who do good (7:19-56).

God created Adam from a handful which he took from the whole of the earth; so the children of Adam are in accordance with the earth, some red, some white, some black, some a mixture, also smooth and rough, bad and good (hadith).

### Noah

We sent Noah to his people (with a mission), "I have come to you with a clear warning: that ye serve none but God. Verily I do fear for you the penalty of a grievous day." But the chiefs of the unbelievers among his people said, "We see (in) thee nothing but a man like ourselves. . . . Nor do we see in you (and your followers) any merit above us, in fact we think ye are liars!" He (Noah) said, "O my people! See ye if I have a clear sign from my Lord, and that He hath sent mercy unto me from His own presence, but that the mercy hath been obscured from your sight? Shall we compel you to accept it when ye are averse to it? . . ." They said, "O Noah! Thou hast disputed with us, and (much) hast thou prolonged the dispute with us; now bring upon us what thou threatenest us with, if thou speakest the truth!". . . It was revealed to Noah, "None of thy people will believe except those who have believed already! So grieve no longer over their (evil) deeds, but construct an Ark under Our eyes and Our inspiration, and address Me no (further) on behalf of those who are in sin, for they are about to be overwhelmed (in the flood)." Forthwith he (began) constructing the Ark. Every time that the chiefs of his people passed by him, they threw ridicule on him. He said, "If ye ridicule us now, we (in our turn) can look down on you with ridicule likewise! . . ." At length, behold! There came Our command, and the fountains of the earth gushed forth! We said, "Embark therein, of each kind two, male and female, and your family—except those against whom the word has already gone forth—and the believers." But only a few believed with him. . . . So the Ark floated with them on the waves (towering) like mountains. . . . Then the word went forth, "O earth! swallow up thy water, and O sky! withhold (thy rain)!" and the water abated, and the matter was ended. The Ark rested on Mount Judi, and the word went forth, "Away with those who do wrong!" Such are some of the stories of the unseen, which We have revealed unto thee, before this—neither thou nor thy people knew them. So persevere patiently, for the end (Day of Judgment) is for those who are righteous (11:25-49).

## THE ABRAHAMIC TRADITION

### Abraham

Ye People of the Book (Jews, Christians, and Muslims)! Why dispute ye about Abraham, when the Torah and the Gospel were not revealed until after him? Have ye no understanding? Ah! Ye are those who fell to disputing (even) in matters of which ye had some knowledge! But why dispute ye in matters of which ye have no knowledge? It is God who knows, and ye who know not! Abraham was not a Jew nor yet a Christian; but he was true in faith, and bowed his will to God's; and he was not of the idolaters (3:65-67).

Our messengers came to Abraham with glad tidings. They (greeted him) saying, "Peace!" He answered, "Peace!". . . And his wife, who was standing (there), laughed when We gave her glad tidings of (the coming birth) of Isaac, and after him, of Jacob. She said, "Alas for me! Shall I bear a child, seeing I am an old woman, and my husband here is an old man? That would indeed be a wonderful thing!" They said, "Dost thou wonder at God's decree? The grace of God and His blessings on you, O ye people of the house, for He is indeed worthy of all praise, full of all glory!" (11:69-73).

When a man came to the Prophet and addressed him as "best of all creatures," the Prophet responded saying, "That was Abraham" (hadith).

**Lot**

The thing I fear most for my people is what Lot's people did [in Sodom and Gomorrah][18] (hadith).

**Joseph**

Behold! Joseph said to his father, "O my father! I did see eleven stars and the sun and the moon—I saw them prostrate themselves to me!" Said (the father), "My (dear) little son! Relate not thy vision to thy brothers, lest they concoct a plot against thee, for Satan is to man an avowed enemy! Thus will thy Lord choose thee and teach thee the interpretation of stories (and events) and perfect His favor to thee and to the posterity of Jacob, even as He perfected it to thy fathers Abraham and Isaac aforetime—for God is full of knowledge and wisdom." Verily in Joseph and his brethren are signs (or symbols) for seekers (after truth). [The story is related of Joseph's betrayal by his brothers when he was sold into slavery in Egypt] . . . The man in Egypt who bought him, said to his wife, "Make his stay (among us) honorable; it may be he will bring us much good, or we shall adopt him as a son." Thus did We establish Joseph in the land, that We might teach him the interpretation of stories (and events). And God hath full power and control over His affairs; but most among mankind know it not. When Joseph attained his full manhood, We gave him power and knowledge; thus do We reward those who do right. . . . The king (of Egypt) said, "I do see (in a vision) seven fat cows, whom seven lean ones devour, and seven green ears of corn, and seven (others) withered. O ye chiefs, expound to me my vision if it be that ye can interpret visions." [The story is related of how Joseph was the only person to correctly predict the meaning of the king's dream] . . . So the king said, "Bring him (Joseph) unto me; I will take him specially to serve about my own person." Therefore when he had spoken to him, he said, "Be assured this day, thou art, before our own presence, with rank firmly established, and fidelity fully proved!"

[It is then told how Joseph was given control over all the storehouses in Egypt]. . . . Then came Joseph's brethren, they entered his presence, and he knew them, but they knew him not. [Then the story is related of Joseph's reconciliation with his brothers and his father]. . . . Then when they (Joseph's family) entered the presence of Joseph, he provided a home for his parents with himself, and said, "Enter ye Egypt (all) in safety if it please God." And he raised his parents

[18] Sodom and Gomorrah are the two ancient cities destroyed because of their wickedness. Cf. Genesis 18-19; Koran 15:51-77; and numerous hadith.

high on the throne (of dignity). . . . He said, "O my father! This is the fulfillment of my vision of old! God hath made it come true! [Then Joseph recounts various events and prays.] O Thou creator of the heavens and the earth! Thou art my protector in this world and in the hereafter. Take Thou my soul (at death) as one submitting to Thy will, and unite me with the righteous" (12:4-101).

When God's messenger was asked who among men was most honorable, he replied, "The one who is most honorable in God's estimation is the most pious." On being told that that was not what they meant, he said, "The most honorable was God's prophet Joseph, son of God's prophet Jacob, son of God's prophet Isaac, son of God's friend Abraham" (hadith).

## JUDAISM

### Moses and Aaron

We narrate unto thee some of the story of Moses and Pharaoh with truth, for folk who believe. Verily Pharaoh exalted himself in the earth and broke up its people into sections. A tribe among them he oppressed, killing their sons and sparing their women. Verily he was of those who work corruption. And We desired to show favor unto those who were oppressed in the earth, and to make them examples and to make them the inheritors. So We inspired the mother of Moses, saying, "Suckle him and, when thou fearest for him, then cast him into the river and fear not nor grieve. Verily We shall bring him back unto thee and shall make him (one) of Our messengers." And the family of Pharaoh took him up, that he might become for them an enemy and a sorrow. . . . And the wife of Pharaoh said, "(He will be) a consolation for me and for thee. Kill him not. Peradventure he may be of use to us, or we may choose him for a son." And they perceived not. But there came to be a void in the heart of the mother of Moses—she was going almost to disclose his (case), had We not strengthened her heart (with faith) so that she might remain a (firm) believer. And she said to the sister of (Moses), "Follow him"; so she (the sister) watched him in the character of a stranger. And they knew not. So We restored him to his mother that she might be comforted and not grieve, and that she might know that the promise of God is true; but most of them know not. When he reached full age and was firmly established (in life), We bestowed on him wisdom and knowledge, for thus do We reward those who do good. [The story is related of Moses slaying a wicked Egyptian who was fighting with a Jew, with the result that Moses had to flee for his life] . . . He therefore got away therefrom, looking about, in a state of fear. He prayed: "O my Lord! Save me from people given to wrongdoing." Then . . . he turned his face towards (the land of) Midian. . . . And when he arrived at the watering (place) in Midian, he found there a group of men watering (their flocks), and besides them he found two women who were keeping back (their flocks). He said, "What is the matter with you?" They said, "We cannot water (our flocks) until the shepherds take back (their flocks), and our father is a very old man." So he watered (their flocks) for them; then he turned back to the shade and said, "O my Lord! Truly am I in (desperate) need of any good that Thou dost send me!" Afterwards one of the (damsels) came (back) to him, walking bashfully. She said, "My father invites thee that he may reward thee for having watered (our flocks) for us." So when he came to him and narrated the story, he said, "Fear thou not, (well) hast thou escaped from unjust people.". . . He said, "I intend to wed one of these my daughters to thee, on condition that thou serve me for eight years; but if thou complete ten years, it will be (grace) from thee. But I intend not to place thee under a difficulty; thou wilt find me, indeed, if God wills, one of the righteous."... Now when Moses had fulfilled the term and was traveling with his family, he perceived a fire in the direction of Mount Sinai. He said to his family, "Tarry ye; I perceive a fire; I hope to bring you from there some information, or a burning firebrand, that ye may warm yourselves." But when he came to the (fire), a voice was heard from the right bank of the valley, from a tree in hallowed ground, "O Moses! Verily I am God, the Lord of the worlds.... Now do thou throw thy rod!" But when he saw it moving (of its own accord) as if it had been a snake, he turned back in retreat, and retraced not his steps. "O Moses! Draw near, and fear not, for thou art of those who are secure.... Those are the two credentials from thy Lord to Pharaoh and his chiefs, for truly they are a people rebellious and wicked." He said, "O my Lord! I have slain a man among them, and I fear lest they slay me. And my brother Aaron—he is more eloquent in speech than I, so send him with me as a helper, to confirm (and strengthen) me, for I fear that they may accuse me of falsehood." God said, "We will certainly strengthen thy arm through thy brother, and invest you both with authority, so they shall not be able to touch you; with Our sign shall ye triumph—you two as well as those who follow you." When Moses came to them with Our clear signs, they said, "This is nothing but fabricated sorcery, never did we hear the like among our fathers of old!" [The story is told of Pharaoh's refusal to accept the signs] ... So We seized him and his hosts, and We flung them into the sea. Now behold what was the end of those who did wrong! (28:3-40).

God's messenger (Muhammad) came to Medina and found the Jews observing the fast on the day of Ashura, so he asked them what was the significance of that day. They replied, "It is a great day on which God delivered Moses and his people and drowned Pharaoh and his people; so Moses observed it as a fast out of gratitude, and we do so also." The Prophet said, "We have as close a connection with Moses as you have," so God's messenger observed it as a fast himself and gave orders that it should be observed (hadith).

A man among the Muslims and a man among the Jews hated one another. The Muslim said, "By Him who chose Muhammad above the universe," and the Jew said, "By Him who chose Moses above the universe." Thereupon the Muslim raised his hand and struck the Jew on his face, and the Jew went to the Prophet and told him what had happened. The Prophet summoned the Muslim and confirmed the circumstance. The Prophet then said, "Do not make me superior to Moses, for mankind will fall down senseless on the Day of Resurrection and I shall fall down senseless along with them. I shall be the first to recover and shall see Moses seizing the side of the Throne; and I shall not know whether he was among those who fell senseless and had recovered before me, or whether he was among those of whom God had exempted from [this]"[19] (hadith).

Being given information is not like seeing. God Most High gave Moses information about what his people had done regarding the (golden) calf and he did not throw down the tablets; but when he saw what they did, he threw down the tablets and they were broken (hadith).

[19] Cf. Koran 39:68.

### David

When they advanced to meet Goliath[20] and his forces, they prayed:"Our Lord! Pour out constancy on us and make our steps firm; help us against those that reject faith." By God's will they routed them; and David slew Goliath; and God gave him power and wisdom and taught him whatever (else) He willed. And did not God check one set of people by means of another, the earth would indeed be full of mischief—but God is full of bounty to all the worlds (2:250-251).

We did bestow on some prophets more (and other) gifts than on others, and We gave to David the Psalms (17:55).

The prayer dearest to God is David's and the fasting dearest to God is David's. He would sleep half the night, get up to pray for a third of it, then sleep the remaining sixth; and he would fast on alternate days (hadith).

When God's messenger mentioned David and talked about him, he would say that, "David was, of men, the most devoted to worship" (hadith).

### Solomon

We indeed gave knowledge to David and Solomon, and they both said, "Praise be to God, who has favored us above many of His servants who believe!" And Solomon was David's heir. He said, "O ye people! We have been taught the speech of birds, and on us has been bestowed (abundance) of all things; this is indeed grace manifest (from God)." [The story of Solomon and the queen of Sheba is told]. . . And he (Solomon) diverted her (the queen of Sheba) from the worship of others besides God, for she was of a people that had no faith. She said, "My Lord! Verily I have wronged myself, and I surrender with Solomon unto God, the Lord of the worlds" (27:15-44).

### The Children of Israel

Because of the wrongdoing of the Jews We forbade them good things which were (before) made lawful unto them, and because of their much hindering from God's way, and of their taking usury when they were forbidden it, and of their devouring people's wealth by false pretences. We have prepared for those of them who disbelieve a painful doom. But those of them who are firm in knowledge and the believers (who) believe in that which is revealed unto thee (O Muhammad) and that which was revealed before thee—especially the diligent in prayer and those who pay the poor-due, the believers in God and the Last Day—upon these We shall bestow immense reward (4:160-162).

And verily we gave the Children of Israel the Scripture (Torah) and the Judgment, and prophethood, and provided them with good things and favored them above (all) peoples; and

[20] Goliath is the giant warrior of the Philistines whom David killed with a stone from a sling. Cf. I Samuel 17:48-51.

gave them plain commandments. And they differed not until after the knowledge came unto them, through rivalry among themselves. Verily thy Lord will judge between them on the Day of Judgment[21] concerning that wherein they used to differ (45:16-17).

## CHRISTIANITY

### The Virgin Mary

Behold! A woman of (the family of) Imran[22] said, "O my Lord! I do dedicate unto Thee what is in my womb for Thy special service, so accept this of me—for Thou hearest and knowest all things." When she was delivered, she said: "O my Lord! Behold! I am delivered of a female child! . . . I have named her Mary, and I commend her and her offspring to Thy protection from the Evil One, the rejected." Right graciously did her Lord accept her. He made her grow in purity and beauty. To the care of Zachariah (father of John the Baptist) was she assigned. Whenever Zachariah went in to her in the sanctuary, he found her provisioned. He said: "O Mary! Whence (comes) this to you?" She said, "From God, for God provides sustenance to whom He pleases without measure" (3:35-37).

And (remember) she who guarded her chastity, We breathed into her of Our Spirit, and We made her and her son a sign for all peoples (21:91).

And (remember) Mary, daughter of Imran, who guarded her virginity, so We breathed into her of Our Spirit, and she confirmed the Words of her Lord and His Books, and was one of the devout (66:12).

Many men have been perfect, but among women only Mary, the daughter of Imran, and Asiya, the wife of a Pharaoh (of Egypt),[23] were perfect (hadith).

Except Mary and her son (Jesus), no human being is born without the devil touching him, so that he raises his voice crying out because of the devil's touch (hadith).

### The Story of John the Baptist's Birth

(This is) a recital of the mercy of thy Lord to His servant Zachariah. Behold! He cried to his Lord in secret, praying, "O my Lord! Infirm indeed are my bones, and the hair of my head doth glisten with gray; but never am I unblest, O my Lord, in my calling upon Thee! I fear my kinsfolk after me, since my wife is barren. Oh, give me from Thy presence a successor. (One that) will (truly) represent me, and represent the posterity of Jacob; and make him, O my Lord! one with whom Thou art well pleased!" (His prayer was answered), "O Zachariah! We give thee good news of a son—his name shall be John; on none by that name have We conferred

[21] Various Koranic translators use the terms "Day of Judgment" and "Day of Resurrection" interchangeably to refer to what is commonly known to Christians as the Day of Judgment.

[22] Imran is the father of Mary, mother of Jesus.

[23] Asiya was the woman who saved Moses and raised him as a son.

distinction before." He said, "O my Lord! How shall I have a son, when my wife is barren and I have grown quite decrepit from old age?" God said, "So (it will be)."... (Zachariah) said, "O my Lord! Give me a sign." "Thy sign shall be that thou shalt speak to no man for three nights, although thou art not dumb." [The story of John the Baptist's birth and righteousness is related]. .. So peace on him the day he was born, the day that he dies, and the day that he will be raised up to life (again)! (19:2-15).

**The Story of Jesus' Life**

Behold! The angels said, "O Mary! God hath chosen thee and purified thee—chosen thee above the women of all nations. O Mary! Worship thy Lord devoutly, prostrate thyself, and bow down (in prayer) with those who bow down."... Behold! The angels said, "O Mary! God giveth thee glad tidings of a Word from Him: his name will be Messiah Jesus, the son of Mary, held in honor in this world and the hereafter and of (the company of) those nearest to God. He shall speak to the people in childhood and in maturity. And he shall be (of the company) of the righteous." She said, "O my Lord! How shall I have a son when no man hath touched me?" He said, "Even so. God createth what He willeth. When He hath decreed a plan, He but saith to it, 'Be,' and it is!" And He will teach him (Jesus) the Scripture and wisdom, and the Torah and the Gospel, and (appoint him) a messenger to the Children of Israel, (with this message), "I have come to you, with a sign from your Lord, in that I make for you out of clay, as it were, the figure of a bird, and breathe into it, and it becomes a bird by God's leave. And I heal those born blind, and the lepers, and I quicken the dead, by God's leave; and I declare to you what ye eat, and what ye store in your houses. Surely therein is a sign for you if ye did believe. (I have come to you), to attest the law which was before me and to make lawful to you part of what was (before) forbidden to you; I have come to you with a sign from your Lord. So fear God, and obey me."... When Jesus found unbelief on their part, he said, "Who will be my helpers to (the work of) God?" Said the disciples, "We are God's helpers. We believe in God, and do thou bear witness that we have surrendered (unto Him)...". (And remember) when God said, "O Jesus! Verily I am gathering thee and causing thee to ascend unto Me, and am cleansing thee of those who disbelieve and am setting those who follow thee above those who disbelieve until the Day of Judgment.[24] Then unto Me ye will (all) return, and I shall judge between you as to that wherein ye used to differ" (3:42-55).

They (who) rejected faith—they uttered against Mary a grave false charge. And they said (in boast), "We killed Messiah Jesus, the son of Mary, the messenger of God." But they killed him not, nor crucified him, but so it was made to appear to them; and those who differ therein are full of doubts, with no (certain) knowledge, but only conjecture to follow, for of a surety they killed him not. Nay, God raised him up unto Himself—God is exalted in power, wise—and there is none of the People of the Book but must believe in him (Jesus) before his (own) death; and on the Day of Judgment he will be a witness against them[25] (4:156-159).

[24] This passage clearly refers to the ascension of Jesus prior to the Day of Judgment: "God said, "O Jesus! Verily I am gathering thee and causing thee to ascend unto Me . . . until the Day of Judgment".

[25] The majority of Muslims interpret the phrase, "nor crucified him" to mean that the Jews did not crucify Jesus, ignoring the subsequent phrase, "but so it was made to appear to them," and the context provided by many other

Relate in the Book (the story of) Mary, when she withdrew from her family to a place in the east. She placed a screen (to screen herself) from them; then We sent her our angel, and he appeared before her as a man in all respects. . . . He said, "Nay, I am only a messenger from thy Lord, (to announce) to thee the gift of a holy son." She said, "How shall I have a son, seeing that no man has touched me, and I am not unchaste?" He said, "So (it will be). Thy Lord saith, 'That is easy for Me, and (We wish) to appoint him as a sign unto men and a mercy from Us.' It is a matter (so) decreed." So she conceived him, and she retired with him to a remote place. [The birth of Jesus is related]. . . She pointed to the babe. They said, "a child in the cradle?" He (Jesus) said, "I am indeed a servant of God, He hath given me revelation and made me a prophet. And He hath made me blessed wheresoever I be, and hath enjoined on me prayer and almsgiving as long as I live. . . . Peace on me the day I was born, and the day I die, and the day I shall be raised alive!"[26] Such (was) Jesus, the son of Mary. (It is) a statement of truth, about which they (vainly) dispute. It befitteth not (the majesty of) God that He should take unto Himself a son. Glory be to Him! When He determines a matter, He only says to it, "Be," and it is[27] (19:16-35).

### Jesus

Do not exaggerate in your religion nor utter anything concerning God save the truth. The Messiah, Jesus, son of Mary, was only a messenger of God, and His Word which He conveyed unto Mary, and a Spirit from Him. So believe in God and His messengers, and say not "Three"—cease! (It is) better for you!—God is only One God[28] (4:171).

They surely disbelieve who say, "Verily God is the Messiah, son of Mary." The Messiah (Jesus) said, "O Children of Israel, worship God, my Lord and your Lord. Verily whoso ascribeth partners unto God, for him God hath forbidden Paradise." They surely disbelieve who say, "Verily God is one of three in a Trinity," when there is no God save the One God. If they desist not from so saying, a painful doom will fall on those of them who disbelieve. . . . The Messiah, son of Mary, was no other than a messenger, messengers (the like of whom) had passed away before him, and his mother was a saintly woman—and they both used to eat (earthly) food. See how We make the revelations clear for them, and see how they are turned away! (5:72-75).

One day will God gather the messengers together, and ask, "What was the response ye received

Koranic verses. This issue is also discussed by Martin Lings in "Do the Religions Contradict One Another?" (*A Return to the Spirit: Questions and Answers* [Louisville, KY: Fons Vitae, 2005]) and by Frithjof Schuon in "The Sense of the Absolute in Religions" (*Gnosis: Divine Wisdom* [Bloomington, IN: World Wisdom, 2006]).

[26] Many interpret this statement by Jesus to refer to his resurrection: "Peace on me the day I was born, and the day I die, and the day I shall be raised alive!"

[27] See Reza Shah-Kazemi's article "Jesus in the Qur'an: Selfhood and Compassion—An Akbari Perspective" (*Sufism: Love and Wisdom*, edited by Jean-Louis Michon and Roger Gaetani [Bloomington, IN: World Wisdom, 2006]).

[28] Although the Koran and Hadith accept many basic tenets of Christianity, the Koran identifies the concept that God is one of three in a "Trinity" as an exaggeration. A fundamental principle in Islam is the unity of God, thus any idea that relativizes this primordial Unity is considered an exaggeration. Frithjof Schuon addresses this question in "The Sense of the Absolute in Religions" in *Gnosis: Divine Wisdom.*

(from men to your teaching)?" They will say, "We have no knowledge—it is Thou who knowest in full all that is hidden." Then will God say, "O Jesus, son of Mary! Recount My favor to thee and to thy mother. Behold! I strengthened thee with the Holy Spirit, so that thou didst speak to the people in childhood and in maturity. Behold! I taught thee the Scripture and wisdom, the Torah and the Gospel. And behold! Thou makest out of clay, as it were, the figure of a bird, by My leave, and thou breathest into it and it becometh a bird by My leave, and thou healest those born blind, and the lepers, by My leave. And behold! Thou bringest forth the dead by My leave."... And behold! God will say, "O Jesus, son of Mary! Didst thou say unto men, 'Worship me and my mother as gods in derogation of God'?" He (Jesus) will say, "Glory to Thee! Never could I say what I had no right (to say). Had I said such a thing, Thou wouldst indeed have known it. Thou knowest what is in my heart, though I know not what is in Thine. For Thou knowest in full all that is hidden" (5:109-116).

If anyone testifies that there is no god but God alone, who has no partner, that Muhammad is His servant and messenger, that Jesus is God's servant and messenger, the son of His handmaid, His Word which he cast into Mary and a Spirit from Him, and that Paradise and hell are real, then God will cause him to enter Paradise no matter what he has done (hadith).

All the descendants of Adam have their sides pierced by the devil with two of his fingers at birth, except the son of Mary (hadith).

**Christians**

And with those who say: "Lo! we are Christians," We made a covenant, but they have forgotten a portion of that which they were reminded of—so we estranged them, with enmity and hatred between the one and the other, till the Day of Resurrection; and God will assuredly tell them of the things they have done (5:14).

Thou wilt surely find that the nearest . . . in love to the believers (Muslims) are those who say, "We are Christians"; that is because there are priests and monks among them, and because they are not proud (5:82).

## "PEOPLE OF THE BOOK"

Of the People of the Book are a portion that stand (for the right). They rehearse the signs of God all night long, and they prostrate themselves in adoration. They believe in God and the Last Day; they enjoin what is right and forbid what is wrong; and they hasten (in emulation) in (all) good works. They are in the ranks of the righteous. Of the good that they do, nothing will be rejected of them—for God knoweth well those that do right (3:113-115).

If only the People of the Book would believe and ward off (evil), surely We should remit their sins from them and surely We should bring them into gardens of delight. If they had observed the Torah and the Gospel and that which was revealed unto them from their Lord, they would surely have been nourished from above them and from beneath their feet. Among them there are people who are moderate, but many of them are of evil conduct. . . . Say: O People of the

Book! Ye have naught (of guidance) until ye observe the Torah and the Gospel and that which was revealed unto you from your Lord." That which is revealed unto thee (Muhammad) from thy Lord is certain to increase the contumacy and disbelief of many of them. But grieve not for the disbelieving folk. Verily those who believe, and those who are Jews, and Sabians, and Christians—whosoever believeth in God and the Last Day and doeth right—there shall no fear come upon them, neither shall they grieve (5:65-69).

When the funeral bier of a Jew, a Christian, or a Muslim passes you, stand up for it. You are not standing for its sake, but for the angels who are accompanying it (hadith).

When the Prophet went to his bed he used to say, "O God, Lord of the heavens, Lord of the earth, Lord of everything, who splittest the grain and the kernel, who hast sent down the Torah, the inspired statements of Jesus (Gospel), and the Koran, I seek refuge in Thee from the evil of every evil agent whose forelock Thou seizest. Thou art the First and there is nothing before Thee; Thou art the Last and there is nothing after Thee; Thou art the Outward and there is nothing above Thee; Thou art the Inward and there is nothing below Thee" (hadith).

Does any of you imagine that God has prohibited only what is to be found in the Koran? By God, I have commanded, exhorted, and prohibited various matters as numerous as what is found in the Koran, or more numerous. God has not permitted you to enter the houses of the People of the Book (Jews and Christians) without permission; nor dishonor their women, nor eat their fruits, when they give you what is imposed on them (hadith).

## Appendix of Additional Koranic Verses

**Other Religions:** 2:2-4, 2:87, 2:106, 2:177, 2:213, 3:33, 3:81, 3:161, 3:179, 3:194, 4:41-42, 4:136, 6:34, 6:42-44, 6:39, 10:13, 11:100-108, 11:120, 12:109-111, 13:32, 14:4, 15:10-11, 16:43-44, 16:89, 19:58-60, 19:73-75, 21:7-9, 22:17, 22:42-53, 25:20, 25:35-39, 28:58-60, 30:47, 32:3, 33:7-8, 35:24-26, 37:108-139, 38:12-14, 39:23, 42:51, 43:6-8, 43:23-25, 50:12-14, 51:38-53, 58:21, 72:26-27, 87:17-19
**Adam:** 7:11-17
**Noah:** 10:71-74, 23:23-30, 40:5, 71:1-3
**Hud:** 11:50-59
**Salih:** 11:61-68, 14:5-13, 27:45-53
**Shuaib:** 11:84-95
**Abraham:** 2:124-127, 6:161, 14:35-41, 16:120-123, 19:41-50, 26:69-103, 29:23-29, 29:31, 43:26-29, 60:4, 89:6-13
**Lot:** 11:77-83, 15:51-77, 27:54-58
**Ishmael, Isaac, Jacob, Enoch, Elisha, Ezekiel, and Job:** 19:54-57, 21:83-86, 38:41-48
**Moses:** 2:47-67, 2:92-93, 5:20, 5:44, 7:103-170, 10:74-93, 19:51-53, 20:9-99, 21:48-49, 26:12-67,
27:7-14, 29:39-40, 32:23-25, 40:23-54, 41:45, 45:45-48, 46:12, 61:5, 62:5
**David:** 34:10, 38:17-26
**Solomon:** 21:81, 34:12, 38:30-40
**The Children of Israel:** 2:40-41, 3:93, 5:12, 26:192-199, 27:76-77, 44:31

**Jesus:** 2:253, 3:49, 3:59, 5:17, 5:46-48, 61:6, 61:14
**John the Baptist:** 3:38-41, 21:89-90
**People of the Book:** 2:62, 2:111-113, 3:2-5, 3:199, 4:47, 4:153-155

Become a "hanif", free from restrictions of sect.
Come into the monastery of Faith like a monk.

As long as your vision beholds traces of otherness,
Your being in a mosque is like being in a church.

If your veil of "otherness" is lifted away,
The monastery's form will become a mosque.

It does not matter what state you're in,
Oppose your inverted self and find deliverance.

Idol and belt, Christian and church bell
Are all symbols of rejecting fame and good name.

If you want to become one of the Special Servants,
Become prepared for sincerity and ethical behavior.

Go and pull yourself from the way of selfishness;
At every moment renew your faith in selflessness.

Since our hidden selves are the real infidels,
Don't be satisfied with an outer worship of Islam.

With every new moment turn to refresh your faith,
Be a Muslim, be a Muslim, yes, be a Muslim!

*Mahmūd Shabistarī*

# The God Conditioned by Belief

## *Emir ʻAbd al-Qādir al-Jazāʼirī*

> *Say: we believe in that which has been revealed to us and in that which has been revealed to you: your God and our God are one God, and we surrender* (muslimūn) *to Him.*
>
> (Koran 29:46)

What we are going to say comes from subtle allusion (*ishāra*) and not from exegesis (*tafsīr*) properly speaking.[1]

God commands Muhammadans to say to all the communities who belong to the "People of the Book"—Christians, Jews, Sabeans, and others, "We believe in that which was revealed to us" that is in that which epiphanizes itself to us, namely the God exempt from all limitation, transcendent in His very immanence, and, even more, transcendent in His very transcendence, who, in all that, still remains immanent; "and in that which was revealed to you"—that is, in that which epiphanizes itself to you in conditioned, immanent, and limited forms. It is He whom His theophanies manifest to you as to us. The diverse terms which express the "descent" or the "coming" of the revelation[2] do not designate anything other than the manifestations (*ẓuhūrāt*) or the theophanies (*tajalliyāt*) of the Essence, of His work or of one or another of His attributes. Allah is not "above" anything, which would imply that it is necessary to "climb" towards Him. The divine Essence, His word, and His attributes are not localizable in one particular direction from which they would "descend" towards us.

The "descent" and other terms of this type have no meaning except in relation to the one who receives the theophany and to his spiritual rank. It is this rank which justifies the expression "descent" or other analogous expressions. For the rank of the creature is low and inferior while that of God is elevated and sublime. If it were not for that, there would be no question of descending or "making [the Revelation] descend," and one would not speak of "climbing" or "ascending"; "lowering" or "approaching."

It is the passive form [in which the real subject of the action expressed by the verb remains hidden] that is used in this verse, since the theophany in question here is produced starting from the degree which integrates all the divine Names.[3] Originating from this degree, the only Names

[1] [Editor's Note: all the footnoted text below is by Michael Chodkiewicz, editor of *The Spiritual Writings of Amir ʻAbd al-Kader.*] The distinction between showing the "subtle allusions" (*ishārāt*) and commentary properly speaking (*tafsīr*) is often affirmed by Ibn ʻArabī. In the chapter of the *Futūḥāt* specifically devoted to the *ishārāt* (*Futūḥāt al-makiyya*, vol. 1, p. 278), Ibn ʻArabī emphasizes the fact that spiritual men do not designate as *tafsīr* the interpretation they "see in themselves" (*mā yarawnahu fī nufūsihim*). This not only corresponds to a difference in nature between two modes of intellection, but it also serves as a measure of prudence to avoid controversies with the "literalists" (*ṣāḥib al-rusūm*).

[2] The Arabic text gives the terms *nuzūl, inzāl, tanzīl, ītaʼ* which, although they have certain differences of meaning, are often used interchangeably to designate the "descent" of the Revelation.

[3] This degree is that of the Name *Allāh* insofar as it applies to the *ulūhiyya*, the "function of divinity" (and not insofar as it applies to the divine Essence, which is "anterior" to the distinction of the Names).

which epiphanize themselves are the name of the divinity (the name Allāh), the name *al-Rabb* (the Lord) and the name *al-Raḥmān* (the All-Merciful). [Among the scriptural evidence for the preceding] Allāh has said: "And your Lord will come" (Koran 89:22) and, similarly, one finds in a prophetic tradition: "Our Lord descends. . .".[4] Allāh has further said, "Only if Allāh comes" (Koran 2:210), etc. It is impossible for one of the divine degrees to epiphanize itself with the totality of the Names which it encloses. He perpetually manifests certain of them and hides others. Understand!

Our God and the God of all communities contrary to ours are in truth and reality one unique God, in conformity to what He has said in numerous verses, "Your God is one unique God" (Koran 2:163; 16:22; etc.). He also said, "There is no God but Allāh" (*wa mā min ilāhin illa Llāhu*, Koran 3:62). This is so in spite of the diversity of His theophanies, their absolute or limited character, their transcendence or immanence, and the variety of His manifestations. He has manifested Himself to Muhammadans beyond all form while at the same time manifesting Himself in every form, without that involving incarnation, union, or mixture. To the Christians He has manifested Himself in the person of Christ and the monks, as He said in the Book.[5] To the Jews, He has manifested Himself in the form of 'Uzayr [Ezra] and the Rabbis. To the Mazdeans He has manifested Himself in the form of fire, and to the dualists in the form of light and darkness. And He has manifested Himself to each person who worships some particular thing—rock, tree, or animal—in the form of that thing, for no one who worships a finite thing worships it for the thing itself. What he worships is the epiphany in that form of the attributes of the true God—May He be exalted!—this epiphany representing, for each form, the divine aspect which properly corresponds to it. But [beyond this diversity of theophanic forms], He whom all of these worshippers worship is One, and their fault consists only in the fact that they restrict themselves in a limiting way [by adhering exclusively to one particular theophany].

Our God, as well as the God of the Christians, the Jews, the Sabeans, and all the diverging sects, is One, just as He has taught us. But He has manifested Himself to us through a different theophany than that by which He manifested Himself in His revelation to the Christians, to the Jews, and to the other sects. Even beyond that, He manifested Himself to the Muhammadan community itself by multiple and diverse theophanies, which explains why this community in its turn contains as many as seventy-three different sects.[6] Indeed, within each of these it

4 The *ḥadīth* evoked here is that, reported in most of the canonical collections (for example, Bukhārī, *tawhīd*, 35, *da'awāt*, 13, etc.) according to which: "Each night, Our Lord descends to the heaven of this lower world, where He remains only during the last third of the night and says: 'Is there someone who invokes Me, that I may respond to him? Is there someone who addresses a prayer to Me, that I may answer it? Is there someone who asks Me for pardon, that I may pardon him?'"

5 This phrase alludes to verse 31 of Sura 9 where it is said of the Christians: "They have taken their doctors and their monks, along with Jesus, son of Mary, as Lords alongside of Allāh." For 'Abd al-Qādir, the "error" of the Christians is relative and not absolute. It does not consist in the fact of recognizing the created beings as manifestations of the divine Names, but in the reductive identification of God with one or another of His theophanies. The same remark is valid in reference to the Jews, envisaged in the following phrases, where the reference is to the Koran 9:30 ["And the Jews say: Ezra is the son of Allāh"]. This interpretation of "infidelity" (*kufr*) is analogous to that which Ibn 'Arabī gives in the *Fuṣūṣ al-ḥikam* with respect to Jesus (vol. 1, p. 141) where he says that the error of the Christians does not reside in the affirmation that "Jesus is God" nor that "He is the son of Mary," but in the fact of "enclosing" (*taḍmin*) the vivifying power of God in the human person of Jesus.

6 According to a *ḥadīth* (Ibn Ḥanbal, 3, 145) the Muhammadan community is divided into 71 or 73 sects.

would be necessary to distinguish still other sects, themselves varying and divergent, as anyone who is familiar with theology can confirm. Now, all of that results only from the diversity of theophanies, which is a function of the multiplicity of those to whom they are destined and to the diversity of their essential predispositions. In spite of this diversity, He who epiphanizes Himself is One, without changing, from the eternity without beginning to the eternity without end. But He reveals Himself to every being endowed with intelligence according to the measure of his intelligence. "And Allāh embraces all things, and He is All-Knowing" (Koran 2:115).

Thus the religions are in fact unanimous regarding the object of worship—this worship being co-natural to all creatures, even if few of them are conscious of it—at least insofar as it is unconditioned, but not when it is considered in relation to the diversity of its determinations. But we, as Muslims, as He has prescribed, are subject to the universal God and believe in Him. Those who are destined for punishment are so destined only because they worship Him in a particular sensible form to the exclusion of any other. The only ones who will understand the significance of what we have said are the elite of the Muhammadan community, to the exclusion of the other communities.[7] There is not a single being in the world—be he one of those who are called "naturalists," "materialists" or otherwise—who is truly an atheist. If his words make you think to the contrary, it is your way of interpreting them which is flawed. Infidelity (*kufr*) does not exist in the universe, except in a relative way. If you are capable of understanding, you will see that there is a subtle point here, which is that someone who does not know God with this veritable knowledge in reality worships only a lord conditioned by the beliefs which he holds concerning him, a lord who can only reveal himself to him in the form of his belief. But the veritable Worshipped is beyond all of the "lords"!

All this is part of the secrets which it is proper to conceal from those who are not of our way. Beware! He who divulges this must be counted among the tempters of the servants of God. No fault can be imputed to the doctors of the law if they accuse him of being an infidel or a heretic whose repentance cannot be accepted. "And God says the Truth, and it is He who leads on the straight way" (Koran 33:4).

*Translated by a team under the direction of*
*James Chrestensen and Tom Manning*

[7] This remark should be understood as follows: just as the Prophet Muḥammad is the "Seal of Prophethood," to whom "the knowledge of the first and the last" was given, so his community—in the person of its spiritual elite—inherits, by reason of its function at the end of the human cycle, the privilege of recapitulating, and thus validating, all the modes of knowledge of God corresponding to the specific perspectives of previous revelations.

# The Shaykh Ahmad al-'Alawī and the Universalism of the Qur'ān: A Presentation and Translation of His Commentary on Verse 2:62

*Tayeb Chouiref*

## Introductory Study

The Shaykh Ahmad al-'Alawī (1869-1934) was one of the greatest spiritual masters of Islam in the 20th century. During his life, his personal radiation was immense, not only in Algeria and within the Arab world but also well-beyond, for some among his hundred thousand disciples resided in Europe and others in South-East Asia.

His intellectual radiation was no less considerable: besides the works he published on Sufism,[1] he founded a newspaper, *al-Balāgh al-jazā'irī*, where he dealt at times with spiritual matters, and at other times with social matters, always from a strictly traditional perspective.[2]

Among the Islamic sciences, the Shaykh al-'Alawī had a particular affinity with Qur'ānic exegesis. Evoking his relationship with the Qur'ān, he says of himself in a poem:

> It [The Qur'ān] hath taken up its dwelling in our hearts and on our tongues and is mingled with our blood and our flesh and our bones and all that is in us.[3]

This inner relationship with the Qur'ān led him to compose a commentary in which he could communicate to the reader a part of what his "spiritual opening" allowed him to grasp of the divine Word. He entitled his commentary—unfortunately unfinished—*al-Bahr al-masjūr*,[4] a Qur'ānic expression that may be rendered as "the boiling ocean." This commentary distinguishes itself from classical works in that it approaches each verse in four steps: the Commentary (*tafsīr*) in which he explains the meaning of the words and sheds light on the circumstances of the revelation (*asbāb al-nuzūl*); the Deduction (*istinbāt*) where he expounds the rules and principles that may be drawn from the verse; the Spiritual Allusion (*ishāra*) that allows him to enunciate spiritual truths which appear to be far removed from the literal text; and, finally, the Language of the Spirit (*lisān al-Rūh*) where he provides insights into Sufi metaphysical doctrine.

The passage of the *Bahr al-masjūr* which we have translated below, and which we introduce here, is a commentary upon verse 2:62:

> Lo! Those who believe, and those who are Jews, and Christians, and Sabaeans—whoever believeth in Allah and the Last Day and doeth right—surely their reward

[1] See the list of his works as edited and commented on by Martin Lings in *A Sufi Saint in the Twentieth Century: Shaikh Ahmad al-Alawi, His Spiritual Heritage and Legacy* (Cambridge: The Islamic Texts Society, 1993), p. 230.

[2] A large number of thee articles were included in two volumes: *al-Balāgh al-jazā'irī* (Mustaghānim, 1986).

[3] Quoted by Martin Lings in *Sufi Saint*, p. 23.

[4] *al-Bahr al-masjūr fī tafsīr al-Qur'ān bi-mahd al-nūr*, 2 vols. (Mustaghānim, 1995).

is with their Lord, and there shall no fear come upon them neither shall they grieve.[5]

This verse that the Shaykh al-'Alawī characterizes as enigmatic (*lughz*) enunciates clearly the universal perspective of the Qur'ān. It must, however, be noted that the universalism of the Book, as well as that of the Prophet, was harmed by the historical evolution of the Muslim community: political stakes, theological controversies, the social impact of the Crusades, etc. contributed greatly to the withdrawal of the universalist spirit in Islamic lands. To this must be added the complex evolution and the often ill supported extension of the theory of abrogation. In what follows, we will thus briefly remind our reader of the essential points of this theory in order better to bring to light the theological stakes that lie at the core of the Shaykh's argumentation in his commentary.

Although the Prophet expressly affirmed the right of Christians and of Jews to practice their respective religions in Islamic lands, theologians developed the theory of abrogation (*naskh*) according to which the Qur'ānic revelation supersedes all other religions. Historically, the phenomenon of abrogation pertains, in Islam, to the very process of the revelation of the Qur'ān. Certain verses were, in fact, replaced by others, thereby losing all legal import. It is in such a way that verse 2:240, stipulating that the period of abstinence (*'idda*) of a widow must last one year, is abrogated by verse 234 of the same surah which reduces this period to four months and ten days. One of the reasons that led theologians to affirm the abrogation of the previous revealed Laws is the Qur'ānic affirmation according to which the Jews and the Christians have altered their Scriptures (*tahrīf*). The Qur'ān reproaches them, for example, for having eliminated the announcement of the coming of the prophet Muhammad.[6]

The diversity of the positions of theologians concerning the abrogation by Islam of the other Abrahamic religions can be summarized by four theses:[7]

1. The Law of Muhammad abrogates all others.
2. The Law of Abraham is still valid with the exception of what in it has been abrogated by the Law of Muhammad.
3. With the same exception, the Law of Moses is still valid in addition to Abraham's.
4. With again the same exception, the Law of Jesus is still valid in addition to Abraham's.

Those who hold the three last theses base themselves on the verses inviting Muslims to follow the "guidance" that certain ancient prophets received (Qur'ān, 6:90 and 16:123).

However, the thesis of abrogation raises quasi-insoluble theoretical problems: When does the Qur'ānic Revelation abrogate the other Laws? From the moment of the first revelation in the Cave of Hira? At the time of the Hegira? Upon the death of the Prophet? At which precise moment does a Jewish or Christian believer cease to practice a religion accepted by Heaven?

[5] All English translations of the Qur'ān appearing in this article are taken from Mohammed Marmaduke Pickthall's classic *The Meaning of the Glorious Koran.*

[6] See verse 4:46.

[7] We draw this summary from Eric Chaumont's article "Abrogation", in *Dictionnaire du Coran*, ed. Mohammad Ali Amir-Moezzi (Paris: Robert Laffont, 2007), pp. 14-17.

Why would a believer be rejected by God for an event of which he may be totally unaware? For theologians seeking not to attribute to God an utter lack of mercy the only tenable position is that of the "transmission of the message" (*tablīgh*): the religion of the Christian and the Jew ceases to be valid from the moment when he receives the message of Islam. This position allows one to prolong the validity of these religions well beyond the life of the Prophet, but it poses other problems: What should one understand by "transmission of the message"? Does knowledge of the existence of Islam necessarily mean that one has received and understood its message?

Thus, the theory of the abrogation of previous religions by Islam, as useful as it may be for the social cohesion of the Muslim community, is hardly satisfying from the point of view of spiritual coherence and the legitimate needs of thought. This theory seems more rooted in the development of a *contra errores infidelium* apologetics than it is the fruit of a literal reading of the sacred texts of Islam.

Moreover, Ibn Hazm (d. 1063), one of the most important representatives of the "literalist" school of jurisprudence (*madhhab zāhirī*), gives this recommendation:

> Put your trust in the pious man, even if he does not share your religion, and distrust the impious, even if he belongs to your religion.[8]

It is not surprising, therefore, that it was above all the mystics who insisted on the universalist dimension of the Qur'ānic message. They seem in this closer to the positions of the Prophet than were the theologians. In fact, far from announcing to them the abrogation of their religion, the Prophet invited a delegation of Christians from Najrān to perform their rites within the very walls of the mosque of Medina, something which greatly surprised certain of the Companions.[9] Concerning the attitude of a Muslim faced with what may disconcert him in other religions, the Prophet recommends a pious suspension of judgment: "Do not say that what is related by the people of the Book is true, do not say either that it is false, but say: 'We believe in Allah and that which is revealed unto us and that which was revealed unto Abraham and Ishmael and Isaac and Jacob and the tribes, and that which was vouchsafed unto Moses and Jesus and the prophets from their Lord. We make no distinction between any of them, and unto Him we have surrendered.'"[10] These words of the Prophet seem to guard the common believer against two opposite pitfalls: syncretism and peremptory rejection. Nevertheless, this *hadīth* of the Prophet undeniably establishes a certain "right" to religious exclusivism. Exclusivism is not simply a sign of human limitation, for it also results from the divine origin of a religion:

> In normal times a man's religion is *the* religion, and in fact each religion addresses itself to a humanity which, for it, is humanity as such. The exclusivism of a religion is a symbol of its divine origin, of the fact that it comes from the Absolute,

[8] Quoted by Eric Geoffroy in *Initiation au soufisme* (Paris: Fayard, 2003), p. 273.

[9] Concerning this event, see Martin Lings, *Muhammad: His Life Based on the Earliest Sources* (Cambridge: Islamic Texts Society, 1995), p. 326.

[10] *Hadīth* transmitted by Abū Hurayra and validated by Bukhārī; and quoting the Qur'ān verse 3:84.

of its being in itself a total way of life.[11]

It is through the initiatic development and the opening of the "eye of the heart" that the Sufis will seek to avoid the two previously mentioned pitfalls:

> Because it is concerned with the inner meaning (*ma'nā*) through the penetration of the outward form (*nām*), Sufism is by nature qualified to delve into the mysterious unity that underlies the diversity of religious forms."[12]

Ibrāhīm Ibn Adham (d. 777), a mystic belonging to the era of the Predecessors (*salaf*), did not hesitate to acknowledge that he had a Christian monk among his spiritual masters:

> I received gnosis (*ma'rifa*) through the teaching of a monk named Father Symeon.[13]

What do the first mystical commentaries of the Qur'ān say about the verse of interest to us here? 'Abd al-Karīm al-Qushayrī (d. 1072), author of the famous Risāla, comments upon it thus:

> The divergence of ways, since they derive from the same Principle (*asl*), does not endanger the obtainment of divine Acceptance. Whoever believes in the words of the Real—may He be Exalted—concerning what they teach on His Nature and His Attributes will receive divine Satisfaction (*Ridwān Allāh*), whatever be the divine Name that he may invoke and the sacred Law that he may follow.[14]

A few centuries later, Ismā'īl Haqqī (d. 1724), in his mystical commentary of the Qur'ān entitled Rūh al-bayān, will justify the universalism of his commentary on verse 2: 62 by an allusion to the immutable Religion that he calls the "Religion of Truth" (*al-Dīn al-Haqq*):

> Know that the beauty of the Religion of Truth is present in all souls: what leads away from it is nothing other than human limitations (*āfāt bashariyya*) and blind imitation (*taqlīd*). In fact, every man is born in accordance with the primordial nature (*fitra*) as the Prophet has said, peace and blessing be upon him. . . . According to Ibn al-Malik, one must understand by "primordial nature" the "Yes" that every man, before coming into this world, answered to God's question: "Am I not your Lord?" Every man has, therefore, affirmed his faith in God following a direct contemplation of the Real.[15]

[11] Seyyed Hossein Nasr, *Sufi Essays* (Albany, NY: SUNY, 1973), p. 175.

[12] Ibid., p. 123.

[13] Concerning his teaching see Tayeb Chouiref, *Les Enseignements spirituels du Prophète* (Lille: Editions Tasnīm, 2008), vol. I, p. 183.

[14] *Latā'if al-ishārāt* (Dār al-kutub al-'ilmiyya), vol. I, p. 50.

[15] *Rūh al-Bayān* (Dār al-fikr), vol. I, p. 153.

The forgetfulness or rejection of the universalist spirit of Islam leads to what Ibn 'Arabī (d. 1240) called the withdrawal into the worship of "the god created by beliefs." In this connection, he offers the following recommendation:

> Beware not to bind yourself to a particular belief by denying others, for you would lose a great good; and what is more, the true nature of things would[16] inevitably elude you! Let your soul be the substance of all beliefs, for Allāh the Most-High is too vast and too immense to be enclosed in one belief to the exclusion of others.[17]

Moreover, Ibn 'Arabī underlines that the people of the Book are shown to be integrated and protected under the Muslim Law by the per capita tax called *jizya*, thereby demonstrating what Michel Chodkiewicz terms a "derived validity."[18]

Sufi masters have sometimes accepted that non-Muslims, attracted by the aura of their sanctity, may benefit from their teachings. The great mystical poet Jalāl al-Dīn Rūmī (d. 1273) evidenced a great openness in this domain. He himself relates the following anecdote:

> I was speaking one day amongst a group of people, and a party of non-Muslims were present. In the middle of my address they began to weep and to register emotion and ecstasy.
>
> Somebody asked: What do they understand and what do they know? Only one Muslim in a thousand understands this kind of talk. What did they understand, that they should weep?
>
> I answered: . . . After all, everyone acknowledges that He is the Creator and the One who provides for everything, that He is the Master of all, that to Him all things shall return, that it is He who punishes and forgives. When anyone hears these words, which are a description and a remembrance of God, a universal commotion and ecstatic passion supervenes, for the fragrance of their Beloved emanates from these words.[19]

For his part, the Shaykh al-'Alawī always showed a keen interest in all religions, and we know that he particularly appreciated the Gospel of John.

Expressing himself in Algeria, where Muslims were suffering greatly from French colonization, the Shaykh had to be careful in his formulations concerning his approach to other religions, and particularly so with respect to Christianity. Indeed, for the Algerian movements of reformist Islam (*islāh*),[20] any universalist perspective was nothing but a disguised form of a willingness to collaborate with the enemy. The Shaykh's prudence, however, does not exclude clarity: the translation of the following commentary is one more proof of the religious universality of the Shaykh and one of the expressions of his profound understanding of the Qur'ān.

16 *al-'ilm bi-l-amr 'alā mā huwa 'alayhi.*

17 *Fusūs al-hikam*, p. 113.

18 See Michel Chodkiewicz, *Le Sceau des saints* (Paris: Gallimard, 1986), p. 101.

19 Quoted by Seyyed Hossein Nasr in *Sufi Essays*, p. 149. We have slightly modified the translation of Rūmī's text.

20 On the relationships of the Shaykh with these movements see Martin Lings, *Sufi Saint*, pp. 114-116.

## Translation[21]

### Qur'ān (2:62)

> Lo! Those who believe, and those who are Jews, and Christians, and Sabaeans—whoever believeth in Allah and the Last Day and doeth right—surely their reward is with their Lord, and there shall no fear come upon them neither shall they grieve. (Qur'ān 2:62)

### Commentary (*tafsīr*):

Whoever meditates on the Qur'ān realizes that God is more merciful toward the servant than the latter could be toward himself. Thus God, after having struck the sons of Israel with deafness as a punishment for their unfaithfulness, describes these men in all of their perversity. But He then shows Himself under His Attribute of Mercy, for this prevails over His Wrath.[22] Henceforth the sons of Israel were encompassed in this Mercy and placed among the number of those who have faith among other traditional communities: there is no greater sweetness than that! . . .

### Deduction (*istinbāt*):

We can draw three deductions from this verse:

— The traditional communities (*firaq*)[23]—including Islam—are, in themselves, equal since they form the object, in this verse, of a single enumeration.
— A man having faith in what is taught by Islam could be considered as belonging to the people of the Book, even if he does not accomplish the pious actions that must, in principle, accompany his faith. This will not be the case if his actions are contrary to his faith.
— The Sabaeans possess a sacred Law since they are mentioned among the traditional communities who possess one.

### Spiritual Allusion (*ishāra*):

The fact of mentioning side-by-side the different traditional communities while not distinguishing Muslim believers from other believers must lead us to consider no one, be he a Muslim or an infidel (*kāfir*), pious or sinful, as being inferior to us, and this throughout our entire life. In fact, our destiny is unknown to us and it is our state at the moment of death that matters: such is the lot of all mankind.

### Language of the Spirit (*lisān al-Rūh*):

Thus I have understood from this enigmatic verse that all aforementioned traditional commu-

[21] See *al-Bahr al-masjūr*, vol. I, pp. 145-148.

[22] Allusion to a famous *hadīth*: "Indeed, God Most-High wrote for Himself, when He created the world: 'Indeed, My Mercy prevails over My Wrath'" (quoted by Tirmidhī).

[23] The term refers here to revealed religions and therefore to those which possess a holy Scripture.

nities possess a genuine validity in Religion (*makāna fī l-Dīn*). One may draw from the order of the enumeration a certain preeminence of the first over the last, but it remains nonetheless that a traditional community will always be of an incomparably higher rank than pagan cults.

*Translated by Patrick Laude and Joseph Fitzgerald*

Earnest for truth, I thought on the religions (*tafakkartu fī al-adyān*):
They are, I found, one root with many a branch.
Therefore impose on no man a religion,
Lest it should bar him from the firm-set root.
Let the root claim him, a root wherein all heights
And meanings are made clear, for him to grasp.

*Mansūr al-Hallāj*

# Religion Is One in Its Essence: The Spiritual Teaching of Tierno Bokar[1]

*Amadou Hampaté Bâ*

Tierno rebelled against the idea that any being could be excluded from God's love. He scorned the distinctions made by those "attached to the letter" and chose to ignore those who make this love the privilege of only orthodox believers.

For my own part, I could not understand how only Muslims could be the beneficiaries of the mercy of God. I reflected on the smallness of their number in relation to the whole of humanity, both in time and in space, and I said to myself: "How could God, in front of a mound of seeds, take only one handful of these seeds and reject all the others, saying: 'Only these are my favorites'?"

I had often heard around me, especially from certain marabouts, that non-Muslims were *kuffār* (infidels) and that they would go to hell. This angered me, as if I myself had been one of those unhappy infidels. So one day I took advantage of a class to ask him about this subject that was troubling me:

### Does God Love Infidels?

"Tierno, you always speak of God's love which embraces everything. But does God also love infidels?" He answered:

> God is Love and Power. The creation of beings comes from His love and not from some constraint. To detest that which is the result of the Divine Will acting through love, is to take a position against the Divine Will and dispute His wisdom. To imagine the exclusion of a being from primordial Love is proof of fundamental ignorance. Life and perfection are contained in Divine Love, which manifests Itself in a radiating Force, in the Creative Word that brings the living Void to life.[2] From this living Void, He makes forms appear that He divides into kingdoms.
>
> May our love not be centered upon ourselves! May this love not incite us to love only those who are like us or to espouse ideas that are similar to our own! To only love that which resembles us is to love oneself; this is not how to love.
>
> Being a man, the infidel cannot be excluded from the Divine love. Why should he be excluded from ours? He occupies the rank which God has assigned to him. The act of a man debasing himself can bring about a punishment for him, but without thereby provoking an exclusion from the Source from which he came.

[1] Editor's Note: The following selections are from Amadou Hampaté Bâ, *A Spirit of Tolerance: The Inspiring Life of Tierno Bokar*, edited by Roger Gaetani (Bloomington, IN: World Wisdom, 2008), pp. 122-134. Bâ was a student and disciple of the Malian Sufi master, Tierno Bokar, who become known as "the sage of Bandiagara," the town in Mali where he lived for most of his life. The editor's notes below are all by Roger Gaetani.

[2] Tierno compared this living Void, pure potentiality, to the mathematical notion of zero, the starting point containing the seed of all numbers that emerge from it. He does not mean here "nothingness," but rather "non-manifested."

> It is necessary to reflect upon the legend of Korah and Moses.[3] Korah was the most perverse of beings. He had received his share of the finest riches that a man can enjoy on earth. From these, he had made a paradise for himself, access to which, he said, was forbidden to Moses and to his God. Moses asked God to chasten Korah.
>
> God replied, "I have entrusted the earth to you. Act as you see fit."
>
> The Prophet Moses then addressed Korah, "O infidel! Mend your ways and return to your Lord, otherwise you shall receive a punishment that will be cited as an example."
>
> "Call upon me all the misfortunes you want, I fear nothing," replied Korah.
>
> So Moses ordered that the earth swallow up Korah and all of his possessions. Korah, ensnared by his feet and unable to loosen the hold, understood that he was lost. He repented and asked Moses to forgive him.
>
> "You believed yourself to be stronger than God," Moses replied to him. "You have rejected the Eternal, and me, His Messenger. Now you are defeated and your riches are no more. The earth will swallow you up slowly; you shall be subjected to this punishment until the end of time."
>
> It was thus that Moses excluded the infidel from God's love. He caused him to perish after having pronounced his judgment, and he expected the approval of the Almighty. But the ways of God are impenetrable and the Lord reproached him severely, saying, "O Moses! Korah called upon you seventy times in repentance and you remained deaf to his plea. If he had called upon Me but one time, I would have saved him."
>
> Moses was confused. God added, "Do you know why you did not have compassion for Korah? It is because to you he is neither your son, nor a being that you have created."[4]
>
> This intentional juxtaposition of "son" with "created being" clearly shows us that God, Who has not engendered and Who was not engendered,[5] has for those He created the same love that a father has for his children. He was generous to the children of Adam, without differentiating amongst their states.

In this regard, Tierno told us about a major event in the life of Shaykh Ahmad al-Tijani when he was living in Morocco, where he benefited from the protection of the Sultan. During a public talk, a troublemaker who wanted to embarrass him asked him a trick question. He asked, "Does God love infidels?"

Basing his response on commentaries of the Koran, the Shaykh dared to answer, "Yes, God loves infidels." This was an unexpected answer at that time. There was a great outcry. Indignant, the audience left the room. Only eleven faithful disciples remained around the Shaykh,

[3] Editor's Note: This story of Korah (called Qarun in the Koran) is constructed of elements from the Koran, which mentions him very briefly, the Old Testament, and other legends whose source we do not know.

[4] Editor's Note: Whereas, for God, even one as wicked as Korah is still considered as a "son" and one of His created beings.

[5] An allusion to a phrase in the Koran 112:3.

those very ones who later would see the birth of the Tijani order.

Marcel Cardaire, himself a fervent Catholic, had been touched by the attitude of openness and love that radiated from the teachings of Tierno Bokar. Let us allow him to speak:

> The first lesson that the "brothers in God" learnt was a lesson of religious tolerance.
>
> In the small rooms of Tierno's disciples, the teaching that was described to us took on new dimensions according to the rhythm of the seasons. It became true nourishment. In this country of simple technologies, we heard simple sentences fall from simple lips. The words penetrated better than if they had been pronounced in one of those temples or mosques that give homage more to the prowess or refinement of man than to the majesty of the Creator. And moreover, these words that we have collected in no way resemble what one hears in other places of worship. These were words in their pure state, words spoken not to exalt man, neither speaker nor listener, but rather truly animating words, spoken with such sincere feeling for the other as to cause God to live in the heart of the unbeliever, to vivify his faith, and to give a meaning to the lives of everyone.
>
> In these small rooms we heard maxims that we would have liked to see engraved in golden letters on the portals of all the places of worship in the world. What religious university, what al-Azhar, could match the Sage of Bandiagara?[6]

Among those who came to listen to Tierno, not all were from the Tijani order. One day several Qadiri, members of the Qadiriyya brotherhood, one of the most ancient orders in Islam, came to listen to his classes. When the time came to carry out the great *dhikr* (the common chanting of the Name of God) one student asked Tierno, "Are those who are not Tijani going to take part in the *dhikr*?"

"Make the *dhikr* without worrying about them," he replied. "If some of them want to participate, you have no right to forbid them. And if they prefer to leave, you have no right to restrain them."

The *dhikr* took place, in the presence of numerous Qadiri. When it had finished, Tierno spoke:

### The Rainbow

> The rainbow owes its beauty to the variety of its shades and colors. In the same way, we consider the voices of various believers that rise up from all parts of the earth as a symphony of praises addressing God, Who alone can be Unique. We bitterly deplore the scorn that certain religious people heap on the form of divine things, a scorn that often leads them to reject their neighbor's hymn because it contrasts with theirs. To fight against this tendency, brother in God, whatever be the religion or the congregation to which you are affiliated, meditate at length on this verse:

[6] *Tierno Bokar, le Sage de Bandiagara*, p. 80.

"The creation of the heavens and the earth, and the diversity of your languages and of your colors are many wonders[7] for those who reflect" (Koran 30:22).

There is something here for everyone to meditate upon.

During a certain period, American Protestant missionaries had come to the Soudan. They liked to preach in the areas where the Catholic Church had not been able to establish itself. Because Bandiagara was one of these places, the head of this Protestant mission arrived one day in the town, set himself up on the market square, and began to speak of God in the Bambara language.

Astonished, or at least amused to hear a foreign pastor express himself thus in their language, large numbers of curious people surrounded him. When he started to speak of God with warmth and strength, and above all when he translated the psalms of David into Bambara, people were moved. Muslims are always moved by Biblical language, especially when it is translated into their tongue. But there were a few bigots in the audience who took offense to the scene and who tried to turn the crowd away crying, "It's a Christian! It's a Christian!"

One of Tierno's students had been present at the scene. When he arrived in class, he reported these facts to us, exulting in a malicious way what had happened to the pastor. "Today," he said, "a pastor wanted to talk to us about God. But we made so much fun of him that he was obliged to leave."

Tierno was revolted by this behavior. Wanting to put his students on guard against disrespectful behavior towards men who spoke in the name of God, he launched an out-and-out call for tolerance on that day:

**Children of the Same Father**

> Are children of the same father, although physically different from one another, any less brothers and legitimate sons of he who fathered them? In accordance with this law-truth, we pity those who deny believers from different confessions a spiritual identity and brotherhood under one single God, the unique and immutable Creator.
>
> Although it may not please those attached to the letter,[8] for us one thing alone counts above all others: to profess the existence of God and His unity. So, brother in God who comes to the threshold of our *zāwiya*, which is a center of love and charity, do not harass the follower of Moses. God Himself witnesses that He has said to His people, "Implore God for assistance, and be patient. The earth belongs to God and He bequeaths it to whom He will among His servants. A blissful end

[7] The Arabic word *aya* signifies at once "marvel," "miracle," "sign," and "verse." If the revealed verses are "signs" of God, in an inverse manner one can also say that all the "marvels" that exist in creation are also "signs," therefore another mode of divine Revelation. According to this perspective, everything is Revelation. It is we who do not know how to read.

[8] Editor's Note: That is, to outward forms, as in "the letter of the law." The exoteric form of a religion will necessarily exclude other possible forms, but here Tierno is suggesting that the central tenet of Islam, God's unity, implies for those with the virtues of love and charity that they must expand these virtues to encompass other children of God, through that very principle of God's unity, which encompasses all.

will be for those who fear Him" (Koran 7:128).

Neither should you harass the follower of Jesus. God, in speaking of the miraculous child of Mary, the Virgin Mother, said, "We granted to Jesus, son of Mary, the gift of miracles and We comforted him through the Holy Spirit" (Koran 2:253).[9]

And the other human beings? Let them enter, and even greet them in a brotherly way in honor of that which they have inherited from Adam, of whom God has said, addressing the angels, "When I have perfected him and breathed into him of My Spirit, then fall down before him prostrate as a sign of your veneration" (Koran 38:72)._

This verse implies that every descendant of Adam is the repository of a particle of the Spirit of God. How would we therefore dare to scorn a receptacle that contains a particle of God's Spirit?

Moreover, Tierno often said:

> You who come to us and whom we esteem, not as a student, but as a brother, reflect! Meditate on this verse from the Book of Guidance:
>
> "There is no compulsion in religion. The Truth distinguishes itself from error. He who rejects false deities in order to believe in God has grasped a handhold that is firm, unbreakable. And God is All-hearing, All-knowing" (Koran 2:256).

**Relations with Other Religions**

"Tierno," I asked him one day, "is it good to converse with people of another faith to exchange ideas and better understand their god?" He answered:

> Why not? I will tell you: one must speak with foreigners if you can remain polite and courteous. You will gain enormously by knowing about the various forms of religion. Believe me, each one of these forms, however strange it may seem to you, contains that which can strengthen your own faith. Certainly, faith, like fire, must be maintained by means of an appropriate fuel in order for it to blaze up. Otherwise, it will dim and decrease in intensity and volume and turn into embers and then from embers to coals and from coals to ashes.
>
> To believe that one's race or one's religion is the only possessor of the truth is an error. This could not be. Indeed, in its nature, faith is like air. Like air, it is indispensable for human life and one could not find one man who does not believe truly and sincerely in something. Human nature is such that it is incapable of not believing in something, whether that is God or Satan, power or wealth, or good or bad luck.
>
> So, when a man believes in God, he is our brother. Treat him as such and do not be like those who have gone astray. Unless one has the certitude of possess-

[9] Editor's Note: This Koranic passage is usually translated as: "We gave Jesus, the son of Mary, clear signs [or 'proofs'], and strengthened [or 'confirmed,' or 'supported'] him with the Holy Spirit."

> ing all knowledge in its entirety, it is necessary to guard oneself against opposing the truth. Certain truths only seem to be beyond our acceptance because, quite simply, our knowledge has not had access to them."

He added:

> Avoid confrontations. When something in some religion or belief shocks you, instead seek to understand it. Perhaps God will come to your aid and will enlighten you about what seems strange to you. . .

Not only would Tierno Bokar not prohibit his students from interacting with believers of other faiths, but he also considered this practice an actual therapy for the soul. He asked people to make the necessary mental effort and to struggle against what is holding them back so as to better understand.

Along these same lines, one day he told us about a vision he had had:

> In my mind, I saw a gigantic man lying on his back. People of various religions and faiths were bustling about him. Some were speaking into his ear, others were opening his mouth, others were making him breathe in various perfumes, others were applying an eyewash, etc.
>
> "What is this that I am seeing, who is this man?" I cried out to myself.
>
> A voice answered me, "This is the blessed man who reminds himself of the Unity of God and of the brotherhood that should unite His worshipers, wherever they may come from. He is receiving, as you see, all the teachings. The result is better for him. He is porous, like sand. God gave him the power to conserve and to assimilate."

He added:

> The religious teaching given by a Prophet or by an authentic spiritual master is like pure water. One can absorb it without danger to one's spiritual or moral health. Such a teaching will be intelligible and of a superior order. Like clear water, it will contain nothing that can change it by modifying its flavor, its odor, or its color. It will mature the mind and purify the heart because it does not contain any external pollutant that could have the effect of obfuscating the soul or hardening the heart. We cannot overemphasize the benefits of studying the teachings of revealed religions. They are, for everyone, like potable water. We advise, however, that they be assimilated slowly, and to avoid murky theology that is likely to contain a spiritual Guinea worm.[10] The saying goes, "When you are sweating, do not

[10] Guinea worm, also called in French "filaire de Medine" (*dracunculus medinensis*). The larvae live in stagnant water. They implant themselves into humans, live in subcutaneous cellular tissues, and develop particularly in the legs, where they appear as enormous abscesses which in fact are made up of the implantation of the female and the accumulation of microfilaria. Upon the slightest contact with water, the sore opens and the female releases the mass of microscopic worms which renew the cycle.

> take in cold water." We recommend that "When your soul is in mystical fervor, do not read anything."

He constantly tried to inculcate into us the spirit of tolerance and make us understand that it was only the intrinsic spiritual quality of a man that mattered:

> Our planet is neither the largest nor the smallest of all those that our Lord has created. Those who inhabit it can therefore not escape this law: we should not believe ourselves to be superior, nor inferior, to other beings in the universe, whatever they be.
>
> The best of created beings amongst us will be those who live in Love and Charity and in respect for their neighbor. Upright and radiant, they will be like a sun that rises and that goes straight up towards the sky.

**Religion is One in Its Essence**

One can see that for Tierno Bokar there existed but one eternal Religion, unalterable in its fundamental principles but varying in its forms of expression and corresponding to the conditions of time and place of each Revelation. This primordial Religion was, for him, comparable to a trunk from which the known historical religions branch off like the branches of a tree.

It was this eternal Religion which was taught by all the great Messengers of God and which was molded to serve the necessities of each epoch. Too often, however, most people had only understood or retained the outward forms, in the name of which they entered into conflict with each other.

This concept is in conformity with the teachings of the Koran itself, which emphasizes the unity of the divine Revelation throughout time:

> Say ye: We believe in God and that which has been revealed unto us and that which was revealed unto Abraham and Ishmael and Isaac and Jacob and unto the tribes; and that which was given unto Moses and Jesus; and unto that which was given unto the Prophets from their Lord. We show no preference between any of them, and unto God we submit ourselves (Koran 2:136).[11]

> Lo! Those who believe, those who practice Judaism, those who are Christians or Sabaeans, those who believe in God and the Last Day, those who do right—these are the ones who will find their reward beside their Lord. They will know no fear, nor will they grieve (Koran 2:62).

> Set your face to the pure Religion, the religion of the *fitra* (original primordial nature) through/for which God created mankind. There is no changing God's creation. That is the immutable religion, but most men know not (Koran 30:30).

[11] Editor's Note: The final sentence of this verse is usually translated as "We make no distinction [or, 'difference'] between any of them, and unto Him we surrender."

> O Messengers of God. . . . This your religion (*dīn*) is One. I am your Lord, fear Me (Koran 23:51-52).[12]

Tierno elaborated on this:

> That which varies in the diverse forms of Religion—for there can only be one Religion—are the individual contributions of human beings interpreting the letter with the laudable aim of placing religion within the reach of the men of their time.
>
> As for the source of religion itself, it is a pure and purifying spark that never varies in time or space, a spark which God breathes into the spirit of man at the same time as He bestows speech upon him.
>
> Contrary to what usually happens, one should therefore not be surprised to find spiritual riches in someone from a people considered as backward, but one should instead be troubled at not finding them in civilized individuals who have long worked on developing their material lives. . . .
>
> In its Essence, Faith is one, whatever the religion that conveys it might be. But in its manifestations, it presents, as we have seen, three fundamental states: solid, liquid, and gaseous. Faith is the essence of religion, which can then be seen as an atmosphere surrounding a universe populated with three categories of men: the believing masses, preachers blinded by parochialism, and finally initiates who have found God and worship Him in truth and in silence.

*Translated by Fatima Jane Casewit*

[12] Editor's Note: Other translations would render this section of the two verses as "O Messengers of God. . . . This your community [or 'nation' or 'brotherhood') is One and I am your Lord, therefore fear [or 'keep your duty unto'] Me." The Arabic word *umma* can imply all these meanings of "religion," "nation," "community," or "brotherhood."

# An Interview on Islam and Inter-religious Dialogue

## *Seyyed Hossein Nasr*

***What do you see as the main challenges to religions today?***

The main challenges are first of all the creation by and for modern man of a world that is based on the forgetting of God, a world that man has made and removed from virgin nature by means of a technology that is based on the quantification of the natural world, and therefore creation of spaces, of forms, in which people live every day and of sounds that they hear that are all cut off from the Divine Origin of things. Such a world therefore makes the reality of religion in a sense alien or unreal in everyday life, especially for those who live in urban environments, completely cut off from the world of nature, where the realities of religion are manifested in every natural form for those who can see. This element is complemented by the domination over the modern and now post-modern world of the modernistic paradigm (to which also the post-modern world really belongs), that is, a worldview in which at best God is a deistic God, originator of things but now far away. And at worst, of course, His reality is denied completely.

The challenge to religion is a worldview in which everything is envisaged within a closed material universe independent of transcendence, you might say, that is, the presentation of the view of a universe that is expected to explain everything and encompass everything within and by itself without opening unto transcendence. There is much to say about this matter philosophically that I cannot go into now, but let me just say that the paradigm, worldview or *Weltanschauung* as the Germans say, that was forged in Europe during the Renaissance and in the seventeenth century, and which became crystallized during the Age of Enlightenment, especially in France, this worldview clearly holds enmity *vis-à-vis* all authentic religions, because it is based on the self-sufficiency of the material, physical world. It does not see and therefore refutes the ontological dependence of the world in which we live upon the Divine Principle. And even if it accepts the Divine Principle, that Principle and its ontological independence are considered to be secondary and more or less irrelevant to man's everyday life. It is not accidental that Europe has produced the largest number of atheists as far as we know of any continent of the world, at least during the last three centuries. It is difficult to give an exact account, you might say, of what was going on in the loss of religious faith and the rise of agnosticism as far as quantitative estimates are concerned at the end of the late Egyptian civilization and later developments of the Greek and Roman civilizations in the Mediterranean world, and to count heads. But certainly since the establishment of the modernist outlook, this has been the case.

***What are the main contemporary opportunities, in your view, for religions to have their voice heard and their relevance recognized?***

The most important opportunity that has arisen for religion in the modern world during the last century, including not only the West but also its spread into other parts of the globe, is the cracks that have appeared in the veneer of this modernistic worldview—that is, the gradual crumbling of the way of looking at things which itself has prevented people over several centuries in the West and a century or two in many other parts of the world from taking religion seriously. The idols of the new pantheon of atheism and agnosticism have to a large extent been broken. Of course we now see this virulent response of a new blatant atheism that has grown up in the last two or three decades in England and America. But that is, I think, more than anything else a kind of death-cry. It is not that serious; it is not going to last. The earth is now shaking under the feet of people who thought they stood on the earth without any need of Heaven. Therefore, many heads are now turning upward toward the sky. And this is a natural human response. This breaking of the idols of the new "age of ignorance" provides, I think, the most important opportunity for religion to remanifest itself.

There is also a second important opportunity, and that is the following: traditionally, each religion was a world unto itself. And when it talked about "the world," it meant *its* world. And its world was, for its followers, *the* world. When it talked about "humanity," it meant really its own followers. That is understandable and has been in fact throughout history the norm. There were exceptions, as when Islam and Hinduism met in Kashmir, or someplace like that, or Islam and Christianity and Judaism in Iberia; but by and large, that was the rule. Today that boundary has been broken to some extent. There are two forces that have penetrated into the previously homogenous space of various religions—first occurring in the West, but now it is also occurring more and more elsewhere. The first is the forces of secularism, rationalism, materialism, and the like: the whole atheistic, agnostic worldview. And the second is other religions. There now are two "others." And the second "other," which is other religions, can help to a great extent overcome the lethal effect of the first "other," that is, it provides the opportunity for a particular religion to find an ally in other religions of the world, speaking different languages, having different forms, different symbols, but nevertheless, confirming a spiritual view of existence. This is a very important opportunity in the world in which we live. It is in a deep sense a dispensation from God to compensate for the withering effect of the spirituality-denying worldview that has surrounded modern human beings for the last four centuries or five centuries in the West, and is now doing so more and more in other continents.

***Do you perceive dangers in contemporary religious pluralism?***

I do not believe there is any danger at all if this religious pluralism is understood in the metaphysical sense based on the doctrine that there is the Absolute, a single Divine Principle (whether considered objectively or subjectively) upon which all authentic religions are based. There is nothing pluralistic about this doctrine; there is nothing relative about it. There is one Divine Principle that manifests Itself in different religious universes through which there is created religious pluralism. You have differences of religious forms, of sacred forms, of theologies and languages, and so forth. These are, however, elements that contribute to the plenitude of the garden of religion rather than simply relativizing religion.

The danger comes from the idea that has already been mentioned by Karl Marx and other opponents of religion, the idea that since there is more than one religion, all religions must be false. Seen in this way, religious pluralism has been taken as proof that there is nothing absolute in a particular religion and that all religious truth claims are therefore relative. I believe that one of the great achievements in the twentieth century in the field of religion has been the very explicit and succinct formulation of the doctrine of the transcendent unity of religions made by Frithjof Schuon, and with another language by René Guénon, as well as by many others since those great figures appeared. I must also mention here Ananda Coomaraswamy who wrote many notable works about this truth. These remarkable figures wrote mostly in the mid- and late twentieth century. Since then, as a result of their achievement, we can turn the presence of more than one religion in our sight, in our experience—that is, what we call "religious pluralism"—into a very positive element, and avoid the danger faced by people who equate pluralism with relativism. That is the danger that existed from the eighteenth century onward in the West, and it was made use of a great deal by opponents of religion to combat the claims of a particular religion, in this case primarily Christianity, to the truth.

***When considering the disconcerting diversity of religious faiths among religions that range from monotheism to non-theistic and polytheistic, what can we see as common grounds?***

What we can see as common grounds are many—much more than one would think. First of all, between theism and non-theism: what is common between them is, you might say, the *Urgrund*, the Supreme Ground of Being, the absolute Divine Reality, which might be seen only in an objective manner, or in a subjective manner, as in Buddhism. But in any case, as far as religions such as Taoism, Buddhism, or Confucianism are concerned, and from another perspective in *Advaita Vedānta*, they do not speak of the personal aspect of the Divine. In such traditions there is no *theos* in the usual sense that the Abrahamic religions and many schools of Hinduism understand the Divine Reality. Nevertheless, there is the absolute Divine Reality, the Source of all reality, the Source of Being, and so forth. I have no difficulty myself, whatsoever, in finding this common ground between the monotheistic and non-theistic expressions of metaphysics at the heart of various traditional religions.

As for polytheists, there must be a distinction made between religions that speak of the gods but remain fully grounded in the doctrine of Unity (such as Hinduism) and the practice of polytheism based on the loss of the vision of Divine Unity, a kind of decadence that has taken place over and over again in human history, as we see in the ancient Babylonian religions. And once that occurs, of course, there is no longer any common ground between monotheism or non-theism and polytheism. It is important to emphasize that polytheism in the Hindu sense must not be confused with this latter form of polytheism. Hinduism is based on the manifestation of one single Divine Principle in multifarious forms, which we in Islam do not accept to be legitimate in physical form, albeit one can say that the Divine Names in Islam are realities of different aspects of Divinity but not in physical forms, whereas in Hinduism, especially in its popular dimension, these realities are envisaged in the physical forms of the gods. That is where the difference comes from. Nevertheless, polytheism of the Hindu kind is based on a single Divine Reality, and that single Divine Reality would be the common ground between monotheism, which denies any possibility of any *theos* other than the Divine Reality in Itself, and what we call "polytheism" in its non-decadent form.

Putting this metaphysical question aside, there is no doubt that in all authentic religions, whatever form they have externally, there is also a common ground as far as many ethical and aesthetic teachings are concerned, attitudes towards good and evil, towards nature, towards a vision of a spiritual reality that transcends the material, the possibility of spiritual wayfaring, spiritual realization, the sense of the sacred and many, many other elements which are remarkable when seen in their deeper similarities, cutting across the theological distinctions of monotheism, non-theism, and polytheism.

***How would you define the main goals of religion, or religions? Is it possible to define commonalities in this respect?***

This question is somewhat ambiguous, but I think I understand to what it is alluding. You can talk about *religion*, and you can talk about *religions*. This is also a modern problem. If in the thirteenth century in Paris you talked about *religion*, that meant most likely Christianity, and you did not speak about *religions*. Today it becomes more and more difficult to speak about religion without also considering other religions, and therefore having to speak in the plural. But it is still possible. For many ordinary believers in a more insulated Christian, Muslim, Jewish, or Hindu community, it is still possible to speak about religion, and be speaking about the particular religion of those people without having to direct attention or make references to other religions. This becomes more and more difficult to the degree that that insularity is removed. And in both cases, whether you speak of religion or religions, there are many common goals including the ultimate goal of human life, whether seen as salvation or deliverance that one finds in the teachings of religions as different as Mahāyāna Buddhism and Kabbalistic Judaism.

There is also another issue that is involved here. In teaching *religion* in modern institutions of learning in the West today, and now more and more in other places where modernism has spread, it is very difficult not to also speak about *religions* and to ignore other religions. One can teach about religion in two different ways: one is to speak about religion in general as a whole field of human experience, or experience of the Divine and of Divine manifestations, and elements common to religions. Let us say, you can teach that religious people have a firm belief in God's Will acting in their lives. Now, that sentence pertains to Jews, Muslims, and Christians but it would have a different meaning in, let us say, Buddhism. So, when you talk about *religion*, you talk about an element which is common in different religions but with different meanings and applications. The second is to teach about religion as *my* or *our* religion as they do in seminaries. In this case you can also be exclusivist and say, "This is the *only* authentic religion worthy of study." And that is where, of course, the problem for the world in which we live comes in. This exclusivist view is, however, being challenged more and more these days because you do have other religions and you can hardly deny that they *are* also religions if you want to be intellectually honest. And I believe that the teaching of religion in academic settings—not in churches and synagogues and mosques and temples, but in academic settings—will have to deal more and more with *religions* as well as *religion* as such rather than just "*my*" or "*our*" religion. Let us hope that also more and more the teaching of religion in Western academic settings will be done from the point of view of religion itself rather than a non-religious or anti-religious perspective as we find so often today in the West.

***What do you see as the specific function of Islam and Muslims in interreligious dialogue?***

My view of the specific function of Islam and Muslims is not the same as some of my co-religionists who are not aware of the specific function that Islam has in interreligious dialogue. I believe that Islam is the final religion for the present humanity: the final plenary revelation. Finality always implies integration. That is why the Quran is perhaps the most religiously universalist, and least exclusive, of all sacred scriptures. It keeps talking about other *religions* all the time. And even the definition of "faith" is *īmān bi'Llāh*, "faith in God," "His *books*" and "His *messengers*," and not in the singular, *book* and *messenger*. So to accept other prophets, other sacred scriptures, is part and parcel of Islam's definition of itself. This is extremely significant and also providential. I believe that Muslims have a providential role to play in bringing out the significance of interreligious dialogue, of accepting the books, prophets, and messengers of God who preceded Islam, whether they be Christian, or Jew, or anybody else. The 124,000 prophets mentioned in *ahādīth* are also *our* prophets and messengers.

Islam also provides the universalist, metaphysical knowledge or worldview which makes this acceptance possible. It is not by any means accidental that in the twentieth century the great expositions of the universality of revelation, which we see in the writings of traditional authors, came for the most part from an Islamic background, not completely, to be sure, for some also came from a Hindu background. Most of the great recent expositors of the doctrine of the universality of religion, however, have belonged to the Islamic tradition, starting with Guénon himself, who although he began with the exposition of Hindu doctrines—and there already he speaks of the universality of revelation—lived the last part of his life in Cairo as a Muslim and died as a Muslim. And this is not at all, by any means, accidental. But there are many Muslims today who do not understand this particular function of Islam to which Schuon has alluded in some of his writings. It is for scholars, for those who do understand, to make this matter better known in Islamic circles. One certainly does not become any less of a Muslim by taking the Quranic message of universality seriously, when over and over again the Quran asserts that "A messenger has been sent to every people" and other verses with the same message. The Quran states that God could have created us all as a single nation, but He decided to create us as different people with different paths to God so that we could vie with each other in wisdom. A faithful Muslim cannot just admire that message asserted repeatedly in the Quran without taking it to heart. Those like myself, who take this aspect of the Quran very seriously, do not believe that we are in any way betraying Islam, to put it mildly, by remaining so faithful to the teachings of the Quran on this crucial matter.

***What would you say to Muslims who are reticent toward interreligious dialogue?***

What I say here concerns a large body of Muslims, who have in fact increased in number in recent times because of outside pressures which have threatened the very fabric of Muslim life and made them more exclusivist in self defense. When a creature is threatened from the outside, it usually withdraws unto itself. I believe that a century ago, ordinary Muslims praying together in mosques were a lot more universalist than their grandchildren. My advice to Muslims today is to become more aware of this reality and study more the Islam practiced by their traditional ancestors. Despite the rise of exclusivism, there are, nevertheless, today many faithful people in the Islamic world who are becoming aware of the importance of interreligious dialogue, including a number of formal religious scholars (*'ulamā'*) such as muftis, theologians, and the like. When you see the King of Saudi Arabia, a country that in its Islamic interpretation of things is Wahhābī, which is the most exclusive and closed towards other religions of all the schools of Islamic thought, calling for interreligious dialogue, you understand that this is really a very deep need of the Islamic world.

What I would furthermore say to Muslims who are reticent toward interreligious dialogue is as follows: this is really what is called in Arabic *fard kifāyah*, that is, it is obligatory for the community as a whole, but not for a particular person, not like the daily prayers that are obligatory for each individual, *fard 'ayn*. The carrying out of religious dialogue today is like the study of the science of *Hadīth* that is obligatory for the Islamic community as a whole, but is not incumbent upon every individual. In the same way interreligious dialogue is not incumbent upon every individual. Some people do not understand it; some people are not comfortable with it. Fine. *Allāh ta'āla* does not expect it of everyone. And in the case of those people, what I would say to them is that they should leave judgment of other religions in the Hands of God, and not try to prejudge with their incomplete knowledge what God will ultimately judge. They should have the attitude of not being aggressively against other religions and interreligious dialogue, because they themselves do not feel comfortable dealing with other religions. They should follow Islam with sincerity and surrender to God and leave judging other religions in His Hands. As the Quran says, *lakum dīnukum walī dīn*, that is, "to you, your religion, and to me, my religion." As for other groups of people who have the capability to participate meaningfully in dialogue, who can be enticed, or even transformed, you might say, by interreligious dialogue, one should make them understand first of all why interreligious dialogue is so important, why it concerns the very survival of religion in the future, why, if their children begin to go to a modern university, whether in the Islamic world or in the West, interreligious dialogue is the best guarantee that they will remain interested in religion itself, and will not simply turn away from it altogether. There are many other issues of this kind that can be explained. There are many arguments that have to be made.

And also in this domain there is need for courage. People who are devoted to interreligious dialogue must have the courage to withstand the criticisms that will be made of them. I have experienced that many times in my own life and I speak from experience here. One has to have the courage to stand one's ground, to be honest, to be sincere, and to remain devout, so that interreligious dialogue does not dilute one's own devotion to one's own faith. This is what many people in the Islamic world fear, as do also many in the Christian and Jewish worlds. There are many Orthodox Jews who refuse to have dialogue; there are many Catholics and Protestants who refuse to have dialogue. It is not unique to Muslims. This is one of the consequences that they all fear. It is very important therefore that those who carry out interreligious dialogue do so religiously, and not simply as secular scholars in a university, so that they can demonstrate to their coreligionists that they have not become any less pious, whether they are Muslims or otherwise, because of carrying out interreligious dialogue and talking to followers of other faiths in order to gain deeper knowledge of and empathy for the other.

***What are the main obstacles to interreligious engagement in the Muslim world and in the West?***

In the Islamic world, the main obstacles are not only theological but also political because in some Muslim countries these kinds of dialogues are usually guarded over carefully by political authorities, and certain types are encouraged, while certain kinds are discouraged. And there are also the obstacles coming from what are usually called "fundamentalist" groups—I do not like this term—but anyway from exclusivist groups, people who are strongly bound to only the external, exterior, exoteric teachings, forms and aspects of their religion without looking at the inward, the spiritual, the esoteric where real understanding of the other is to be found. They put an obstacle before interreligious engagement in many parts of the Islamic world, as you can see, in fact even discouraging individuals from such activities. You see that in Egypt, and in a country very different from Egypt, in Saudi Arabia, you see it in Pakistan as well as you see it in Iran at least in certain cases; you see it all over the Islamic world.

But such opposition is not the same everywhere. There are many Islamic countries in which there are not insurmountable obstacles out there in the social and political order. Rather, the obstacles come from within, and from the fact that, until now, most Muslims have not felt the need for interreligious engagement. Let us not forget the Muslim experience of the Ottoman-style system in which you had Christians and Jews living in peace in the community with their own laws and yet interacting with the Muslim majority. Of course that is a different kind of engagement with the "other" than what we are talking about now, when there is also the need of an interreligious dialogue that must be based on discussing theological issues and penetrating to some extent into the intellectual and spiritual world of the other side. But the historical memory of such a situation remains and makes many Muslims feel that the presence of other religions is nothing new and therefore there is no need for interreligious dialogue on their part. It is true that this had not been necessary in traditional times, with certain exceptions noted already, but it is now becoming more and more necessary. In many places such historical experiences whose memory survives are among the main obstacles. But there is also the fact that some people *feel* that there is an obstacle coming often from a kind of inertia or lack of need of dialogue resulting from the earlier history of their family or their town, or people whom they knew, or the intellectual history that they follow. There are even some people who feel that religious dialogue is part of the Christian agenda with which Muslims need not be concerned. I repeat, I do not believe that serious and profound interreligious dialogue is meant to be carried out by every follower of Islam or other religions. Such an assertion would be absurd. The important thing is to cultivate a sense of respect of the other on the basis of the teachings of those who can provide keys for the understanding of the other, people who because of their virtue and knowledge of their own tradition as well as of other religions can be a respected and trustworthy voice within their own community.

As for the West, the obstacles there are very different. In the West, there is no direct political obstacle to interreligious dialogue or engagement. Or perhaps one should say, to be sure, that there is no political obstacle except in some fundamentalist circles in America. There are some religious constraints with a political dimension within certain Christian communities which would correspond to certain exclusivist groups in the Islamic world—some Protestant fundamentalists, or certain Catholic groups who are very strongly opposed to interreligious dialogue with other religions, especially Islam, but even Judaism. Also within Judaism, there are many Orthodox and very serious Jewish groups who are opposed to dialogue but, by and large, there is no political opposition to serious dialogue in the West. The much more subtle obstacle that exists in the West is that there has developed this century-old school or discipline of the study of religion and religions, what the Germans called *Religionswissenschaft*, based on a non-religious or even anti-religious and secularist study of religion. This academic approach to the study of religion is based on historicism or a phenomenology that pays no attention to the noumena, to the inner reality of things. It has dominated religious studies in the West and especially in universities in recent times. That is why many of the interreligious dialogues that have been carried out have also been combined with a dilution or rejection of the traditional formulations of various religions. This is a very serious obstacle because it will end ultimately in either this kind of least-common-denominator idea of the goal of religious dialogue which is so much around us today, or even in the dissolution of the idea of the sacred, which is at the heart, of course, of all religions. Of course, the least common denominator approach to religion is not the fruit of the academic study of religion alone. In fact, many academic studies have criticized the emotional pseudo-universalism seen in certain circles, but the academic study of religion has certainly played an important role in the destruction of the sense of the sacred in religions and their dilution as faith systems, therefore making it possible by certain people to argue for a least common denominator "world religion."

***Modern men tend to look at the past in a somewhat stereotyped way, as ages of exclusiveness and intolerance, while there are actually historical precedents for interreligious engagement from which we may learn.***

Not only are there lessons or historical precedents from which we can learn, but I would say that, in fact, if we look at the world as a whole in older days there was a great deal less exclusivism and intolerance than there is today, if you consider the amount of knowledge that people had of the "other." While this may not have been true of much of Western Christianity, it is certainly true of the Islamic world, which is located in the middle of globe, and in which there was a lot more knowledge of Christianity and Judaism on the one hand, and Hinduism and Buddhism on the other hand, with Zoroastrianism and Manichaeism in the middle, than one finds in the pre-modern West of other religions. Even today, I think a simple villager near the city of Shiraz in Iran has more knowledge and awareness of other religions than many people do in certain parts of the United States. I have seen that from experience. So yes, there is certainly a very unfortunate stereotyping of ages gone by.

But in addition to that, we have some remarkable instances of the deepest kind of interreligious engagement before modern times which can serve as models for us. Let me just mention a few cases. The first—let us start from the West—is the case of Andalusia. In the Iberian Peninsula—but especially Andalusia, where Christians, Jews, and Muslims lived side by side—there were a lot of interactions, too many to enumerate, but that world produced, on the one hand, a figure such as Muhyī al-Dīn ibn 'Arabī, who is one of the greatest expositors of the metaphysics of religious diversity, especially in his book *Fusūs al-Hikam, The Bezels of Wisdom.* And on the other hand, it led to the rise of a person such as St. John of the Cross on the Christian side, who although a Christian saint, was deeply influenced by Sufi poetry. We can see that truth as we study more fully his relation to Islam.

Then we have in the Ottoman world many instances of this harmonious engagement of religions, at least the Abrahamic ones. In Iran it has been the same way with Zoroastrianism being added to the list of minority religions living in an Islamic community. Between Iran and the Turkish world we have the figure of Jalāl al-Dīn Rūmī, who lived most of his life, of course, before the Ottoman Empire was established, in what later became the heart of the Ottoman world, that is, Anatolia. In the writings of Jalāl al-Dīn Rūmī we have some of the greatest and most beautiful expositions of what Schuon called the "transcendent unity of religions," the doctrine that all authentic religions come from God, that their differences are based on differences of perspective and the formal order and that each religion issues from and focuses upon that one Divine Reality on which all authentic religions are based. In fact, the whole Sufi literature and tradition, going back to Hallāj, and especially Persian Sufi literature, are impregnated by the doctrine of the Oneness of the Origin of all religions and are full of references to this transcendent unity, from Bābā Tāhir 'Uryān to Sanā'ī to Jalāl al-Dīn Rūmī to many other later figures, all of whom speak of the unity of the essence of religions and diversity of religious forms.

Then there is the example of India where we see numerous meetings between Sufis and Hindu yogis and pandits and their interreligious discourses. It was in India where some four centuries ago there took place a major event, the translation of the *Upanishads* from Sanskrit into Persian, which finally brought this text through Anquetil-Duperron to Europe when he translated the Persian text into Latin and presented it to Napoleon in 1804, and from there the *Upanishads* became well known in Europe. There are many instances like that which have not even been fully studied. I find in my humble study of both the philosophical and Sufi or gnostic mystical traditions within Islam remarkable instances of this interreligious engagement—not to talk about all the theological discussions held in Islam, but in the context of many religions, such as in the book *al-Milal wa'l-nihal*, of Shahrastānī, etc. Certainly our ancestors have left us many historical, theological, and metaphysical precedents of the greatest importance which could act as a guide for us today, as a model for us in our search for profound and serious inter-religious dialogue and understanding.

*Gnosis*
The eye of certainty is like the sun —
There is no veil through which it does not see.
The center dwells in the periphery,
And as each ego thinks itself alone
All numbers must contain the number one.

The depth of God is more than we can tell;
Next to the deepest knowledge of the Real
Every religion is a heresy.
Eckhart, from whom God nothing hid, knew well:
*To reach the kernel you must break the shell.*

And Ibn 'Arabi, absorbed in prayer,
Saw nothing but an ocean without shore —
Its waves are flowing still through every soul:
There is no part that does not touch the whole.

*Barry McDonald*

# The Koran as the Lover's Mirror

*William C. Chittick*

It is well known that Sufism places a premium on love, but Western observers rarely associate love with Islam itself. This no doubt helps to explain the tendency to see Sufism as somehow tangential to the tradition. I would argue rather that love for God is every bit as central to the Islamic perspective as it is to a tradition like Christianity, though the rhetorical stress is by no means the same. In the present context, one piece of evidence will have to suffice: Islamic praxis is based on following the Sunnah of Muhammad—that is, imitating his conduct, his customs, and his character traits. The Koran is of course utterly basic to Islamic ways of seeing and doing things, but the Koran is known and interpreted first of all through the manner in which it was embodied and acted out by Muhammad. Following the Prophet provides the parameters for the Muslim understanding of the Koran and of all things. But what exactly is the rationale for following the Prophet? A most succinct expression is found in surah 3:31: "Say [O Muhammad!]: 'If you love God, follow me, and God will love you.'" If you do not love God, there is no reason to follow the Prophet. This has hardly been lost on practicing Muslims.

If it is not obvious to outsiders that Muslims have been motivated by love for God, this has something to do with the many directions in which Islamic civilization developed—literature, law, art, philosophy, theology, political institutions. Modern scholarship has been much more interested in these observable aspects of culture than in psychological or spiritual motives. Nonetheless, most scholars recognize that Islamic civilization has always been concerned with unpacking the teachings of the Koran and applying them to diverse realms of human endeavor. In other words, expressions of Islamic civilization and culture flesh out the ways in which people imitate the Prophet, who embodied the Koran. And Muslims in turn are motivated to imitate the Prophet by love for God and the desire to call down God's love upon themselves.

Although Muslims have followed Muhammad in order to attract God's love, they have also recognized that God loves human beings in any case. Sufi authors commonly highlight the notion that the divine motivation for creating the universe is love. What makes human beings special, among all God's creatures, is that they have the capacity to love God freely in response to His love for them. All other things simply serve God as they were created to serve Him, with no free choice on their parts.[1] As Rūmī puts it,

Choice is the salt of worship—
    the spheres turn, but not because they want to.
Their turning is neither rewarded nor punished,
    for, at the time of reckoning, choice bestows excellence.[2]

1 Theologically, this distinction is often drawn in terms of God's two commands: He issues the command "Be!" (*kun*) to all things, and they can do nothing but obey; this is the creative or "engendering" command (*al-amr al-takwīnī*). To human beings (and jinn) he also issues the command, "Do this and don't do that," and they accept or reject it on the basis of their own free choice; this is the "prescriptive command" (*al-amr al-taklīfī*).

2 *Mathnawī* (Nicholson edition), Book 3, vss. 3287-88.

So, to say that God created the universe out of love means that the divine love brings into existence the ugly along with the beautiful, the bad along with the good. Only within the context of such an apparently mixed-up universe can free choice have any meaning. And only those who choose freely to love God can love Him with worthy love. If love were to be coerced, it would not be love. This is one reason why the Koran says "There is no compulsion in the religion" (2:256). The religion—the right path taught by the Koran and the Prophet—is precisely to live up to the requirements of love for God and to do so by putting the Sunnah into practice. If the religion were coerced, it would not be love, and it would not be the religion.

In short, although God loves humans beings and created them to love Him, they are free *not* to love Him. So, a second sort of divine love responds to the free choice of human beings to love God, a choice that demands following the divine guidance as embodied in the prophets. And, God says in the often cited *ḥadīth qudsī*, "When I love My servant, I am the hearing with which he hears, the eyesight with which he sees, the hand with which he grasps, and the foot with which he walks." When love reaches its culmination, the divine Lover is none other than those he loves, and the human lovers are none other than the divine Beloved. This is one of the meanings that Sufis see in the verse, "He loves them, and they love Him" (Koran 5:54).

* * *

I chose to talk about the Koran as a "mirror" because I wanted to stress the role of the interpreter in understanding scripture. The fact that people see the Koran through their own specific lenses is especially clear when one surveys the vast number of Koranic commentaries written over the centuries—not to mention the critiques and studies written by non-Muslims. Jurists have found in the Koran a book of law, theologians see all sorts of God-talk, philosophers find the guidelines for wisdom and virtue, linguists uncover fascinating intricacies of Arabic grammar, biologists find theories of life. As for Western scholarship, nothing is more obvious than that scholars reach different conclusions on the basis of diverse premises and prejudices.

When I first chose the topic for this paper, I immediately put into the relevant file a statement from the *Maqālāt* of Shams-i Tabrīzī, Rūmī's famous companion. In that book we learn that Shams used to make his living as a teacher of the Koran. He tells us repeatedly that the path to God is that of following (*mutābaʿat*) the Prophet—having in mind, of course, the already mentioned Koranic verse, "If you love God, follow me." In one explanation of the central importance of the Koran, he says,

> For the travelers and the wayfarers, each verse of the Koran is like a message and a love-letter [*ʿishq-nāma*]. They know the Koran. He presents and discloses the beauty of the Koran to them.[3]

I suppose that nowadays not too many people read the Koran as a love-letter. But, is this because of the contents of the Koran? Or is it because of the contents of the readers' souls? Shams thinks the answer is obvious: "The flaw is that people don't look at God with the gaze of love."[4]

[3] Chittick, *Me & Rumi: The Autobiography of Shams-i Tabrizi* (Louisville: Fons Vitae, 2004), p. 156.

[4] Ibid., p. 228.

The issue is not only interpretation of scripture, of course, since the same argument applies to our views on everything. Our understanding of the world and of our own role within it depends on where we are coming from. And with even more reason, how we understand "God" depends on who we are. This should be obvious—everyone has a different understanding of the word "God." Ibn ʿArabī, the "Greatest Master" of Sufi teachings, makes the point by arguing that absolutely no one can worship God as such. All people without exception worship the god or gods of their beliefs (*al-ilāh al-muʿtaqad*). Given that the term "god" can designate the point of reference for one's attitudes and activities, even those who claim not to worship any gods are deceiving themselves. All of us have points of reference and orientations.

I do not want to claim that interpretation of scripture is totally subjective, but it does seem clear that scripture has the capacity to allow people to see into their own souls. When people read scripture, they find themselves. If they do not like what they are seeing, they should—in the traditional way of looking at things—try to dissolve the knots in their souls that prevent them from seeing the beauty of the Divine Word. Needless to say, the modern response is somewhat different.

* * *

One needs to remember that Muslims never considered the Koran a book among other books, any more than the Bible was simply a classic for Christians. The Koran was the Word of God, God's own self-expression with the purpose of guiding those whom He loves. People read and recited the Koran not to entertain themselves with old stories, nor to edify themselves, but to bring themselves into conformity with the divine reality that is disclosed in the text. The purpose of engaging with the Koran was to transform the soul. Reciting the text and conforming oneself to its teachings was a way to express one's love for God and to make oneself worthy for God's love.

The idea that reciting the Koran and observing the Sunnah are transformative goes back to Islamic teachings about what it means to be human, teachings with which the Koran is saturated—that is, if one is looking for them. People can become transformed because they can come to know God and love Him, and this is possible because human beings are not fixed in their status. It may be true that the God whom people worship is always the God of belief, and it may also be true that God in Himself is always beyond the capacity of created beings to understand. But, this does not mean that the God of my belief today is the same as the God of my belief tomorrow, quite the contrary. Understanding and worship of God change constantly in keeping with the growth and development of the human self.

Ibn ʿArabī points out that the uniqueness of human beings goes back to the fact that they cannot be pinned down. Just as God cannot be defined, so also the creatures whom He created in His own image cannot be put into a box. In other words, the "definition" of what it means to be human has everything to do with indefinability.

In the Koran, the angels say, "Each of us has a known station" (37:164). This suggests that the angels are all different and that each has a specific function. None of the angels can do the job of any other angel. Ibn ʿArabī argues that the rule expressed in this verse applies to all created things; each thing in the universe is exactly what it is meant to be and is doing precisely what it was created for—with the partial exception of human beings. In their case, human status depends upon not having a fixed station in this life, because only nonfixity can allow for freedom. People can develop and grow as they attempt to make themselves worthy for God's love.

Humans, in short, cannot be defined in any more than a general way. No one can know what he or she really is, because each of us is a work in progress. What we do in our daily activities constantly brings about changes in our psychic and spiritual make-ups. We remain indefinable until death, at which point we enter into our own fixed stations, like the angels and other creatures.

When we apply the rule of nonfixity and indefinability to our own beliefs and practices—whether these be religious or non-religious—we see that our understandings, words, and deeds are always in the process of changing, for better or worse. Moreover, we reap the fruits of these changes—the law of karma is ineluctable. Reality itself holds us responsible for what we think and do. Death is simply the point at which all this becomes obvious.

Given that people are constantly developing and changing, they should be concerned with making sure that they develop in a worthy and congenial way. Love for God provides the necessary focus. Following the Prophet, one needs to remember, does not simply mean performing certain acts. More than anything else it means assuming certain attitudes toward God and the world.

Islam provides the basic guidelines for the proper attitudes in the testimony of faith, the Shahadah: "There is no god but God, and Muhammad is God's messenger." I have already indicated something of the importance of God's Messenger for actualizing love. The role played by the first Shahadah is less obvious, but in fact, the declaration of divine unity—*tawḥīd*—is in some ways even more basic.

The statement "There is no god but God" is typically considered an expression of belief. For Muslims, it is more like a statement of fact, or a self-evident truth. Even more than that, it is a methodology. Specifically, it responds to the human limitation of always seeing God and scripture in our own measures, and it provides the means to bring our measures into conformity with God's measure. Given that our beliefs and attitudes alter and change day by day and even moment by moment, we need a method of focusing, training, and guiding them and allowing them to develop in a direction that will lead to long-term happiness.

The first Shahadah provides a way of thinking about God. What it basically says is that every thought about God needs to be negated. Whatever god we conceive of is not God in Himself, who alone truly is. Whatever interpretation we make of the Koran—which is God's self-expression—does not live up to the reality of God. There can be no definitive and final answers in our minds and souls. To say definitive and final is to say "absolute," and God alone is absolute, God alone is definitive and final. As Shams puts it, "It is God who is God. Whatever is created is not God—whether it's Muhammad or other than Muhammad."[5] The definitive and final God is not the God that we can understand. Our God of our beliefs is always tentative.

In other words, the Shahadah provides a method to help people avoid trying to size up God. The great lovers of Islamic civilization say that if people want to understand God in God's measure, they need to look upon Him with the eye of love and strive to conform to His wishes. As a methodology for lovers, the Shahadah tells them that there is nothing worthy of love but God, because God alone is adequate to the ever-changing and unlimited substance of the hu-

[5] Ibid., p. 71.

man soul. God alone can fill up the divine image that is the human self. As for what is less than God, love for it is legitimate and desirable only to the degree in which the object of love is recognized as God's good and beautiful face (*wajh*) shining in the created realm. The principle of unity demands that all things be seen as signs and marks of God's goodness.

* * *

There is a hadith that can help us understand the role of love in interpreting the Koran: "Your love for a thing makes you blind and deaf." A typical way of reading this is to say that loving what is less than God makes people blind and deaf to the guidance provided by the Koran and the Sunnah. This will have ill consequences for the soul because, if people love something other than God, they will not follow Muhammad, and then God will not love them and will not bring them into His proximity after death.

This saying, however, can be read in other ways as well. We can take it not as a criticism of misguided love, but as a statement of fact concerning all love, guided or misguided. Love for the ugly and vicious makes people blind and deaf to the beautiful and the virtuous, and love for the beautiful and good turns them away from the ugly.

If we acknowledge that love makes us blind, it becomes obvious that all scriptural interpretation is inadequate. Why? Because every interpreter loves something, some god, some principle, some goal. And the love that drives us—the love for whatever it is that we worship—makes us blind and deaf to other gods and other loves. If our god is history, or psychology, or physics, for example, this would make us blind and deaf to metaphysics, not to mention "mysticism." This is obvious; we meet it in every facet of life, especially life in the academy. People not only do not see things the same way, they *cannot* see things in the same way, because they are blinded by their loves.

So, every interpreter of scripture is a lover—of something or other—and every lover sees scripture as his own mirror. For those who love the God of *tawḥīd*, the God described in the first Shahadah, their love makes them blind and deaf to every negative attribute that might be applied to God, for they can only see that He is adorned with every positive attribute. Love makes them give all credit for good to God, and all credit for evil to ourselves.

If human beings were fixed in status like other creatures, it would be a waste of breath even to mention the fact that they are blinded by their loves and obsessed by their own interpretative stances. It is precisely because we are not fixed in status and are constantly changing that we need to remember our own limitations. We can always strive to lift our gazes higher and see through better lenses.

* * *

I am not arguing, by the way, that "love for God" is necessarily a good thing. That all depends upon the god of belief. If the god of belief does not conform with God as He truly is, what people call "love for God" can easily be hatred for the Beautiful, the Good, and the True. This is one reason that Islamic texts never divorce love for God from knowledge of God. Real faith cannot be a leap into the unknown, because it is impossible to love something that you do not know. This is the problem, precisely: we cannot know God in Himself, so we can only love Him in the degree that we know Him. It becomes all important to expand our own measure in knowledge and understanding so as to achieve as close an approximation as possible to the divine measure.

In texts that discuss love for God, the expression "lover" and "knower" are often synonyms. Or, if love is taken as higher—as is done typically in Sufi poetry—knowledge becomes the means for achieving true love. Al-Ghazālī often makes the connection between love and knowledge in his *Iḥyāʾ*. He does so, for example, in a passage found at the beginning of a section on the heart's illness, mentioned in the Koran:

> Every part of the body was created for its own specific act. The illness of each part is for it not to be able to perform the act for which it was created, or to perform the act but in a disrupted manner. The illness of the hand is for it not to be able to grasp. The illness of the eye is for it not to be able to see.
>
> In the same way, the illness of the heart is for it not to be able to perform the specific act for which it was created. This act is knowledge, wisdom, recognition, love for God, worshiping Him, and taking joy in remembering Him. The heart should prefer these over every other desired thing and utilize all desires and all bodily parts in this path. . . .
>
> So, in each bodily part there is a benefit, and the benefit of the heart is wisdom and knowledge. This is the specific characteristic of the human soul through which human beings are distinguished from the beasts. For, they are not distinguished from them by the power of eating, sexual intercourse, eyesight, and so on—only through knowing things as they are. And the Root of things, the one who brings them into existence and devises them, is God. It is He who made them things. So, if a man were to know all things but not to know God, it would be as if he knew nothing.
>
> The mark of knowledge is love. He who knows God loves Him. The mark of love is that he does not prefer this world or any other loved thing over Him. . . . Whenever anyone loves something more than he loves God, his heart is ill. It is as if his stomach loved clay more than it loved bread and water, or as if it ceased to have any desire for bread and water. Hence, the stomach is ill, and this is the mark of its illness.
>
> Thus it is known that all hearts are ill, except as God wills.[6]

* * *

I can sum up in these terms: Love for God pushes the lover to follow the Prophet, who embodies the message of the Koran. One cannot love God properly, however, without knowing God, and to know God one needs to have a sound knowledge of God's self-expression, which is precisely the Koran and its embodiment in Muhammad. In order to know and understand the Koran correctly, one needs to read it with the eye of love. As an interpretive method, love demands that the reader look at God in terms of the Shahadah, which negates every blame-

[6] *Iḥyāʾ ʿulūm al-dīn*, Volume 3, Book 2, section on "The marks of the illnesses of the hearts" (Beirut: Dār al-Hādī, 1992, vol. 3, pp. 96-97).

worthy attribute from God and ascribes every praiseworthy attribute to him. This demands that interpreters understand every verse in the best light—in view of the real nature of God's wisdom, compassion, mercy, and guidance.

* * *

All these remarks are meant to provide a brief introduction to my favorite Koran commentator, one of those who treated the Koran as a love-letter. This is Rashīd al-Dīn Maybudī, who was a contemporary of al-Ghazālī. His commentary has not been well known to Western scholarship, perhaps because it is written in Persian. He took inspiration from ʿAbdallāh Anṣārī, a scholar of Ḥanbalī jurisprudence who wrote a number of classic Sufi texts in both Arabic and Persian and who died about forty-five years before Maybudī completed his commentary in 520/1126.[7]

The commentary is called *Kashf al-asrār wa ʿuddat al-abrār*, "The unveiling of the secrets and the provision of the pious." It is one of the longest commentaries in the Persian language, though, like many classical Persian texts, a good percentage of the book is in fact in Arabic. For many centuries, it was one of the best known and most popular commentaries on the Koran wherever Persian was a significant language of learning. It was published in ten volumes in the 1950s.

Maybudī's commentary has a unique arrangement. The author takes ten or so verses at a time, and then explains their meaning in three stages. In the first stage, he provides a literal Persian translation. In the second, he offers grammatical clarifications, explains the circumstances of the revelation, and gives detailed accounts of interpretations provided by the Prophet, the Companions, and other commentators. In the third stage he chooses one or more of the verses and suggests something of their more inner meanings. He follows the path of what has commonly been called commentary by "allusion" (*ishāra*). Literally, the word means "to point." Technically it designates a meaning that is not expressed directly but needs to be brought out by reflection and meditation. In this third stage he demonstrates how the Koran addresses the dynamics of spiritual development and the unfolding of the human soul. Love, of course, comes up repeatedly.

The first two stages of the book are written in a style that is dry, precise, and sometimes pedantic. In contrast, the third stage provides some of the most beautiful examples of early Persian prose and, in contrast to the other two sections, frequently cites Persian and Arabic poetry and often quotes the words of Anṣārī. Here I will look at the third-stage commentary on three verses. It should be kept in mind that these three passages represent a tiny fraction of the explanations by "allusion" that are offered in the ten volumes.

The first passage pertains to the second verse of the second surah. The first verse of the surah is simply the enigmatic letters "*alif lām mīm*," concerning which diverse interpretations have been offered, some of which Maybudī cites. The second verse is translated by Arberry in this way: "This is the book, wherein is no doubt, a guidance to the godfearing."

In stage two of the commentary Maybudī follows the typical reading by explaining that the

[7] I first wrote these sentences before the appearance of Annabel Keeler's ground-breaking study, *Sufi Hermeneutics: The Qur'an Commentary of Rashīd al-Dīn Maybudī* (Oxford: Oxford University Press, 2006), which throws a great deal of light on Maybudī and his work.

verse refers to the Koran. In stage three, however, he looks for allusions. He takes the word *kitāb*, which is usually translated as "book," in its literal sense, which is "writing." He understands the verse to say, "This is the writing wherein is no doubt." He then explains the meaning in terms of two other Koranic verses where writing is mentioned. Then he offers a brief meditation on the verse:

> It is said that "This is the writing" is an allusion to what God has written against Himself for Muhammad's community: "Surely My mercy takes precedence over My wrath." God does that in His words, "Your Lord has written mercy against Himself" [6:54]. It is also said that the verse is an allusion to the faith and knowledge that God has written upon the hearts of the believers. Thus He says, "He wrote faith in their hearts" [58:22].
>
> In this verse, it is as if God is saying, "My servant, I have written the outline of faith in your heart, I have mixed in the perfume of love, I have decorated paradise for you, I have adorned your heart with the light of knowledge, I have lit up the candle of union with Me, I have stamped the seal of kindness on your heart, and I have written the characters of love in your awareness."
>
> "He wrote faith in their hearts": [God is saying,] "I wrote in the Tablet,[8] but what I wrote there was only your description. I wrote in your hearts, and what I wrote there was only My description. I wrote your description in the Tablet, and I showed it to Gabriel. I wrote My description in *your* heart. Would I have shown it to an enemy?
>
> "In the Tablet I wrote your cruelty [*jafāʾ*] and faithfulness [*wafāʾ*]; in your heart I wrote laudation and knowledge. What I wrote about you has not changed. How could what I wrote about Myself change?
>
> "Moses carved out a stone from the mountain, and, when I wrote the Torah therein, the stone turned into emerald. The knower's heart was made of harsh stone—when I wrote My name therein, it turned into an exalted book."[9]

* * *

The next verse is the first half of 2:148, which reads, "Everyone has a direction to which he turns." This is often understood as explaining the diversity of creation. In stage two of the commentary, Maybudī reads the verse as referring to the "kiblah" of people, their orientation in their worship. Each of us has a god on which our aspirations are focused, and that god is determined by our created nature, which was given to us by our Creator. This idea is commonplace in Islamic thought, and is alluded to in Koranic verses like 25:43, "Have you seen the one who has taken his own caprice as his god?" I have already explained how Ibn ʿArabī develops some of its implications in terms of "the god of belief." Here are Maybudī's words in stage two:

[8] This is of course the Guarded Tablet (*al-lawḥ al-maḥfūẓ*), within which God writes with the Highest Pen (*al-qalam al-aʿlā*). The Pen and Tablet are also known as the First Intellect and the Universal Soul.

[9] *Kashf al-asrār*, edited by ʿA. A. Ḥikmat (Tehran: Dānishgāh, 1952-60), vol. 1, pp. 54-55.

> Everyone has a kiblah toward which he turns. The folk of falsehood have turned their faces toward a crooked kiblah—by [God's] decree and abandonment. The folk of truth have turned their faces toward a straight kiblah—by [God's] decree and giving success. And the whole affair is in God's hand.[10]

In this straightforward interpretation, Maybudī takes the verse as a statement of the actual situation, of the static relationship between creatures and the Creator. But our situations are not in fact fixed, so we can always do something to change them. The fact that we are abandoned today does not demand that we will be abandoned tomorrow, nor does the fact that we receive success today mean that we have a lock on success. If we look with the eye of love, we can see that the verse is urging us to recognize our true Beloved and turn away from all the false objects of love that attract us. This is the way Maybudī interprets it in the third stage:

> He [God] says by way of allusion: "All people have turned away from Me. They have become familiar with others instead of Me. They have made the ease of their hearts to lie in something less than Me and accepted it as their beloved."
>
> You, who are the nobles on the Path, you, who claim to love Me—lift up your eyes from anything less than Me, even if it be the highest paradise. Then you will walk straight, following the Sunnah and the conduct of Muhammad, and you will fulfill completely the duty of emulating that greatest man of the world. For, his conduct, as the greatest of the prophets, was to turn his eyes away from all beings and not to see any refuge or to accept any resting place other than the shelter of Unity [*aḥadiyyat*].
>
> When a man wears down his soul in the path of love
> he'd better not incline to anyone less than the Friend.
> In the path of love the lover must never
> give a thought to paradise or hell.
>
> When someone puts himself right by following [Muhammad], the candle of his love for God will be lit in his path such that he will never fall away from the road of love. To this is the allusion in the verse, "Follow me, and God will love you" [3:31]. Whenever someone goes straight on the avenue of love, he will be secure from the varied directions that are the kiblahs of the shallow-minded. One fervent lover has said in his state,
>
> No matter that I don't have the world's kiblah—
> my kiblah is the Beloved's lane, nothing else.
> This world, that world, all that exists—
> lovers see the Beloved's face, nothing else.

[10] Ibid., p. 407.

Al-Ḥallāj alluded to the kiblahs of the shallow-minded when he said, "The desirers have been turned over to what they desire." In other words, everyone has been placed with his own beloved.

The reality of this work is that all creatures have claimed love for the Real, but there was no one who did not want to be *somebody* in His court.

> Whoever found himself a name found it from that Court.
> Belong to Him, brother, don't think about anyone else!

Since everyone claimed to love the Real, He struck them against the touchstone of trial to show them to themselves. He threw something into them and made it their kiblah, so they turned their face to it, rather than to Him. In one it was possessions, in another position, in another a spouse, in another a beautiful face, in another vainglory, in another knowledge, in another asceticism, in another worship, in another fancy. He threw all of these into the creatures, so they busied themselves with them. No one spoke of Him, and the path of seeking Him stayed empty.

This is why Abū Yazīd said, "I walked up to His gate, but I didn't see any crowding there, because the folk of this world were veiled by this world, the folk of the afterworld were veiled by the afterworld, and the claimants among the Sufis were veiled by eating, drinking, and begging. There were others among the Sufis of a higher level—but they were veiled by music and beautiful faces. The leaders of the Sufis, however, were not veiled by any of these. I saw that they were bewildered and intoxicated."

It was in accordance with this sort of tasting that the Guide on the Path [Anṣārī] said, "I know the drinking place, but I'm not able to drink. My heart is thirsty and I wail in the hope of a drop. No fountain can fill me up, because I'm seeking the ocean. I passed by a thousand springs and rivers in hope of finding the sea.

"Have you seen someone drowning in fire? I'm like that. Have you seen someone thirsty in a lake? That's what I am. I'm exactly like a man lost in the desert. I keep on saying, 'Someone help me!' I'm screaming at the loss of my heart.'"[11]

* * *

I conclude by citing one more passage, again from the commentary on the second surah, specifically verse 5. At the beginning of this surah, after saying that the Koran is the book within which there is no doubt, the text goes on to say that it is a guidance for the godfearing, and then it describes the godfearing—those who have faith in the unseen and perform the commanded practices. Verse 5 then reads, "Those are upon guidance from their Lord; those are the ones who prosper." The next verse turns to a description of those who do not prosper—those who reject God's guidance.

[11] Ibid., pp. 412-13.

In the third stage of his commentary on verse 5, Maybudī goes into quite a bit of detail to suggest what sort of "prosperity" is at issue:

> Here you have endless good fortune and unlimited generosity. God has opened up the door of their insight and has looked upon their hearts with the gaze of solicitude. He has lit up the lamp of guidance in their hearts so that, what for others is unseen, for them is manifest, what for others is reports, for them is unmediated seeing.[12]

Next Maybudī turns to accounts of the Prophet's Companions and some of the early Sufis to suggest the difference between knowing something by means of transmitted reports, and knowing it by means of direct vision and immediate experience. Then he turns once again to the sayings of Anṣārī and cites a highly poetical dialogue between the spirit (*jān*) and the heart (*dil*), which concludes by reminding us that all this talk of love and transformation represents *tawḥīd* in practice, and it leads to the union in which God becomes the hearing with which the lovers hear and the eyesight with which they see.

> The human substance is like a rusted mirror. As long as it has rust on its face, no forms appear within it. When you polish it, all forms will appear. As long as the opaqueness of disobedience is on the believing servant's heart, none of the mysteries of the spiritual realm [*malakūt*] will appear within it, but, when the rust of disobedience is removed from it, the mysteries of the spiritual realm and the states of the Unseen begin to show themselves. This is precisely the "unveiling" [*mukāshafa*] of the heart.
>
> Just as the heart has unveiling, the spirit has unmediated seeing [*muʿāyana*]. Unveiling is the lifting of the barriers between the heart and the Real, and unmediated seeing is seeing together [*ham-dīdārī*]. As long you are with the heart, you are receiving reports. When you reach the spirit, you arrive at unmediated seeing.
>
> Shaykh al-Islām Anṣārī has let out the secret here in the tongue of unveiling, lifting from it the seal of jealousy. He said:
>
> On the first day of the beginningless covenant a tale unfolded between heart and spirit. No one was there—not Adam and Eve, not water and clay. The Real was present, the Reality was there.
>
> No one has heard such a marvelous tale. The heart was the questioner, and the spirit was the mufti. The heart had an intermediary, but the spirit received the report by unmediated seeing. The heart asked a thousand questions from the spirit, and they all came to nothing. With one word the spirit answered them all.
>
> The heart did not have its fill of asking, nor did the spirit of answering. The questions were not about deeds, nor were the answers about rewards. Whenever the heart asked about reports, the spirit answered from unmediated seeing. Finally, the heart came to unmediated seeing, and it brought back the report to water [and clay].

[12] Ibid., p. 58.

If you have the capacity to hear, listen. If not, don't hurry to deny, just stay silent.

The heart asked the spirit, "What is faithfulness [*wafāʾ*]? What is annihilation [*fanāʾ*]? What is subsistence [*baqāʾ*]?"

The spirit answered, "Faithfulness is to bind the belt of love, annihilation is to be delivered from your own selfhood, subsistence is to reach the reality of the Real."

The heart asked, "Who is the stranger, who the mercenary, who the familiar?"

The spirit replied, "The stranger has been driven away, the mercenary remains on the road, the familiar is called."

The heart asked the spirit, "What is unmediated seeing? What is love [*mihr*]? What is unneedingness [*nāz*]?"

The spirit replied, "Unmediated seeing is the resurrection, love is fire mixed with blood, unneedingness is the handhold of need [*niyāz*]."

The heart said, "Add to that."

The spirit answered, "Unmediated seeing does not get along with explanation, love is paired with jealousy [*ghayrat*], and wherever there is unneedingness, the story is long."

The heart said, "Add to that."

The spirit replied, "Unmediated seeing cannot be analyzed, love takes the sleeper in secret, and he who reaches unneedingness in the Beloved will never die."

The heart asked, "Has anyone ever reached that day by himself?"

The spirit replied, "I asked that from the Real. The Real said, 'Finding Me is by My solicitude [*ʿināya*]. Thinking that you can reach Me by yourself is your sin.'"

The heart asked, "Is there permission for one glance? I'm tired of interpretation and reports."

The spirit replied, "Here we have a sleeper, running water, his fingers in his ears. Will he hear the sound of the Pool of Paradise?"

The discussion of heart and spirit was cut off. The Real began to speak, and the spirit and heart listened. The tale unfolded until the words rose high and the place was emptied of listeners.

Now the heart finds no end to unneedingness, and the spirit none to gentleness. The heart is in the grasp of Generosity, the spirit in the shelter of the Holy. No mark of the heart appears, no trace of the spirit. Nonexistence is lost in existence, reports in unmediated seeing. From beginning to end this is precisely the tale of *tawḥīd*. To this "I am his hearing with which he hears" gives witness.[13]

[13] Ibid., pp. 59-60. I have taken a bit of help in reading this passage from parts of it that are also found in *Majmūʿa-yi rasāʾil-i fārsī-yi Khwāja ʿAbdallāh Anṣārī*, edited by M. Sarwar Mawlāʾī (Tehran: Tūs, 1377/1998), pp. 367-77.

# *Civilizational Dialogue and Sufism: The Holy Qur'ān and the Metaphysics of Ibn al-'Arabī*

*Reza Shah-Kazemi*

## 1. "Civilized Dialogue" and the Holy Qur'ān

The notion of "civilizational dialogue" has been proposed in recent years as an antidote to the poison disseminated by the sensational prophecy of "the clash of civilizations" made by Samuel Huntington. What is meant by a dialogue between civilizations is of course simply "civilized dialogue", that is, a mode of dialogue between individuals of different cultures and religions which seeks to accept the Other within a civilized framework; a mode of dialogue which respects diversity and difference, and upholds the rights of all individuals and groups to express their beliefs and to practice their faith without hindrance. In the Holy Qur'ān one finds a clear enunciation of the manner in which civilized dialogue should take place in a context of religious diversity; it does so in several verses, some of the most important of which we shall cite here as the essential background against which one should view the metaphysical perspectives on the Other opened up by Ibn al-'Arabī, verses to which we will return in the course of presenting these perspectives:

> *For each of you We have established a Law and a Path. Had God willed, He could have made you one community. But that He might try you by that which He hath given you* [He hath made you as you are]. *So vie with one another in good works. Unto God ye will all return, and He will inform you of that wherein ye differed.* (5:48)

> O *mankind, truly We have created you male and female, and have made you nations and tribes that ye may know one another.* (49:13)

> *And of His signs is the creation of the heavens and the earth, and the differences of your languages and colors. Indeed, herein are signs for those who know.* (30:22)

> *Truly those who believe, and the Jews, and the Christians, and the Sabeans—whoever believeth in God and the Last Day and performeth virtuous deeds—surely their reward is with their Lord, and no fear shall come upon them, neither shall they grieve.* (2:62)

> *Say: We believe in God, and that which was revealed unto Abraham, and Ishmael, and Isaac, and Jacob, and the tribes, and that which was given unto Moses and Jesus and the prophets from their Lord. We make no distinction between any of them, and unto Him we have submitted.* (2:136)

> *And do not hold discourse with the People of the Book except in that which is finest, save with those who do wrong. And say: We believe in that which hath been revealed to us and revealed to you. Our God and your God is one, and unto Him we*

> *surrender.* (29:46)
>
> *Call unto the way of thy Lord with wisdom and fair exhortation, and hold discourse with them* [the People of the Book] *in the finest manner.* (16:125)

It is on the basis of such verses as these that Martin Lings asserted that, whereas the universality proper to all true religions can be found within each religion's mystical dimension, or esoteric essence, one of the distinctive features of Islam is the fact that universality is indelibly inscribed within its founding revelation—as well as within its esoteric essence. "All mysticisms are equally universal ... in that they all lead to the One Truth. But one feature of the originality of Islam, and therefore of Sufism, is what might be called a secondary universality, which is to be explained above all by the fact that as the last Revelation of this cycle of time it is necessarily something of a summing up."[1]

The extent to which the religions of the Other are given recognition, and indeed reverence, in the Qur'ān does indeed render this scripture unique among the great revelations of the world. It is thus a rich source for reflection upon the most appropriate way to address the various issues pertaining to dialogue with the religious Other. The Qur'ānic message on religious diversity is of particular relevance at a time when various paradigms of "pluralism" are being formulated and presented as a counter-weight to the "clash of civilizations" scenario. In the last of the verses cited above, 16:125, "wisdom" (*ḥikma*) is given as the basis upon which dialogue should be conducted. The whole of the Qur'ān, read in depth and not just on the surface, gives us a divine source of wisdom; imbibing from this source empowers and calibrates our efforts to engage in meaningful dialogue and to establish authentic modes of tolerance; it thus provides us, in the words of Tim Winter, with a "transcendently-ordained tolerance."[2] Wisdom is a quality and not an order: it cannot be given as a blue-print, a set of rules and regulations; it calls for human effort, a readiness to learn, it needs to be cultivated, and it emerges as the fruit of reflection and action. As the words of verse 16:125 tell us, we need wisdom and beautiful exhortation, and we also need to know how to engage in dialogue on the basis of that which is *aḥsan* "finest" "most excellent", or "most beautiful" in our own faith, if we are to authentically invite people to the path of the Lord. In other words, we are being encouraged to use wisdom, rather than any pre-determined set of instructions, in order to discern the most appropriate manner of inviting people to the "way of thy Lord", thus, how best to engage in *da'wa.* But we also need wisdom in order to discern that which is "most excellent" in the faith of our interlocutors in dialogue. This creative juxtaposition between *da'wa* and dialogue indicates implicitly that, rather than being seen as two contrasting or even antithetical modes of engaging with the Other, these two elements can in fact be synthesized by wisdom: if one's dialogue with the Other flows from the wellsprings of the wisdom of one's tradition, and if one makes an effort to understand the wisdom—that which is "most excellent"—in the beliefs of the Other, then this kind of dialogue will constitute, in and of itself, a "most beautiful" form of *da'wa.* For one will

1 Martin Lings, *What is Sufism* (London: George Allen & Unwin, 1975), pp. 22-23. For further discussion of this theme, see our *The Other in the Light of the One: The Universality of the Qur'an and Interfaith Dialogue* (Cambridge: Islamic Texts Society, 2006).

2 Tim Winter, "Islam and the Threat of Europe" in *World Faiths Encounter*, no. 29, 2001, p. 11.

be making an effort to allow the wisdom of one's tradition to speak for itself; to "bear witness" to one's faith will here imply bearing witness to the wisdom conveyed by one's faith-tradition, that very wisdom which, due to its universality and lack of prejudice, allows or compels us to recognize, affirm and engage with the wisdom contained within and expressed by other faith-traditions. For, as the Prophet said, "Wisdom is the lost camel (*ḍālla*) of the believer: he has a right to it wherever he may find it."[3]

If wisdom is the lost property of the believer, this means that wherever wisdom is to be found, in whatever form, in whatever religion, philosophy, spirituality, or literature—that wisdom is one's own. It is thus an inestimable tool in the forging of an authentic civilization. One has to be prepared to recognize wisdom, as surely as one would recognize one's own camel, after searching for it. This translates into the attitude: whatever is wise is, by that very fact, part of my faith as a "believer": my belief in God as the source of all wisdom allows or compels me to recognize as "mine" whatever wisdom there is in the entirety of time and space, in all religions and cultures. This does not mean that one appropriates to one's own self—whether individual or social or religious—the wisdom of the Other; rather, it means that one recognizes the wisdom of the Other as being an expression of the wisdom of God, the one and only source of wisdom, however it be expressed. How, then, is it "mine"? Insofar as one's identity is defined by one's relationship with God as the source of all truth, beauty and wisdom, one's "self" will be, in that very measure, inextricably bound up with the wisdom one perceives, however alien be the context or culture in which it is expressed. On the specifically Islamic level, such an approach produces this open-minded attitude: that which is wise is—by its essence if not its form—"Islamic". It "belongs" to us, and we identify with it. This contrasts with the prejudiced attitude: only that which is Islamic—in its form—is wise.

One should note that the universal vision of wisdom was at its strongest when Islamic civilization was at its most authentic and confident—witness the extraordinary assimilation and transformation of the various ancient forms of wisdom in the early 'Abbāsid period; this was an exemplification of the calibrated appropriation and creative application of wisdom—from the intellectual legacy of the Greeks, and the Persians, Indians and Egyptians, Mesopotamians, Assyrians, etc.—on a grand, civilizational scale, transforming and enriching Muslim philosophy, science, and culture.[4] By contrast, it is the exclusivist, prejudiced approach to wisdom that prevails today, when Islamic "civilization" can hardly be said to exist anywhere. It would also appear to be the case that when Islamic civilization existed, *da'wa* was not invested with the emotional intensity which it has acquired in our times. Modernism—with its highly developed tools of propaganda, its tendencies of ideologization, bureaucratization, and uniformalization—has influenced Muslim thought and behavior and made Muslim *da'wa* much more like Christian missionary movements; in traditional Islam, the *da'wa* that existed was far more low-key, personal and took the form of preaching through personal example—it is not accidental, that,

[3] This saying, cited in the collections of al-Tirmidhī and Ibn Mājah, complements other well-known sayings of the Prophet concerning the need to search for knowledge from the cradle to the grave, even if the knowledge be in China, etc. See al-Ghazzālī's collection of such sayings, together with Qur''ānic verses and sayings of the sages, in his *Kitab al-'ilm*, the first book of his monumental *Iḥyā 'ulūm al-dīn* ("Enlivening of the sciences of religion") translated by Nabih Amin Faris as *The Book of Knowledge* (Lahore: Sh. Muhammad Ashraf, 1966).

[4] See the masterful work by Seyyed Hossein Nasr, *Science and Civilization in Islam* (Cambridge: Islamic Texts Society, 1987, "Introduction", pp. 21-40.

as Thomas Arnold's masterly study reveals, the main "missionaries" of traditional Islam were mystics and merchants.[5] The emotional intensity with which *da'wa* is invested in our times would appear to be, on the one hand, a function of the very weakness of Islamic culture, a defensive reflex used to disguise one's "civilizational" deficiencies; and on the other, it is a kind of inverted image of the missionary Christian movements to which the Muslim world has been subjected in the past few centuries, a mimetic response to one's erstwhile colonizers.

One cannot deny, however, that *da'wa* has always played a role in Muslim culture, and that it has a role to play today. To ignore *da'wa*, within a Muslim context, is to render questionable one's credentials as a "valid interlocutor" on behalf of Islam. But one ought to be aware of the kind of *da'wa* that is appropriate in our times, and to seek to learn from the most subtle and refined spirituality of the Islamic tradition in order to make wisdom the basis of one's *da'wa*. The kind of *da'wa* being proposed here is one which seeks to be true to the wisdom which flows from the Qur'ānic message of religious diversity, a message read in depth, according to Sufi hermeneutics, and in particular the metaphysics of Ibn al-'Arabī.[6] This would be a form of *da'wa* which contrasts sharply with the kind of triumphalist propaganda with which we are all too familiar in our times: a disdainful and arrogant call, issuing from harshly exclusivist attitudes which manifest the claim that "my" religion is alone right and all others are wrong. A dialogue based on wisdom would also be a form of dialogue which contrasts quite sharply with a relativistic pluralism which, by reducing all religious beliefs to a presumptuous lowest common denominator, ends up by undermining one's belief in the normativity of one's religion—a belief which is so central to the upholding of one's faith with integrity. The kind of *da'wa*-as-dialogue being proposed here charts a middle path, avoiding two extremes which are in fact closer to each other than is immediately obvious: a fundamentalist type of *da'wa* which alienates the Other on account of its blatant exclusivity, and a pluralistic mode of dialogue which corrodes the Self on account of its thinly veiled assault on normativity. An effective, realistic, and practical mode of dialogue must do justice both to the Self which one ostensibly represents, and to the Other with whom one is in dialogue; there has to be room for the expression of one's belief in the normativity of one's tradition—the belief that one's religion is the best religion, failing which, one would not adhere to it.[7] The right of the Other to bear witness to his faith should, likewise, be respected.

The question might then be asked: how can these competing truth-claims be reconciled with the needs of dialogue—will the result not simply be two mutually exclusive monologues engaging in an unseemly type of competitive religion rather than respecting each other in an enriching dialogue of comparative religion? There is an existential argument one can make, whatever be the faith adhered to, on behalf of this "exclusivist" claim, and this argument is

[5] See Thomas Arnold, *The Preaching of Islam* (London: Luzac, 1935).

[6] See for a more extended discussion of Ibn al-'Arabī's principles of exegesis, in the context of Sufi and postmodern hermeneutics, *The Other in the Light of the One*, chapter 1, "The Hermeneutics of Suspicion or of Sufism?", pp. 1-73. See also our paper, "Beyond Polemics and Pluralism: The Universal Message of the Qur'ān", delivered at the conference: "Al-Azhar and the West: Bridges of Dialogue", Cairo, 5 January, 2009.

[7] As Frithjof Schuon observes: "Every religion by definition wants to be the best, and 'must want' to be the best, both as a whole and in its constitutive elements; this is only natural, or rather 'supernaturally natural'" ("The Idea of 'The Best' in Religions", in his *Christianity/Islam: Essays on Esoteric Ecumenism* [Bloomington: World Wisdom, 2008], p. 91).

based on the fact that religion is not simply a conceptual schema, it is a transformative power. In the "clash" between rival religions, one is not only confronted by competing, mutually exclusive truth-claims; one is also presented with alternative paths to realization of a Reality which radically transcends all conceptually posited truths. One's perception of the "truths" which fashion and delineate one's path to Reality will be deepened, and the truth-claims will be correspondingly corroborated, in proportion to one's progress along that path: therefore the claim that one's religion is "more true" than other religions is a claim about the transformative power which one has directly experienced, and it is this which bestows an existential certainty—rather than any kind of logical infallibility—about one's claim on behalf of the spiritual power of one's religion, a degree of certainty which is absent from a purely conceptual truth-claim one might make on behalf of the dogmas of one's religion. Religion is more about realization than conceptualization; or rather, it is about an initial set of concepts which call out for spiritual action,[8] and which find their consummation in spiritual realization.[9]

The Buddhist notion of doctrine—all doctrine—as an *upāya*, a "saving strategy" is an example of a wise doctrine which we might use here to help explain this point. This notion means, essentially, that all doctrines are veils which transmit some aspects of the truth while obscuring others: the communicable aspect of the truth in question is transmitted, but at the price of obscuring its incommunicable dimension, if it be taken too seriously, that is: if the communicable aspect of the truth be taken as the whole truth. The key spiritual function of doctrine is to point to a reality beyond itself, and is likened, within Buddhism, to a finger pointing at the moon: one is urged to look at the moon indicated by the finger, and not focus exclusively on the finger.[10] This reduction of the spiritual end to the conceptual means is what fanatical dogmatism does; by contrast, a more supple approach to dogma results in seeing it as a means to an end: the dogma as theory leads to spiritual praxis, and moral transformation, thanks to which the "eye of the heart" is opened up, enabling it to "see" that Reality to which the dogma bears witness, but which it cannot encompass or exhaust.

In regard to the function of language in the search for truth, Rūmī makes this point, which

[8] "Knowledge calls out for action", says Imam 'Alī; "if it is answered [it is of avail], otherwise it departs." Cited in the compilation by 'Abd al-Wāḥid Āmidī, *Ghurar al-ḥikam wa durar al-kalim* (given together with the Persian translation, under the title, *Guftār-i Amīr al-mu'minīn 'Alī*, by Sayyid Ḥusayn Shaykhul-Islāmī) (Qom: Intishārāt-i Anṣariyān, 2000), vol. 2, p. 993, no. 21.

[9] In the words of Frithjof Schuon: "The true and complete understanding of an idea goes far beyond the first apprehension of the idea by the intelligence, although more often than not this apprehension is taken for understanding itself. While it is true that the immediate evidence conveyed to us by any particular idea is, on its own level, a real understanding, there can be no question of its embracing the whole extent of the idea, since it is primarily the sign of an aptitude to understand that idea in its completeness. Any truth can in fact be understood at different levels and according to different conceptual dimensions, that is to say according to an indefinite number of modalities that correspond to all the possible aspects, likewise indefinite in number, of the truth in question. This way of regarding ideas accordingly leads to the question of spiritual realization, the doctrinal expressions of which clearly illustrate the dimensional indefinitude of theoretical conceptions" (*The Transcendent Unity of Religions* [Wheaton, IL: Quest Books, 1984] p. 1).

[10] After mentioning this analogy, Sakyamuni Buddha continues: "Words are the finger pointing to the meaning; they are not the meaning itself. Hence, do not rely upon words" (cited by Eisho Nasu, "'Rely on the Meaning, not on the Words': Shinran's Methodology and Strategy for Reading Scriptures and Writing the *Kyōgōshinshō*" in *Discourse and Ideology in Medieval Japanese Buddhism*, eds. Richard K. Payne and Taigen Dan Leighton [New York: Routledge, 2006], p. 253).

resonates with the idea of an *upāya*, and which highlights the need for spiritual action as an accompaniment to doctrinal learning:

> Someone asked: Then what is the use of expressions and words?
>
> The Master [i.e. Rūmī] answered: The use of words is that they set you searching and excite you, not that the object of the quest should be attained through words. If that were the case, there would be no need for so much striving and self-naughting. Words are as when you see afar off something moving; you run in the wake of it in order to see it, it is not the case that you see it through its movement. Human speech too is inwardly the same; it excites you to seek the meaning, even though you do not see it in reality.

Rūmī then reinforces the point, stressing the incommensurability between the kind of learning that comes through reading, on the one hand, and the understanding that arises from the spiritual discipline of self-transcendence, on the other:

> Someone was saying: I have studied so many sciences and mastered so many ideas, yet it is still not known to me what that essence in man is that will remain forever, and I have not discovered it.
>
> The Master answered: If that had been knowable by means of words only, you would not have needed to pass away from self and to suffer such pains. It is necessary to endure so much for yourself *not* to remain, so that you may know that thing which *will* remain.[11]

Similarly, another great Persian poet ʻAbd al-Raḥmān Jāmī (d.1492), who masterfully synthesized the esoteric teachings of the school of *waḥdat al-wujūd* in his, *Lawāʾiḥ*, expresses succinctly the transcendence of this higher wisdom, in terms of which thought—all thought, including the mentally posited conceptions of the dogmas of religion—is not just surpassed, it is even rendered "evil":

> O heart, how long searching for perfection in school?
> How long perfecting the rules of philosophy and geometry?
> Any thought other than God's remembrance is evil suggestion.[12]

It is this perspective which enables one to reconcile competing truth claims within a unique Reality which transcends all such claims, that Reality to which the "truths" bear witness, to which they lead, and from which they receive all their value. The following words of the Qur'ān bear witness to the unique Reality from which all religions derive: *Our God and your God is One* (29:46); as for leading back to the same Reality: *For each of you We have established a Law and a Path* (5:48).

[11] *The Discourses of Rūmī* (Fīhi mā fīhi), tr. A.J. Arberry (London: John Murray, 1961), p. 202.

[12] This is from William Chittick's translation of the *Lawāʾiḥ*, in *Chinese Gleams of Sufi Light* by Sachiko Murata (Albany: SUNY, 2000), p. 138.

If the paths revealed by God are different and divergent, then they cannot but be accompanied by divergent truth-claims, that is, claims pertaining to ways of conceiving and realizing the truth; yet insofar as this truth is but the conceptual expression of an ultimate Reality, and insofar as this Reality is posited as the alpha and omega of all things, the divergent conceptual claims to truth converge on a unique Reality—that of God, the ultimate truth, the ultimate Reality—both truth and reality being in fact synthesised in one of the most important names of God in Islam, *al-Ḥaqq*, "The Real/The True". If the source and the summit of the divergent paths is a single, unique Reality, it is this oneness of the Real which must take ontological precedence over the competing "epistemological" claims to truth. In other words, Being precedes thought; thought is consummated in Being.[13] The mutually exclusive truth-claims, in their purely conceptual form, might be seen as so many unavoidable shadows cast by the divinely-willed diversity of religious paths; these diverse paths, in turn, can be envisaged as so many "lights" emanating from the one and only Light, this unique Light being refracted into different colors by the prism of relativity, and these differently colored lights then crystallising in the forms of the various religions, according to this symbolism.[14]

Red, blue, and yellow lights remain lights even while of necessity excluding each other: no light can be identified with another, except insofar as each is identified with light as such, and not as such and such a light. Here, the Essence of the Real, or the Absolute, is represented by light as such, and the religions can be seen as colors adding to that light something of their own relativity, even while being the vehicles of that light. As will be seen below, this means of reconciling outwardly divergent religious forms within a unitive spiritual essence evokes Ibn al-'Arabī's image of the cup being colored by the drink it contains. The water—standing here for the Absolute—within the cup—the particular religion—becomes 'colored' by the color of the cup; but this is so only extrinsically, and from the human point of view; for intrinsically, and from the divine point of view—*sub specie aeternitatis*—the water remains colorless.

Returning to the idea of *da'wa*-as-dialogue, in the Christian context, those most opposed to the reductionistic tendencies of the kind of pluralism associated with John Hick argue forcefully that a Christian has both the right and the duty to "bear witness" to his faith: to some degree at least, and in some manner, implicit or explicit, it becomes one's duty to invite others to study and investigate the wisdom that is available within one's own faith. As mentioned above, this is a crucial prerequisite for anyone who wishes to engage in dialogue on behalf of a particular faith: to represent that faith must mean to "re-present" it, to present its wisdom, beauty—but also, its *normativity*, failing which one will not be seen as a "valid interlocutor" within the tradition one seeks to represent.

[13] This is the very opposite of the Cartesian axiom: 'I think, therefore I am'. Here, thought trumps being, individual conceptualisation precedes universal reality. Subjectivism, individualism, rationalism—all are contained in this error, and reinforce its basic tendency, which is to reverse the traditional, normal subordination of human thought to divine Reality.

[14] Schuon refers to the distinction between metaphysics and ordinary religious knowledge in terms of uncolored light, and particular colors: "If an example may be drawn from the sensory sphere to illustrate the difference between metaphysical and theological knowledge, it may be said that the former, which can be called 'esoteric' when it is manifested through a religious symbolism, is conscious of the colorless essence of light and of its character of pure luminosity; a given religious belief, on the other hand, will assert that light is red and not green, whereas another belief will assert the opposite; both will be right insofar as they distinguish light from darkness but not insofar as they identify it with a particular color" (*Transcendent Unity*, p. xxx).

It might be objected here: it is impossible to meet every type of criterion which the different schools of thought within any given religious tradition may propose for one to be deemed a "valid interlocutor" on behalf of that faith. Whilst this is true, it is nonetheless worth making the effort to reduce as far as possible the basis upon which one's credentials as a valid interlocutor would be rejected by one's co-religionists. And one of the main bases for this rejection is, without doubt, the perception that those engaged in dialogue are so intent on reaching out to the Other that they do not sufficiently respect the integrity of the Self—that is, they inadequately uphold the normativity of the tradition ostensibly being represented in dialogue. This is a factor which cannot be ignored if one is concerned with a dialogue that aims to be effective, not just in the debating halls of academia, but also in the wider world, wherein the overwhelming majority of believers within the various religions believe deeply in the normativity of their particular religion.

How, then, can the Muslim engaged in dialogue cultivate that wisdom which perceives the truth, the holiness, and the beauty that is contained within the religions of the Other, whilst simultaneously upholding the normativity of his faith, and the specificity of his identity? [15] The perception of the validity of other, alien forms of religious belief acquires a particular acuteness in the light of the following strongly authenticated saying of the Prophet; it is transmitted by Abū Sa'īd al-Khudrī"

> God appears to the Muslims on the Day of Judgment and declares:
> "I am your Lord." They say: "We seek refuge in God from you, and do not associate anything with God." They repeat this twice or thrice, such that some of them would be about to return. God asks: "Is there any sign between you and Him, by means of which you would recognize Him?" They reply: "Yes"; then the reality is laid bare. . . . Then they raised their heads and He transformed Himself (*taḥawwala*) into the form (*ṣūra*) in which they had seen Him the first time. He then said: "I am your Lord". They said: "You are our Lord".[16]

How, then, is one to recognize the divine "face" in the traditions of the Other; how does one recognize this "lost camel"—the wisdom contained within the religions of the Other? For this wisdom may well be expressed in forms of divine self-manifestation which are not only alien, but, in addition, so unlike one's own received wisdom that one takes refuge from them in one's own "God". If believers on the Day of Judgment are unable to recognize God in anything other than the "sign" furnished by their own beliefs, through the blinkers of their own prejudices, how can believers, here and now, ensure that they do not fall into this same trap?

Evidently, prejudice is one of the main obstacles in the path of any dialogue which aims at discovering the wisdom of the Other; however, one of the principal problems arising out of the removal of prejudice towards the Other is the weakening of the identity of the Self.[17] How

[15] This is one of the central questions which we posed and tried to answer in *The Other in the Light of the One*, pp. 117-139; 185-209; 234-266.

[16] This is part of a long saying concerning the possibility of seeing God in the Hereafter. It is found in the "sound" collection of Muslim, *Ṣaḥīḥ Muslim* (Cairo: 'Īsā al-Ḥalabi, n.d.), vol. 1, p. 94.

[17] Self is given in capitals only as a parallel to the use of the capital O for "Other"; what is meant here is the empirical self, the individual as such, and its communitarian extension, and not the universal Selfhood of the Real

can we reach out to the Other in an unprejudiced manner, without this absence of prejudice diluting or subverting our own sense of identity? Or again: How can we be universalist in our spiritual vision, without sacrificing the specificity of our faith and praxis?

It is our contention here that in the Islamic tradition, the Sufi school of thought associated with Muhyī al-Dīn Ibn al-ʿArabī, known in Sufism as "the greatest shaykh" (al-Shaykh al-Akbar)[18] can be of considerable value in helping to cultivate the wisdom which synthesizes the two principles in question here: an unprejudiced, universalist, supra-confessional view of spirituality, on the one hand; and a normative approach to the specificity and particularity of one's own faith, praxis, and identity on the other. It is possible to arrive at an inclusive perspective, one which, however paradoxically, includes exclusivism; this is a perspective which transcends the false dichotomy, so often encountered in our times, between a fanatical exclusivism which disdains all but one's own faith, and a relativistic inclusivism which fatally undermines the integrity of one's own faith. Upholding the integrity of one's faith is difficult if not impossible without a definitive, clearly delineated identity, which in its very specificity and particularity cannot but exclude elements of the Other on the plane of religious form; by "religious form" is meant not just legal and ritual forms but also conceptual and doctrinal forms. However, all such forms are radically transcended, objectively, by the divine essence of the religions; and all the modes of identity commensurate with these forms are just as radically dissolved, subjectively, within the consciousness of one whose soul has been effaced within that essence. These are natural corollaries of Ibn al-ʿArabī's complex and challenging perspective on the dynamics of religious consciousness.

This metaphysical—or supra-confessional—perspective of Ibn al-ʿArabī should be seen as the result of following faithfully and unreservedly certain spiritual trajectories opened up by the Qur'ān, and not simply as the product of his own speculative genius, however undeniable that genius is. Within this perspective there is a clearly defined relationship between form and essence; as will be demonstrated below, his elaboration on this basic distinction flows from the clear distinction established in the Qur'ān between the essence of religion—which is unique—and its forms—which are diverse. Verses such as the following should be borne in mind as the rest of this paper proceeds:

> *He hath ordained for you of the religion* (min al-dīn) *that which He commended unto Noah, and that which We reveal to thee* [Muḥammad], *and that which We commended unto Abraham and Moses and Jesus, saying: Establish the religion, and be not divided therein.* (42:13)

> *Say: We believe in God and that which is revealed unto us, and that which was revealed unto Abraham and Ishmael and Isaac and Jacob and the tribes, and that which was given unto Moses and Jesus and the prophets from their Lord. We make no distinction between any of them, and unto Him we have submitted.* (3:84)

(*nafs al-ḥaqq*, as Ibn al-ʿArabī calls it), at once transcendent and immanent.

18 For the most comprehensive biography of this seminal figure, see Claude Addas, *Quest for the Red Sulphur*, tr. Peter Kingsley (Cambridge: Islamic Texts Society, 1993); for a concise overview of Ibn al-ʿArabī's thought, see Seyyed Hossein Nasr, *Three Muslim Sages* (Lahore: Suhail Academy, 1988 repr), ch. 3, "Ibn ʿArabī and the Sufis", pp. 83–121.

> *Naught is said unto thee* [Muḥammad] *but what was said unto the Messengers before thee.* (41:43)

It is that essential religion (*al-dīn*) which was conveyed to all the Messengers, whence the lack of differentiation between them on the highest level: the Muslim is not permitted to make an essential distinction between any of them: *we make no distinction between any of them* (3:84; 2:285, et passim)

Understanding this distinction between the essence of religion and its forms is crucial for those engaged in dialogue; a correct understanding of this fundamental distinction enables one to engage in dialogue with wisdom, and on the basis of a principled universality; this, in contrast to an unprincipled or rootless syncretism, and in contrast to a well-meaning but ultimately corrosive relativistic pluralism. Syncretistic universalism stems from a sentimental and superficial assimilation of the sacred; it thus has no intellectual or metaphysical principle which can discern authentic religion from spurious cults, on the one hand, and, on the other, maintain a total commitment to one's own religion whilst opening up to the religions of the Other. In syncretism, indiscriminate openness to all sacred forms in general—or what are deemed to be such—cannot but entail a disintegration of the specific form of one's own religion. Principled universality, by contrast, leads to an intensification of commitment to one's own religion; the sense of the sacred and the need to follow the path delineated by one's own religion not only coexist, but each may be said to be a *sine qua non* for the transformative power of other. For effective access to the sacred is granted, not by an abstract, purely discursive conception of the sacred in general, but by entering into the concrete, specific forms of the sacred which are bestowed by the grace inherent within one's own sacred tradition. From this spiritual process of plumbing the depths of the sacred emerges the comprehension that there is no access to the essence of the sacred, above all religious forms, except by means of those authentic formal manifestations of the Essence: the divinely revealed religions. Such a perspective flows naturally from reflection upon the meaning of the verses from the Qur'ān cited above, and in particular, 5:48: *For each of you We have established a Law and a Path. Had God willed, He could have made you one community. But that He might try you by that which He hath given you* [He hath made you as you are]. *So vie with one another in good works.*

This minimal definition of authenticity—"true" religion being that which is divinely revealed—derives from the Qur'ān and is reinforced by what Ibn al-'Arabī says about obedience to God determining one's salvation: "He who prostrates himself to other than God seeking nearness to God and obeying God will be felicitous and attain deliverance, but he who prostrates himself to other than God without God's command seeking nearness will be wretched".[19] We are using this criterion to distinguish true from false religion, in the full knowledge that authenticity or orthodoxy as defined within each true religion will have its own distinctive and irreducible criteria. In this connection it is worth noting that there was never any central ecclesiastical authority in Islam, comparable to the papacy in Catholicism, charged with the duty of dogmatically imposing "infallible" doctrine. According to a well-known saying in Islam: "The

[19] Cited in William C. Chittick, *The Sufi Path of Knowledge: Ibn al-'Arabī's Metaphysics of Imagination* (Albany: SUNY, 1989), p. 365.

divergences of the learned (*al-'ulamā'*) are a mercy".[20] This saying can be seen as manifesting the ecumenical spirit proper to Islam; orthodoxy qua doctrinal form has a wide compass, its essence being the attestation of the oneness of God and of Muḥammad as His messenger, these comprising the *shahādatayn*, or "dual testimony". Accordingly, in Islamic civilization, a wide variety of theological doctrine, philosophical speculation, mystical inspiration, and metaphysical exposition was acceptable so long as the *Sharī'a*, the Sacred Law, was upheld. We might speculate here that the principle of the saying quoted above can also, by transposition, be applied to the religions themselves: the divergences of the religions constitute a "mercy". This mercy is expressed in the divine will for religion to be characterised by a diversity of paths: *Had God willed, He could have made you one community.*

The capacity to recognise other religions as valid, without detriment to the commitment to one's own religion, evidently requires a certain spiritual suppleness; minimally, it requires a sense of the sacred and an inkling of the universality of revelation; at its most profound, it is the fruit of spiritual vision. With the help of Ibn al-'Arabī's doctrine, itself evidently the fruit of just such vision,[21] we can arrive at a conception of a principled universality, that is, an awareness of the universality of religion which neither violates the principles of one's own religion, nor dilutes the content of one's own religious identity.

## 2. Universality and Identity

The relationship between the perception of religious universality and the imperatives of one's identity is brought into sharp focus by Ibn al-'Arabī in his account of his spiritual ascension (*mi'rāj*), an account describing one of the peaks of his inner life.[22] In this spiritual ascent—distinguished from that of the Prophet, which was both bodily and spiritual—he rises up to a spiritual degree which is revealed as his own deepest essence. But one can hardly speak of personal pronouns such as "his" at this level of spiritual experience: whatever belongs to him, whatever pertains to "his" identity, is dissolved in the very process of the ascent itself. At the climax of this ascent, he exclaims: "Enough, enough! My bodily elements are filled up, and my place cannot contain me!", and then tells us: "God removed from me my contingent dimension. Thus I attained in this nocturnal journey the inner realities of all the Names and I saw them returning to One Subject and One Entity: that Subject was what I witnessed and that Entity was my Being. For my voyage was only in myself and pointed to myself, and through this I came to know that I was a pure 'servant' without a trace of lordship in me at all."[23]

[20] *Ikhtilāf al-'ulamā' raḥma.* This is often cited as a *ḥadīth*, but is more authoritatively ascribed to al-Shāfi'ī.

[21] Ibn al-'Arabī claims that everything he wrote was contained in his first vision of the "glory of His Face"; all his discourse is "only the differentiation of the all-inclusive reality which was contained in that look at the One Reality" (*Sufi Path*, p. xiv).

[22] The following pages contain reflections on material which can be found elaborated in greater detail in our *Paths to Transcendence: According to Shankara, Ibn Arabi, and Meister Eckhart* (Bloomington: World Wisdom, 2006), pp. 69-129.

[23] James W. Morris, "Ibn al-'Arabi's Spiritual Ascension", in Michel Chodkiewicz (ed.), *Les Illuminations de La Mecque/The Meccan Illuminations* (Paris: Sindbad, 1988), p. 380. One is reminded by the words "my place cannot contain me" of Rūmī's lines: "What is to be done, O Muslims? For I do not recognise myself? I am not Christian, nor Jew; not Zoroastrian, nor Muslim." This is a succinct expression of the transcendence of all religious identity in the bosom of the unitive state, which is alluded to later in the poem: "I have put duality

It is of note that immediately following this extraordinary revelation of the deepest reality of "his" selfhood within the divine reality, Ibn al-ʿArabī should proclaim, not the secret of oneness with God, or his "Lordship" in the manner of a Ḥallāj who declared ecstatically *anā 'l-ḥaqq* (I am the Truth), but the very opposite: he came to know through this journey that he was a pure servant (*ʿabd*), without any trace of lordship (*rubūbiyya*). The highest realization is accompanied by the deepest humility. Self-effacement, rather than self-glorification, is the fruit of this degree of spiritual station, the very opposite to what one might have imagined. It is the essence or *sirr*—"secret" or "mystery"—of consciousness within the soul of the saint that, alone, can grasp the truth that it is not conditioned by the soul. The consciousness *within* the soul knows that it is not *of* the soul—this being one of the reasons why this inmost degree of consciousness is referred to as a "secret": its immanent, divine identity is veiled from the soul of which it is the conscious centre. Herein lies one of the meanings of the Sufi saying: the Sufi is in the world but not of it.

The particular dynamics of being within the ontology of Ibn al-ʿArabī helps us to understand why specificity and self-effacement should be the natural expressions of universality and self-realization; these dynamics also help us to see the intimate relationship between the deconstruction of identity and the perception of the universality of religion, as well as the necessity for the reconstruction or restitution of identity within a specific religious matrix. These "religious" corollaries of Being will be explored later in this section. For the moment, attention is to be focused on the fact that at the very summit of this spiritual ascent to ultimate reality and self-realization, Ibn al-ʿArabī receives from that Reality the verse of the Qur'ān (cited above):

> *Say: We believe in God and that which is revealed unto us, and that which is revealed unto Abraham and Ishmael and Isaac and Jacob and the tribes, and that which was given unto Moses and Jesus and the prophets from their Lord. We make no distinction between any of them, and unto Him we have submitted.* (3:84)

He then adds these words: "Henceforth I knew that I am the totality of those (prophets) who were mentioned to me (in this verse)"; and also: "He gave me all the Signs in this Sign".[24]

Since the word for "sign" is the same as that for "verse" (*āya*), this can also be taken to mean that all revealed verses are implicitly contained in this verse which establishes the universality and unity of the essence of the religious message, despite the outward differentiation of its formal expression. This last point is clearly implied in another account of a spiritual ascent, in which Ibn al-ʿArabī encountered the Prophet amidst a group of other prophets and is asked by him: "What was it that made you consider us as many?" To which Ibn al-ʿArabī replies: "Precisely (the different scriptures and teachings) we took (from you)".[25]

Heavily implied in the Prophet's rhetorical question is the intrinsic unity of all the revelations. This principle is expressed in the following verse of the Qur'ān (cited above), which Ibn

aside. . . . / One I seek, One I know, One I see, One I call. / *He is the First, He is the Last, He is the Outward, He is the Inward.*" [paraphrasing 57:2]. (*Selected Poems from the Dīvān-i Shamsi Tabriz*, [ed. and tr. R.A. Nicholson (translation modified)] [Cambridge: CUP, 1977], pp. 125, 127).

[24] Quoted in James W. Morris, "Ibn al-ʿArabī's Spiritual Ascension", p. 379.

[25] Quoted in James W. Morris, "The Spiritual Ascension: Ibn al-ʿArabī and the Miʿrāj", *Journal of the American Oriental Society*, vol. 108, 1988, p. 75.

al-'Arabī quotes and then comments upon:

> *He hath ordained for you of the religion* (min al-dīn) *that which He commended unto Noah, and that which We reveal to thee* [Muḥammad], *and that which We commended unto Abraham and Moses and Jesus, saying: Establish the religion, and be not divided therein.* (42:13)

Then he quotes from another verse, mentioning further prophets, and concluding: *Those are they whom God has guided, so follow their guidance.* (6:90) He comments as follows:

> This is the path that brings together every prophet and messenger. It is the performance of religion, scattering not concerning it and coming together in it. It is that concerning which Bukhārī wrote a chapter entitled, "The chapter on what has come concerning the fact that the religions of the prophets is one". He brought the article which makes the word "religion" definite, because all religion comes from God, even if some of the rulings are diverse. Everyone is commanded to perform the religion and to come together in it.... As for the rulings which are diverse, that is because of the Law which God assigned to each one of the messengers. He said, *For each of you We have established a Law and a Path. Had God willed, He could have made you one community.* (5:48). If He had done that, your revealed Laws would not be diverse, just as they are not diverse in the fact that you have been commanded to come together and to perform them.[26]

One sees clearly that Ibn al-'Arabī is suggesting here a distinction between religion as such, on the one hand, and such and such a religion, on the other; it is religion as such that warrants the definite article (*al-dīn*). But such and such a religion, far from being marginalised in this perspective, is endowed with an imperatively binding nature by virtue of the absoluteness of its own essence, that is, by virtue of being not other than religion as such. For, on the one hand, religion as such, *al-dīn*, is the inner substance and inalienable reality of such and such a religion; and on the other, it is impossible to practise religion as such without adhering to such and such a religion. Apprehending the universal essence of religion, far from precluding particularity and exclusivity of formal adherence, in fact requires this adherence: to attain the essence one must grasp, in depth, the form by which the essence reveals itself. This is why, in the passage quoted above, Ibn al-'Arabī continues by stressing the specific path proper to the final Prophet. It is that path "for which he was singled out to the exclusion of everyone else. It is the Koran, God's firm cord and all-comprehensive Law. This is indicated in His words, 'This is My straight path, so follow it, and follow not diverse paths, lest they scatter you from its road' (6:153)".[27]

This "straight path" both excludes and includes all other paths: excludes by way of specific beliefs and practices, and includes by virtue of the single Essence to which the path leads, and from which it began. But one cannot reach the end of the path without traversing its specific trajectory, without keeping within its boundaries, and thus making sure that one does not

[26] Cited in *Sufi Path*, p. 303 (translation modified).

[27] Ibid.

stray into other paths: *And each one has a direction* (wijha) *toward which he turns. So vie with one another in good works* (2:148). One is instructed to turn towards one's particular goal, in a particular direction, and this is despite the fact that the Qur'ān tells us that *Wherever ye turn, there is the Face of God* (2:115). The ubiquity of the divine Face, then, does not imply that, in one's formal worship, the direction in which one turns to pray is of no consequence. For the Qur'ān also says: *Turn your face toward the sacred mosque, and wherever you may be, turn your faces toward it* [when you pray]. (2:144)

For Ibn al-'Arabī, such combinations of principial universality and practical specificity are paradoxical expressions of a principle that goes to the very heart of his ontology, his understanding of the nature of reality: for "part of the perfection or completeness of Being is the existence of imperfection, or incompleteness within it (من کمال الوجود وجود النقص فیہ)"[28]—failing which Being would be incomplete by virtue of the absence of incompleteness within it. This is an example of the bringing together of opposites (*jam' bayn al-ḍiddayn*) which is emphasised repeatedly in the writings of Ibn al-'Arabī, pertaining to the paradoxes required on the level of language, if one is to do justice to the complexities of existence. Just as completeness requires and is not contradicted by incompleteness, so the incomparability (*tanzīh*) of God requires and is not contradicted by comparability (*tashbīh*), universality requires and is not contradicted by particularity, inclusivity requires and is not contradicted by exclusivity, and nondelimitation (*iṭlāq*) requires and is not contradicted by delimitation (*taqyīd*).

Returning to the direction in which one must pray: on the one hand, the instruction to turn in a specific direction "does not eliminate the property of God's Face being wherever you turn." On the other, the fact that God is there wherever one turns nonetheless implies the bestowal of a specific "felicity" (*sa'āda*) as the consequence of turning in a particular direction for prayer. "Hence for you He combined delimitation and nondelimitation, just as for Himself He combined incomparability and similarity. He said; 'Nothing is like Him, and He is the Hearing, the Seeing' (42:11)."[29]

Nothing is like Him: this denial of similarity, this expression of pure *tanzīh* or transcendence, is immediately followed by an apparent contradiction of this very incomparability, for "He is the Hearing, the Seeing". As human beings also hear and see, this statement inescapably entails establishing modes of similarity or comparability between man and God. Ibn al-'Arabī, however, does not allow the mind to be restricted by this conceptual antimony, but rather takes advantage of the appearance of contradiction, using it as a platform from which to rise to an intuitive synthesis between these two opposing principles: the divine incomparability is perfect only when it is not conditioned by the very fact of being unconditioned by similarity, and vice versa. The divine nondelimitation is only properly grasped in the light of delimitation, and vice versa. This paradox is powerfully delivered in the following passage:

> He is not declared incomparable in any manner that will remove Him from similarity, nor is He declared similar in any manner that would remove Him from incomparability. So do not declare Him nondelimited and thus delimited by being distinguished from delimitation! For if He is distinguished then He is delimited

[28] Ibid., p. 296.

[29] Ibid., p. 11.

> by His nondelimitation. And if He is delimited by His nondelimitation, then He is not He.[30]

Without possessing or manifesting an aspect of finitude, God cannot be regarded as infinite; without assuming a mode of delimitation He cannot be nondelimited; without the relative, He cannot be Absolute. Without the innumerable manifestations of these apparent contradictions of His own uniqueness, without such multiplicity within unity, and unity within multiplicity, "He is not He". The very infinitude of the inner richness of unicity overflows as the outward deployment of inexhaustible self-disclosures; this process is described as the *tajallī* or *ẓuhūr* (theophanic revelation/manifestation). It is a process wherein no repetition is possible (*lā tikrār fi'l-tajallī*); each phenomenon is unique in time, space and quality. In this complex and subtle conception of *wujūd*, there is no contradiction between asserting the uniqueness of each phenomenon—each distinct locus for the manifestation of Being, each *maẓhar* for the *ẓuhūr* or *tajallī* of the one and only Reality—and the all-encompassing unity of being which transcends all phenomena. Multiplicity is comprised within unity, and unity is displayed by multiplicity.

This ontological perspective is to be applied on the plane of religion: there is no contradiction between asserting the uniqueness of a particular religion, on the one hand, and affirming the all-encompassing principle of religion which transcends the forms assumed by religion, on the other. The transcendence in question leaves intact the formal differences of the religions; for, these differences, defining the uniqueness of each religion, are by that very token irreducible; the formal differences can only be transcended in spiritual realization of the Essence, or at least, an intuition of this Essence. They cannot be abolished on their own level in a pseudo-esoteric quest for the supra-formal essence. For these differences are divinely willed; religious diversity expresses a particular mode of divine wisdom, which man must grasp if he is to do justice both to the formless Essence of religion, and the irreducible uniqueness of each religious form.

Ibn al-ʿArabī's conception of *al-dīn*, or religion as such, a religious essence that at once transcends and abides at the heart of all religions is in complete accord with the Qur'ānic perspective on religious diversity; it helps one to see that an orientation towards this quintessential religion does not in the least imply a blurring of the boundaries between religions on the plane of their formal diversity. For one does not so much conceptually posit as spiritually intuit this essence of religion—in other words, one sees this "heart" of religion with one's own "heart", rather than one's mind:

> My *heart* has become capable of every form: it is a pasture for gazelles and a convent for Christian monks,
> And a temple for idols and the pilgrim's Kaʿba and the tables of the Tora and the book of the Koran.
> I follow the religion of Love: whatever way Love's camels take, that is my religion and my faith. (emphasis added)[31]

[30] Ibid., p. 112.

[31] *The Tarjumān al-Ashwāq: A Collection of Mystical Odes*, tr. R.A. Nicholson (London: Theosophical Publishing House, 1978), p. 52.

The defining spirit of principled universality thus pertains to inner vision and does not translate into any modification of one's outer practice. It is on the basis of this religion of love, perceived by spiritual intuition, not formulated by rational speculation, that Ibn al-ʿArabī can issue the following warning to narrow-minded exclusivists:

> Beware of being bound up by a particular creed and rejecting others as unbelief! If you do that you will fail to obtain a great benefit. Nay, you will fail to obtain the true knowledge of the reality. Try to make yourself a Prime Matter for all forms of religious belief. God is greater and wider than to be confined to one particular creed to the exclusion of others. For He says: "To whichever direction you turn, there surely is the Face of God" (2:115).[32]

One should note that this counsel resonates with a Qur'ānic warning to the same effect. This verse comes just before 2:115, quoted in the previous citation from Ibn al-ʿArabī. Here, the attitude of religious exclusivism is censured, and the Muslim is told transcend the level of inter-confessional polemics and focus on the essential pre-requisites of salvation: not belonging to such and such a religion, but submitting to God through one's religion, and manifesting the sincerity of that submission through virtue:

> *And they say: None entereth Paradise unless he be a Jew or a Christian. These are their own desires. Say: Bring your proof if ye are truthful.*
>
> *Nay, but whosoever surrendereth his purpose to God while being virtuous, his reward is with his Lord; and there shall be no fear upon them, neither shall they grieve.* (2:112)

The Qur'ān excludes this kind of chauvinistic exclusivism by virtue of an implicit, and occasionally explicit, inclusivism; but it also includes its own mode of exclusivism, both implicitly and explicitly, in affirming the need to follow the particular religion of Islam. The Akbarī principle of paradoxical synthesis of two apparently contradictory principles can clearly be seen at this level of revelation, and is indeed the ultimate source of Ibn al-ʿArabī's elaborate metaphysics. In keeping with the spirit of this metaphysical perspective, one must assert: it is only on the basis of the vision of the religion of love that one can be "liberated" from the limitations of one's own faith, for then, the escape is upwards, towards the essence of one's own, and every, faith; any attempt to loosen the bonds of one's own belief system, in the absence of this upwardly and inwardly essentializing movement of consciousness, is tantamount to simply dissolving the roots of one's religious identity, and leaving nothing in its place on the level where one cannot do without a sense of identity, that is, the human personality. The consciousness which is alone capable of transcending the formal limitations of religion is supra-personal: it has nothing to do with the empirical ego.

In passing, one might note that it is this dissolution which postmodern deconstruction engenders, deliberately or otherwise; one aspires to be liberated from the "constructions" of

[32] Cited by Toshihiko Izutsu, *Sufism and Taoism: A Comparative Study of Key Philosophical Concepts* (Berkeley/London: University of California Press, 1983), p. 254. With modifications, see note 15 above.

belief, language, history, tradition, etc. by systematic demolition of these elements. But, in stark contrast to the spiritual "deconstruction" of an Ibn al-'Arabī, there is no reconstruction of thought, belief and identity on a higher plane of being.[33] Here it would be appropriate to return to the spiritual ascent, or *mi'rāj* of Ibn al-'Arabī mentioned earlier. It is important to note that in the course of this ascent, he undergoes a process of dissolution by means of which he is divested of various aspects of his being, such that he becomes aware that "his" consciousness is no longer "his", and the Real is realized as the essence of all consciousness and being. The degrees leading up to this unitive state are given in a description of the "journey" of the saints to God, within God. In this journey the composite nature of the saint is "dissolved", first through being shown by God the different elements of which his nature is composed, and the respective domains to which they belong; he then abandons each element to its appropriate domain:

> [T]he form of his leaving it behind is that God sends a barrier between that person and that part of himself he left behind in that sort of world, so that he is not aware of it. But he still has the awareness of what remains with him, until eventually he remains with the divine Mystery (*sirr*), which is the "specific aspect" extending from God to him. So when he alone remains, then God removes from him the barrier of the veil and he remains with God, just as everything else in him remained with (the world) corresponding to it.[34]

The constitutive elements of human nature are "dissolved" (or deconstructed) through being absorbed by those dimensions of cosmic existence to which they belong. Consciousness becomes rarefied, purified, and disentangled from matter and its subtle prolongations. As seen above, the "culminating revelation" coming just before the experience of extinctive union, was given in relation to the essence of all religions. Just as this realization of the essence of all religions does not entail any diminution of adherence to the form of one's own religion, likewise, as regards consciousness as such, the realization of the essence of the Real in no way entails any diminution of one's slavehood before the Real: "The slave remains always the slave", according to a saying often repeated in Ibn al-'Arabī's works. The ego remains always the ego, and this level of personal specificity cannot but entail what Ibn al-'Arabī refers to as *'ubūdiyya*, slavehood.

In other words, in this process of spiritual ascent there is both *taḥlīl* and *tarkīb*, dissolution and reconstitution, dissolution of all elements pertaining to the ego, and then reconstitution of this same ego, but on a higher plane: that of a conscious realization of one's actual nothingness. The higher the plane reached by essentialized consciousness, the deeper one's awareness of one's slavehood. In contrast to deconstruction, this dismantling of specificity and identity in the movement towards universality and transcendent Selfhood is accompanied by a return to specific identity, which is now vibrant with the spirit of the ultimate Self: the individual sees the Face of God everywhere, because of the very completeness of his self-effacement;

[33] Some have tried to see similarities between this type of spiritual self-denouement and postmodern deconstructionism. See our *The Other in the Light of the One*, pp. 23-58, for a presentation of the irreconcilable differences between the two approaches to reality.

[34] James W. Morris, "Ibn al-'Arabī's Spiritual Ascension", p. 362.

and, on the plane of religion, the specific form of his religion resonates with the universality proper to its essence. One grasps religion as such within such and such a religion; the absolute, nondelimited essence of religion is revealed by and within the relative, delimited religion, just as the Self of the Real (*nafs al-Ḥaqq*) subsists as the ultimate reality within the soul of the individual, who now comes to understand that he is both "He" and "not He". Each religion is both a form, outwardly, and the Essence, inwardly; just as man is "the transient, the eternal".[35]

The religion of love, or the religion of the "heart", thus re-affirms and does not undermine one's particular religion, or any other revealed religion; rather, this conception of "the religion" or religion as such presupposes formal religious diversity, regarding it not as a regrettable differentiation but a divinely willed necessity. The infinite forms of existence are integrated, "made one", according to the unitive principle of *tawḥīd*, in the very bosom, and not despite, this infinite unfolding of Being; we observe an analogous synthesis between multiplicity and unity on the level of religious phenomena: the dazzling diversity of religious forms manifest the principle of inexhaustible infinitude, just as the degree proper to "the religion", or religion as such, is the expression, in religious mode, of the principle of absolute oneness. This synthesis between infinity and oneness on the religious plane implies, then, both diversity of revealed forms, and the uniqueness of each specific revealed form. Each revealed religion is totally unique—totally "itself"—while at the same time being an expression of a single, all-encompassing principle, that of Revelation, a principle within which all religions are integrated, or "made one", in the rigorously metaphysical sense of *tawḥīd*.

To conclude: It is clear that for Ibn al-'Arabī the unity of religions lies in the unity of Revelation, and that this position is rooted in the message of the Qur'ān:

> *Say: We believe in God, and that which was revealed unto Abraham, and Ishmael, and Isaac, and Jacob, and the tribes, and that which was given unto Moses and Jesus and the prophets from their Lord. We make no distinction between any of them, and unto Him we have submitted.* (2:136)

The following verse might well be read as an allusion to the mystery of this unity of the celestial cause and the diversity of terrestrial effects:

> *And in the earth are neighbouring tracts, and gardens of vines, and fields sown, and palms in pairs, and palms single, watered with one water. And we have made some of them to excel others in fruit. Surely herein are signs for a people who understand.* (13:4)

The "water" of Revelation is simultaneously one in its substance and multiple in its forms. In terms of the image of the water and the cup, briefly alluded to above: the cup might be seen to symbolize the form taken by Revelation, while water stands for the Essence of Revelation. Water, in itself, is undifferentiated and unique, whilst undergoing an apparent change of form and color by virtue of the accidental shape and color of the receptacles into which it is poured.

[35] This is from Ibn al-'Arabī's *Fuṣūṣ al-ḥikam*, translated by R.W.J. Austin as *Bezels of Wisdom* (New York: Paulist Press, 1980) p. 51.

The receptacles, the forms of Revelation, are fashioned according to the specificities of the human communities to which the specific revealed message is addressed: *And We never sent a messenger save with the language of his folk, that he might make the message clear for them* (14:4). Just as human communities differ, so must the "language" of the "message" sent to them: the cups cannot but differ. However, the one who knows "water" as it is in itself, that is, the essence of that which is revealed, and not just its forms, will recognize this "water" in receptacles other than his own, and will be able to judge all such receptacles according to their content, rather than be misled into judging the content according to the accidental properties of the container.

To accept God fully, therefore, means to accept His presence and reality in all forms of His Self-disclosure, all forms of revelation, all beliefs stemming from those revelations; while to limit Him to one's own particular form of belief is tantamount to denying Him: "He who delimits Him denies Him in other than his own delimitation.... But he who frees Him from every delimitation never denies Him. On the contrary, he acknowledges Him in every form within which He undergoes self-transmutation."[36]

Nonetheless, the ordinary believer who may thus "deny" God by adhering exclusively to his own belief is not punished because of this implicit denial: since God is Himself "the root of every diversity in beliefs", it follows that "everyone will end up with mercy".[37] Also, in terms of the water/cup image: the water in the cup, however delimited it may be by the container, remains water nonetheless, hence the ordinary believer benefits from his possession of the truth; even if this truth be limited by the particularities of his own conception, it adequately conveys the nature of That which is conceived, but which cannot be attained by concepts alone. Thus one returns to the principle that all "religions" are true by virtue of the absoluteness of their content, while each is relative due to the particular nature of its form.

Each particular religion vehicles the Absolute, even while being distinct from It: the absoluteness of a religion resides in its supra-formal, transcendent essence, while, in its formal aspect, the same religion is necessarily relative; and this amounts to saying, on the one hand, that no one religion can lay claim, on the level of form, to absolute truth, to the exclusion of other religions, and on the other hand, that each religion is true by virtue of the absoluteness of its origin and of its essence. One continues to conform to the dictates of one's own religion, and does so, moreover, with a totality that is commensurate with the absoluteness inherent in the religion;[38] and at the same time one is aware of the presence of the Absolute in all those religions that have issued from a Divine Revelation, this awareness being the concomitant of one's recognition of the formal and thus relative aspect of one's own religion; and this recognition, in turn, arises in proportion to one's ability to plumb the metaphysical implications of the first testimony of Islam, "There is no god but God": only the Absolute is absolute.

This kind of approach to the question of religious diversity and interfaith dialogue ensures that the formal integrity and distinctness of each faith will be respected, and at the same time establishes the proper level at which we can say that all religions are at one. It is not on the level

[36] *Sufi Path*, pp. 339–340. The reference here is to God's capacity to transform Himself in keeping with the "signs" by which the believers can recognise Him, as expressed in the ḥadīth cited earlier in this article, and which Ibn al-'Arabi cites several times in his works.

[37] *Sufi Path*, p. 338.

[38] And, as seen earlier, one can conform to one's religion in the sincere belief that it is the *best* religion, without this detracting from the universality of one's perspective.

of forms that they are one; rather, they are one in God as their source, and they are as one in respect of the substance of their imperative to man: namely to submit to the Divinely Revealed Law and Way. Principles such as these, expounded with subtlety and depth in the metaphysical perspective of Ibn al-'Arabī, can help greatly in avoiding both the pitfalls of bridge-building between faiths and cultures, on the one hand, and the dangers of religious nationalism, on the other: that is, it can help to prevent a fragmentary sense of the sacred from arbitrarily or indiscriminately assimilating apparently "religious" forms out of sentimental desire; and, inversely, it can help prevent an over-zealous sense of orthodoxy from summarily anathematising alien religious forms out of dogmatic rigidity. Such a perspective shows that there is no incompatibility between believing absolutely in one's particular faith and cultivating reverentially a universal sense of the sacred.

*Gnosis*
Revealed faith speaks to every man;
Secret and difficult is the kernel of wisdom.
Gnosis is not form, nor is it time;
The sage is guided by a hidden star.

In one sense gnosis is a part
Of faith, its content finely spun;
And yet the depth of gnosis still remains
Beyond the yoke of pharisaic power.

Who can fathom the word of God's wise men?
I am neither a Jew, nor Muslim, nor Christian,
Rumi said; and my Islam is not
Dogmatic belief; it is that which is.

O light of the heart, shining before the Most High,
Which always was and nevermore shall fade.
*Frithjof Schuon*

# Pluralism or the Consciousness of Alterity in Islam

*Éric Geoffroy*

Within the matrix of the main elements of Islam's foundation, the principle of pluralism affirms itself at times externally (Islam's relations to other religions and cultures) and at times internally (Islam's intra-relations). Moreover, one can distinguish a positive pluralism—one formulated by scriptural sources and thereby advocated by those who have directed the community—and a negative pluralism—one more undergone than undertaken, and which *de facto* has invited itself into Islamic history (and into the history of other religions), bringing along its fate of scissions and tears (*fitna;* pl. *fitan*).

The Islamic doctrine of pluralism follows from a logical principle: since, in Islam, God alone is One and unique, all that is other than Him, namely His creation, is projected into multiplicity. However, the divine mercy, which "embraces all things",[1] ensures that there is no rupture between these two levels. There exists, in fact, an all-pervading, although often underlying, dialectic between divine Unicity and the multiplicity of creation. This is why, in Sufism, the initiate tends to perceive *simultaneously* Unicity in multiplicity, then multiplicity in Unicity.

The cosmos can unfold in multiplicity because it is maintained by the axis of *Tawhīd* (Unicity). In the first surah, God presents Himself as the Lord of *the worlds* (*rabb al-'ālamīn*).[2] The faces of creation are innumerable because they originate from Him and are reabsorbed into Him. A great many Koranic verses express this idea of return/reabsorption in God—reabsorption of human souls, but also of the causes for divergence among these souls during their earthly sojourn. A human being who has reached some level of awakening knows that "by the unicity of multitude, we can know the unicity of the Unique", as affirmed by Ibn 'Arabī.[3] While the divine Essence, in its oneness, is unfathomable, God nevertheless makes Himself multiple in universal Manifestation by making Himself known through His names and His attributes. He thereby places Himself within reach of human intellection, and creates an unseverable solidarity between the divine and human planes. Thus, the "recognition of Unicity (*Tawhīd*)" that is required of the faithful Muslim, should, by direct implication, bring about in his consciousness the recognition of the solidarity and interdependence of all the realms of creation. Let us recall the Prophet's words: "The entire creation is God's family (*al-khalq 'iyāl Allāh*)." Before modern ecologists, the emir 'Abd al-Qadir had already affirmed that "the divine tide that reaches the gnat is the self-same one that flows into the whole universe".[4] The aim of the traditional Islamic sciences, moreover, "is to show the unity and interrelatedness of all that exists, so that, in contemplating the unity of the cosmos, man may be led to the unity of the Divine Principle".[5]

The Koran enunciates, first of all, a *cosmic* pluralism, in which the various realms are bound by a community of worship: "The seven heavens and the earth, and all beings therein proclaim His glory—there is nothing that does not praise Him, but ye [humans] perceive not this

1 Koran 7:156.

2 Koran 1:2.

3 *Al-Futūhāt al-makkiyya* (Cairo, 1329 h.), III, 404.

4 *Kitāb al-mawāqif* (Damascus, 1966), stop no. 368.

5 S. H. Nasr, *Science and Civilization in Islam* (New York: New American Library, 1968), introduction.

incantation."[6] Then, on the human scale, pluralism becomes *ethnic* and *cultural*: "If thy Lord had so willed, He could have made mankind one single community, but they cease not differing, save those on whom thy hath bestowed His Mercy. And it is even for that purpose that He created them. . .";[7] "O mankind, We have created you male and female, and made you into nations and tribes, that you may know each other";[8] then it becomes *linguistic*: "And among His signs is the creation of the heavens and the earth, and the diversity of your languages and your colors. . .";[9] and, of course, *religious*, which is our primary interest here.

* * *

### *The Recognition of Religious Alterity: From Text to Practice*

An unceasing debate has occurred between "inclusivist" Muslim authors, who tend to cite the Koranic verses that open onto other religions, and "exclusivist" authors who base themselves on verses that call for rigor, or even for aggression, towards non-Muslims. Depending upon the spatio-temporal environments in which these authors lived, these were, and are, two opposing visions of the world, or else simply a matter of political strategy. . . . Contemporary exegesis tends consistently toward this statement: the scriptural texts of Islam sanction the interreligious diversity one finds within the Revelation; to be a Muslim means, therefore, to recognize the authenticity of all the religions revealed before Islam. However, the environment of conflict, or at least of rivalry, in which the first generations of Muslims were often involved has partially blocked this opening. "Inclusivist" exegetes seem more objective than others for, whether they be ancient or modern, their conceptual background is richer, and thus the ideological and apologetic element is reduced. The spiritual figures among them add to this a gustative perception of the wealth of meaning of the Koran, an experience that cannot but open the Text to others, and bequeath it to them, as it were.

Islam's universalism finds its origin in the *Fitra*: every human being bears God's imprint within himself, whether he is aware of it or not. It is rooted in prophetology, a major doctrine in Islam, and one clearly delineated: "We inspire thee as we inspired Noah and the prophets after him ... [an enumeration of prophets follows] Of some messengers We have already told thee the story; *of others We have not. . .*";[10] "Each community has received a messenger [prophet]. . ."[11]. In reference to these verses, the Prophet used to affirm that there had been 124,000 prophets among mankind, himself being the last in the historical order. Now, only twenty-seven are mentioned in the Koran; therefore, one must search for the signs of prophecy throughout the whole of mankind. Certain Egyptian Muslim authors, well regarded by al-Azhar, thus identify Osiris with the prophet Idrīs, and the pharaoh Akhenaton with the prophet Job (Ayyūb). For them, the 2,800 deities of the Egyptian pantheon would be none other than representations of the Names and Attributes of the one sole God... This, again, is why, according to some ulemas,

[6] Koran 17:44.

[7] Koran 11:118-119.

[8] Koran 49:13.

[9] Koran 30:22.

[10] Koran 4:163-164.

[11] Koran 10:47.

the Buddha could be integrated into the Islamic structure of Revelation—and this all the more so in that the Koran seems to mention him in an allusive fashion.[12]

In the context of seventh-century Arabia, religious pluralism was imperative for Muslims, given, in particular, the Jewish and Christian presence. Once established in Medina, Muhammad had to create a cohesiveness among Muslims, and above all between the Muslims and the non-Muslims of the region, notably the Jews. A city-state embodying the venture of Islam had to be created. The goal was to institute a pluralistic theocracy, of which Muhammad was the arbiter and guarantor. Islam's recognition of other religions was thus combined with an induced hegemony, at least on the political plane. Be that as it may, the use in the first or second year of the Hijrah of the term *Umma* in the text of Medina's "Charter" (*sahīfah*), bespeaks new bonds of solidarity, bonds which transcend tribal affiliations and which indicate a community of diverse faiths.[13] Several verses echo this context, such as: "Verily, this community of yours is a single community, and I am your Lord. So worship Me! But they diverged in their religious convictions, yet all will return to Us!"[14]

Concern for Islam's placement in history led the Prophet himself to give precedence at times to the political dimension, and it came to pass that the Revelation contradicted him on the matter of interreligious openness. Thus, when Salmān Fārisī asked him about the fate of the deeply pious Mazdeans whom he had frequented in Persia, and who had no knowledge of Islam, Muhammad answered that they were destined for the flames of hell. Verse 2:62 was then revealed, which opened up mercy and salvation to the faithful of other religions: "Indeed, those who believe, Jews, Christians and Sabeans, whoever believes in God and in the Last Day and does good works: their reward is with their Lord, no fear shall come upon them, neither shall they grieve." The same "circumstance of Revelation" is sometimes invoked concerning verses 5:69: "Lo! Those who believe, and those who are Jews, Christians, and Sabeans—whosoever believes in God and the Last Day and performs good deeds—no fear shall come upon them, neither shall they grieve."

The same holds true for verses 2:111-112, which lend to salvation an even wider perspective: "[The People of the Book] said: 'None enters Paradise unless he be a Jew or a Christian'. These are their own desires. Say: Bring your proof if you are truthful. Indeed, whoever submits his face to God while being virtuous will find his reward with God, no fear shall come upon him, neither shall he grieve." The expression "to submit one's face to God" does not define any particular creed; it describes a universal religious attitude, as is implied also by verse 2:148: "There is for each a goal toward which he turns himself. Seek thus to surpass each other in good deeds."

The religious pluralism enunciated by certain verses has made more than one Muslim commentator uncomfortable, but one could not deny the obvious. For instance, verse 5:48: "For each of you, we have given a divine law and a path. Had God willed, He would have made of you a single community, but He wanted to test you by the gift he made to you. So vie with one

[12] On these questions see Éric Geoffroy, *Introduction to Sufism: The Inner Path of Islam* (Bloomington: World Wisdom, 2010), pp. 182-183.

[13] On the "Charter" see in particular M. Hamidullah, *Le Prophète de l'islam, sa vie, son œuvre* (Paris, 1959), pp. 124-129; A.L. de Prémare, *Les Fondations de l'islam—Entre écriture et histoire* (Paris, 2002), pp. 88-89; and S. Stétié, *Mahomet* (Paris, 2001), pp. 135-137.

[14] Koran 21:92-93.

another in good works. Your return will be to God; He will enlighten you, then, about your differences." In the context of the preceding verses (5:44-46), which define the Torah and the Gospels as "guidance" and as "light", the most normative exegetes could only conclude in favor of the diversity of paths that lead to salvation.

Some contemporary Muslim commentators even draw from this the implication that an individual may choose the path toward God that most befits him.[15]

At times, the formulation of a verse is less clear and requires an effort of interpretation (*ijtihād*) if the exegete wants to avoid the easy slide down exclusivism's slippery slope. This is the case for two verses quoted above, the implications of which remain central to internal Muslim debates:

1. "The religion, with God, is Islam" (3:19) This means, for many commentators, that this religion is the adhesion to the principle of Unicity whereof all the prophets have spoken.[16] And while a few authors, such as Ibn Kathīr, limit the "religion" to the revelation given to Muhammad, a later commentator such as al-Alūsī epitomizes previously held opinions according to which the "Islam" that is mentioned in this verse is a generic term that encompasses non-Muslim believers.[17] It is therefore *the principle of trusting abandonment to God and to the cosmic order which is at stake here, and not Islam as a historical phenomenon* which has adopted the vicissitudes inherent to mankind's earthly adventure. A number of modern Muslim exegetes, such as Fazlur Rahman, Hassan Hanafi, Mohamed Talbi, and Farid Esack have endorsed this view.

2. An equivalent effort shatters the restrictive meaning given to verse 3:85: "He who seeks a religion other than Islam will see his choice rejected, and he will be among the losers in the hereafter." Some authors reject the community-centered reading of this verse. They stress that the verse cannot be understood outside of the *context* in which it occurs, that is to say following verses 83 and 84. Verse 83 speaks of the "religion of God" to which the creatures of the heavens and earth submit, and it is this primordial religion that is intended by verse 85. The intermediate verse, 84, corroborates such a view for, after having enumerated the historical procession of prophets, it reminds us that no preference should be given to any among them. The "circumstances of the Revelation" do call, however, for a restriction, given that verse 85 was revealed after twelve men who had become apostates left Medina for Mecca.[18] Even so, one of the first great commentators, Tabarī, reports that the non-Muslim believers who were present, including Jews, saw themselves within this "Islam" which guaranteed them salvation as well, provided they follow their own religious tradition.[19] If one relies on a number of past and modern exegetes, some Sufi, others not, verse 85 receives this inclusive and universalist meaning: *the losers in the hereafter will not be those who adhere to a historical religion other than Islam, but those who deny their spiritual origin and their status as worshippers herebelow.*[20] Here

15 F. Esack, *Qur'ān, Liberation, and Pluralism* (Oxford, 1997), p. 170.

16 Among them Tabarī, *Jāmi' al-bayān 'an ta'wīl āyī al-Qur'ān* (Beirut, n.d.), III, p. 212; Ibn 'Arabī, *Fusūs al-hikam*, éd. 'Afīfī (Beirut, n.d., I, pp. 94-95; al-Qāshānī, *Tafsīr al-Qur'ān al-karīm* (attributed to Ibn 'Arabī) (Beirut, n.d.), I, p. 174; Ibn 'Ajība, *Al-bahr al-madīd fī tafsīr al-Qur'ān al-majīd* (Beirut, 2002), I, p. 300.

17 Alūsī, *Rūh al-ma'ānī*, II, p. 107.

18 *Ibid.*, II, p. 215.

19 Tabarī, *Jāmi' al-bayān*, III, p. 339.

20 From the past: Qāshānī, I, p. 199; Alūsī, II, p. 216; Ibn 'Ajība, I, p. 343. Among modern commentators: R. Ridā, *Tafsīr al-Manār*, the Shiite Tabataba'i, *al-Mīzān fī tafsīr al-Qur'ān*; F. Esack, *Qur'ān*, p. 163.

once again we find ourselves on the fertile ground of the *Fitra*. Is it out of a desire to appropriate them that the Koran refers to Noah, Abraham, Jacob and other prophets as "muslims"? Or, rather, is it because the term *islām* designates first the natural, primordial religion before it designates the religion brought by Muhammad?

**Does Islam Abrogate Prior Religions? The Question of Tolerance**

Can followers of other religions be saved even though Islam is now among us and they have not entered it? What is raised here is the delicate issue of the abrogation of previous religions by Islam, which Muslims consider to be the final expression of the Message addressed to mankind. Once again, opinions are divided among the *ulama*.[21] Some exegetes have proposed that verse 2:62, which we examined earlier ("Lo! Those who believe, and those who are Jews, Christians and Sabeans. . ."), was abrogated by verse 3:85 ("He who seeks a religion other than Islam will see his choice rejected, and he will be among the losers in the hereafter."), although we just examined the sense in which the word *islām* must be taken in this verse. Be that as it may, other exegetes have denied that God could fail to keep the promise of salvation accorded to non-Muslims in verse 2:62.

The various positions on the subject of abrogation are obviously linked to the historical environment of those who adopted them. When, in former times, each religion was focused upon itself, it was difficult not to support, at least publicly, the exclusivist position. Nevertheless, in the midst of the medieval period, a few individuals had the courage to lay claim to the foundational universalism of their religion. Ibn 'Arabī, for example, holds that, although there is abrogation, the prior religions, which are so many "lights", are by no means untrue, for each of them is established in a specific relationship with God.[22] Moreover, contemporary *ulama*[23] do at times acknowledge the Koran's Judeo-Christian "heritage" in cases where some non-Muslims prefer to speak of "borrowing". In this vein, Abdelmajid Charfi affirms that the Koran "has never said that the message of Muhammad abrogates the previous messages: it rather considers it as confirming and dominating them. Now, domination does not mean abrogation!"[24] In fact, some verses imply that Islam, given its nature as the "seal" of Revelation, must protect the various forms of faith. Thus the first authorization Muslims received to resort to defensive armed struggle was aimed at preserving places of worship in general: ". . . If God had not raised some men against each other, hermitages as well as churches, synagogues, and mosques would have been destroyed, in which the Name of God is frequently invoked."[25]

This duty to protect prior religions can easily appear as an hegemonic endeavor on the part of Islam. Moreover, have the precepts that it actuates always been applied by Muslims? Certainly not, for mankind, quite simply—and this everywhere—is weak and fallible. But these precepts clearly constitute the foundations upon which have been nourished the religious ma-

[21] For a summary of this question see E. Chaumont, "Abrogation", *Dictionnaire du Coran*, M.A. Amir-Moezzi (ed.), (Paris, 2007), p. 15.

[22] Ibn 'Arabī, *Al-Futūhāt al-makkiyya*, I, p. 265; C. A. Gilis, *L'Esprit universel de l'Islam* (Paris, 1998), pp. 204-205.

[23] M. Ghazālī, *Al-ta'assub*, p. 82.

[24] A. Charfi, *L'islam entre*, p. 50.

[25] Koran 22:40.

turity opening onto the universal, that is to say the *tolerance* characteristic of classical Islam, as attested to by European philosophers of the 18th century and, later on, by many Orientalists.[26] This tolerance flows from the Koranic teachings of the "Immutable Religion"[27] and from rules such as: "What to them (non-Muslims) is due to us is due, and what upon them is incumbent upon us is incumbent."[28] It is true that each Muslim camp—the inclusivists and the exclusivists—buttresses its own cause by calling on different verses that seemingly contradict each other, some extolling tolerance and others intolerance.[29] The latter verses, in turn, are now made use of by non-Muslim islamophobes who obviously are not at all interested in the "circumstances of the Revelation." In this ideological imbroglio, and to summarize, the position that to me appears the most sound holds that "the verses that extol tolerance and respect for the freedom to believe or not to believe have a universal scope, whereas the so-called 'combative' verses are relative to a particular situation",[30] that is to say to a historical context which is not relevant for us today. For many Sufis, it is not in terms of mere tolerance that one must envisage the universalism of the Revelation, but in terms of a *transcendent unity of religions.*[31] In a logical way, esoterists tend to be inclusivists, since they perceive the weft, the grammar common to all religions, while exoterists tend to be exclusivists, since they are limited by the barriers of dogma.

Certain negative historical contexts (the Crusades, economic and commercial decline, then colonialism. . .) and more generally the slow process of sclerosis of Islamic culture have led to an evermore pronounced withdrawal into the shell of identity. While the first generations of Muslims were open to alterity, eager to assimilate what comes from other civilizations, the rejection of "the other" has now become a symptom of the discontent experienced both collectively and individually in so-called "Muslim" societies. Thus the Indonesian "Council of Ulama" (MUI), in a fatwa of July 27, 2005, has condemned religious pluralism within Indonesian society: it denounced the opinion according to which all religions are equal, and religious truth is relative. However, Indonesian society has always fully accepted the religious and cultural diversity that make up its identity. . .

In this baneful restriction of thought, the Koran, and more generally the ethics of Islam, have been made the servants of interpretations that ignore context, and which deny any intelligence or depth to the text, spurring frustration and resentment. They have been made the subjects of gross confusions that identify, for example, non-Muslim believers with *kuffār* (unbelievers, infidels) whereas this term, which possesses a considerable semantic density, designates above all the disbelieving Meccans hostile to the Prophet. Moreover, Muslims have copiously abused this term internally to disqualify on the dogmatic plane such or such an Islamic group... And, indeed, whether one be Muslim or not, one always more or less "buries" truth or faith, one is

[26] Among modern commentators let us limited ourselves to I. Goldziher, *Le dogme et la loi dans l'islam* (Paris, 2005) (re-ed. of 1920), pp. 29-30; A. Fattal, *Le statut légal des non-musulmans en pays d'Islam* (Beirut, 1958); B. Lewis, *Le retour de l'islam* (Paris, 1985), p. 27 or *Juifs en terre d'islam* (Paris, 1986), p. 71.

[27] Éric Geoffroy, *Introduction to Sufism: The Inner Path of Islam*, pp. 182-183.

[28] A rule reminded, for example, by M. Ghazālī, *Al-ta'assub*, p. 87.

[29] One will find a good summary of it in M. C. Ferjani, *Le politique et le religieux dans le champ islamique* (Paris, 2005), pp. 257-258.

[30] Ibid., p. 259.

[31] See Éric Geoffroy, *Introduction to Sufism: The Inner Path of Islam*, p. 183 ff.

always more or less "ungrateful" towards divine grace: such are the fundamental meanings of the root *kfr*.[32]

However, when one considers this question—a sensitive one for Islam as for other religions—it is important to distinguish the doctrinal background from historical vicissitudes. In spite of the tribulations of history, "the Koranic rule has managed to impose a tolerance which, even in our day, is respected in very few socio-political systems".[33] Thus, while there was a political disagreement at a certain moment between the nascent Muslim community and the Jews of the region of Medina, this did not prevent the Prophet and the generations that followed him from respecting the Jewish religion: it is no coincidence that the Spanish Jews who, like the Muslims, were expelled by the *Reconquista* in 1492, took refuge en masse with the Ottoman sultan of Istanbul. How can a contemporary imam curse all Jews by making the shortcut equation Jew = Zionist extremist, when the Prophet specifically affirmed, "he who harms a Christian or a Jew will be my enemy on the Day of Judgment and will pay for it"? In reality, rather than debating about the hypothetical abrogation of the religions prior to Islam—a topic which, on a theological level, has become obsolete—the contemporary Muslim should focus on the *inner* abrogation of his past, solidified, representations and illusions, those which prevent him from adhering to the Reality (*Haqīqa*) at once perennial and immanent, and renewed at each instant.

*Translated by Patrick Laude and Joseph Fitzgerald*

Differences of opinion among the doctors of the law,
Are a blessing from God, it is said in Islam.
Why? Because the light of the spiritual miracles
That move the heart is inexhaustible.

Our soul too is multiform
In its simplicity. God is One;
And every truth that comes from above,
Whatever be its form, belongs to God.

If God did not wish to dwell in a variety of hearts
Here below, there would be no religions.

*Frithjof Schuon*

32 See Koran 57:20 where the term *kuffār* may be translated by "farmers" or, by semantic derivation by "those who have buried the seed of faith".

33 M. Boisard, *L'humanisme de l'islam* (Paris, 1979), p. 199.

# "Neither of the East nor of the West": Universality in Islam

*M. Ali Lakhani*

*God is the Light of the heavens and the earth.*
*The parable of His Light is as if there were a niche,*
*And within it a Lamp: the Lamp enclosed in Glass,*
*The Glass as it were a glittering star,*
*Lit from a Blessed Tree,*
*An Olive, neither of the East nor of the West,*
*Whose oil is nigh luminous, though no fire has touched it:*
*Light upon Light! God guides to His Light whom He wills.*
*And God strikes similitudes for men, and God has knowledge of everything.*[1]

The idea of universality has an intrinsic metaphysical appeal. It corresponds to an aesthetic sensibility that perceives an underlying order and harmony in the midst of chaos, and to an ethical sensibility that is premised on an inner impulse of peace and goodness. As this paper will attempt to show, it is precisely these sensibilities of Beauty and Virtue that lie at the heart of the message of Islam and that impress it with its ambience and ethos of universality.

But if the idea of universality has an intrinsic metaphysical appeal, in practice it belies a tension that is also metaphysically rooted. This is the tension between the divine archetypes of Rigor and Mercy, between the need to impose universality as outward conformity to rigid laws, and the need to achieve it by accommodation. The former can lead to a homogeneity that sacrifices diversity in the name of universality, while the latter can lead to an outlook of "laissez faire" that sacrifices principles for the sake of peace. As this paper will argue, both these approaches are flawed. Instead, as we will attempt to show, Islam advocates a principled pluralism that springs from the very substance of reality, of the "Hidden Treasure" of the Divine Heart that is the ontological foundation and the Illuminating Lamp of both Beauty and Virtue.

When we speak of the "message" of Islam, this begs the question: where should we look to discern its message? As with all faith traditions, Islam was brought into the world by a messenger, the Holy Prophet Muhammad (peace and blessings be upon him), who first received the divine Word from God through the Archangel Gabriel, and thereafter through a series of intermittent "revelations" that spanned the rest of his life. At one level, therefore, the message can be equated with the codified "revelations" of the Qur'an, which is itself a compendium of

[1] *Surah an-Nur*, 24:35. The author's interpretations of the various Qur'anic *ayats* cited in this article are based on his readings of Qur'anic commentaries, and particularly the texts and translations of Muhammad Asad (*The Message of the Qur'an* [Gibraltar: Dar-al-Andalus, 1980]) and Abdullah Yusuf Ali (*The Holy Qur'an: Text, Translation and Commentary* [McGregor & Werner, 1946]).

the *ayat* or "signs" of God[2] and which describes itself as a "Manifest Light"[3]. In another sense, the Holy Prophet is himself "an Illuminating Lamp"[4], bearing the message that lights the world, and so is also a sign of God. It is noteworthy that both the Messenger (the "Lamp") and the Message (the "Light") are described using the symbol of luminosity and diffusion, which carries the metaphysical connotations of spirituality and universality. But in a broader sense, the "revelation" can be understood in terms of the ever-renewing theophany[5] that is continually destroyed[6] and re-created by the divine fiat[7] in each moment of its existence. Each and every aspect of creation, including oneself, is a translucent "sign" of God, and so humankind is exhorted to discern these signs with "eyes of faith":

> And in the earth are signs for those whose faith is profound—and in yourselves: can you not see?[8]

What we are exhorted to discern is the nature of our existential reality and our existential purpose—those divine messages that are imprinted in the "signs" which are found in "the utmost horizons" and within ourselves[9]. The essence of these messages is contained in the two testimonial declarations or *shahadat* that constitute the basic creed of Muslims, *La ilaha illa' Llah* and *Muhammadun Rasulu 'Llah*: "There is no god but God" and "Muhammad is the messenger of God". The first declaration sums up the doctrine of *tawhid* (the integral Unity of Reality), while the second pertains to the doctrines of *nabuwwah* (Prophecy) and *ma'ad* (the Return to God) and speaks to the salvation and perfectability of man, of the possibilities of Union and Realization. Referring to these two declarations, Frithjof Schuon has commented as follows:

> The first of these certainties is that "God alone is" and the second that "all things are attached to God."... All metaphysical truths are comprised in the first of these Testimonies and all eschatological truths in the second.[10]

"God alone is": this metaphysical truth is the key to a Muslim's discernment of reality. Cognitively, this formula engages the understanding that at its core unity embraces universality, but, more importantly, it signifies a mode of "seeing" in which everything is metaphysically transparent to transcendence. If "God alone is", then "Wherever you turn, there is the Face of

2 *Surah Yunus*, 10:1, "These are the *ayats* of the Book of Wisdom."

3 *Surah an-Nisa'*, 4:174.

4 *Surah al-Ahzab*, 33:46. This is one of five Qur'anic capacities of the Prophethood (see 33:45-46). The Arabic term *siraj* is translated by Asad as "a light-giving beacon." It can also mean the "sun", and is an emblem of the universality of the Islamic message.

5 *Surah al-Baqarah*, 2:115, "Wherever you turn, there is the Face of God."

6 *Surah al-Qasas*, 28:88, "Everything is perishing but His Face."

7 *Surah al-Baqarah*, 2:117, "... when He wills a thing to be, He but says to it, 'Be!'—and it is."

8 *Surah adh-Dhariyat*, 51:20-21.

9 *Surah Fussilat*, 41:53, "In time We shall make them fully understand Our messages in the utmost horizons and within themselves, until it becomes clear to them that it is the Truth."

10 Frithjof Schuon, *Understanding Islam* (Bloomington, IN: World Wisdom Books, 1998), pp. 5-6.

God."[11] This central doctrine of universality is much more than theoretical in a merely conceptual sense. In the deeper sense, where *theoria* denotes "seeing", the doctrine has hermeneutical and phenomenological implications that are rooted in a particular cosmological understanding of creation, which, as we shall see, is itself founded upon the metaphysical structures of Beauty and Compassion.

According to Islamic cosmology, all creaturely qualities and attributes are derived from their divine archetypes residing within the "treasure-house" of God, and are thence deployed within creation in an aggregated measure. Thus, the Qur'an states, "There is nothing whose treasuries are not with Us, and We send it down only with a known measure."[12] All existential qualities are therefore attenuations of the divine archetypes of perfection. These archetypes are attributes (*sifat*) of the Divine Essence, that is, of that quintessential substance of Reality that constitutes its quiddity (or *dhat*). As such, they are aspects of metaphysical Beauty—which is the radiance of the Divine Essence—and so are termed "The Most Beautiful Names."[13] Conventionally known as "The Ninety-Nine Names of Allah", they are to be understood as the limitless archetypal aggregations of existential reality whose source is the divine treasury and, ultimately, the Divine Essence which is the "Hidden Treasure" of the celebrated Hadith Qudsi of Creation, "I was a Hidden Treasure and My loving nature impelled Me to be known, and so I created the world in order to be known."[14] The archetypal qualities and attributes derived from the Divine Essence have both a hierarchy and complementarity. The hierarchy relates to His Essence, Attributes and Acts, while the complementarity pertains to the masculine and feminine polarities inherent in creation, which are themselves archetypally rooted in the hypostases of masculine Absoluteness and feminine Infinitude that pertain to the transcendence and immanence, respectively, of Reality. Thus, "masculine" qualities such as Rigor, Majesty, and Hiddenness, are complemented by "feminine" qualities such as Mercy, Beauty, and Manifestness. All creatures are compounded of these qualities in a divine "measure", and are therefore aspects of the theophany.

Of all the creatures, it is man alone who is graced with knowledge of the Divine Names. In other words, it is man alone who is privileged to know God. The Qur'an discloses that God "taught Adam the names of all things."[15] The Arabic term *ism* ("name") is to be understood here as referring to the Divine Names, that is, to the theophanic attributes of created things. The ability to recognize the attributes and natures of things is a key component of the Adamic heritage of mankind. But, more significantly, the Qur'an also discloses that Adam, exemplifying humanity, was created in the divine form, "proportioned"[16] out of clay, and enlivened with the

[11] See note 5, supra.

[12] *Surah al-Hijr*, 15:21. The "known measure" (*qadar*) refers to both the finitude of God's creation and to the unique combinations of His ever-renewing theophany. See also *Surah al-Qamar*, 54:49, "Indeed, We have created all things in a known measure."

[13] These are termed *al-asma'al-husna*. *Surah al-Araf*, 7.180, "And all the Most Beautiful Names belong to God, so call on Him by them, and quit the company of those who belie or deny His Names." See also *Surah Ta Ha*, 20:8, and *Surah al-Hashr*, 59:24, "To Him belong the Most Beautiful Names."

[14] See note 27, infra.

[15] *Surah al-Baqarah*, 2:31.

[16] See note 17, infra. "Proportioned" here refers not only to the "fashioning" of the clay, but also to the "measuring out" of creaturely attributes from the divine treasure-house of qualities: see note 12, *supra*.

*ruh* or divine spirit, which was blown into him by God.[17] Spiritualized man is thus a microcosm of reality. The Divine Names are ontologically imprinted within him, as they are within the macrocosm that he reflects. There is nothing in creation that does not bear the imprint of its Maker—though it is man alone who is privileged among the creatures to recognize this imprint and thereby to perceive the divine theophany.

We noted earlier that all creation is the existential manifestation of "The Most Beautiful Names", and so everything is an aspect of metaphysical Beauty. There is nothing in creation that cannot be seen, if rightly perceived, as an aspect of Divine Beauty. The Qur'an states, "It is God who made beautiful everything that He created."[18] Creation therefore expresses the divine nature, hence the Hadith, "God is beautiful, and He loves Beauty." Inasmuch as Beauty is the radiance of the divine, the recognition of God is the discernment of God through His Beauty—in other words, through His theophanic Presence in all things. Muslim doctrine is thereby in accord with the Scholastic precept that "beauty relates to the cognitive faculty"[19], but as its cause, because the ability to recognize Beauty extrinsically relates to the intrinsic source of that recognition, which is the presence of inner Beauty, or Virtue. Thus the Arabic root, *hsn*, refers to "Goodness", both intrinsically, as Virtue, and outwardly as its divine radiance, or Beauty. Intrinsic Beauty, or Virtue, is the very substance of the Intellect and so the cause of knowledge. It is the beauty within us, operating through the intelligence of our aesthetic sensibility, which enables us to discern the sacred radiance of the divine. It is through "the eyes of faith", located in the Heart[20]—that is, through the faculty of the transcendent Intellect functioning cognitively as the active intelligence in the receptive mode[21]—that man is able to recognize the Beauty of the "Face of God"[22] in all its primordial manifestations, in Nature and the Self, and in all other earthly reflections of supernatural beauty, such as sacred Art.

The aesthetic sensibility corresponds to the sense of the sacred, to the perception of hierarchical order and harmonious symmetry, and engages the synthesis of being and knowing, and of love and knowledge. It perceives universality as an aspect of unity, as radiance—that is, as a radial effulgence from the Heart-Center. It is this radial connection that engages our perception of things in the profoundly integrative and ontological sense. The aesthetic sensibility also corresponds to the "symbolist spirit", that is, the recognition of the metaphysical transparency of creation—which sees the "signs" of God as pointing to the reality that "God alone is", that principial unity is reflected in the world of manifestation, that Heaven is reflected on Earth, that Adam is a symbolic reflection of God. But these correspondences are more than conceptual—they are more even than ways of "seeing": they are ontological, that is to say, they involve a

[17] *Surah as-Sajdah*, 32:9, "Then He fashioned him in due proportion, and breathed into him the divine spirit. . .".

[18] *Surah al-Sajdah*, 32:7, "'*Ahhazii 'ahsana kulla shay'in khalaqahuu*. . .". The root, *hsn*, refers to "goodness", both intrinsically, as Virtue, and as the divine radiance, or Beauty.

[19] Aquinas, *Summa Theologica*, I,5,4 ad. 1.

[20] *Surah al-Hajj*, 22:46, "It is not the eyes that are blind, but blind are the hearts within the breast." The Heart is the cardial center of man, the locus of spiritual discernment.

[21] For an elaboration on the meaning of the term "faith" from the perspective of Tradition, see the Editorial published in *Sacred Web*, vol. 23, June 2009, titled "The Secularization of Faith in the Modern World" by M. Ali Lakhani, also in M. Ali Lakhani, *The Timeless Relevance of Traditional Wisdom* (Bloomington, IN: World Wisdom, 2010), pp. 154-159.

[22] See notes 5 and 6, supra.

mode of knowledge that is profoundly transformative. This is the effective purpose of prayer and ritual: to be ontologically transformed by our remembrance of, and our ritual participation with, the Presence of God. It is in this sense that *dhikr* (the invocation of God through His Divine Names, and the remembrance that "God alone is"[23]) and the prescribed rituals that are enactments of our intrinsic poverty and our subsistence in God, can be efficacious modes of Self-realization.

We have described how Islamic cosmology relates to Beauty and to universality in the sense of the divine manifestation and resplendence that is the ever-renewing theophany of the "Face of God." But there is a more profound aspect that we need to explore, which relates to another aspect of the divine substance. If Beauty is the effulgent radiance of the Divine Essence through His creation, the intrinsic nature of the Divine Substance is Compassion. As Adam—or Universal Man—is the microcosm and the reflection of God, so the intrinsic substance of God is reflected in the human soul as Virtue. The realization of this is the *métier* of man: the enactment of the truth of the second *shahadah*: that "all things are attached to God." And to enact and achieve this realization, man must engage in the task of "self-beautification" which is the essence of *ihsan* or Virtue. This truth provides a metaphysical foundation for an objective ethics grounded in the ontological reality of man, and is another aspect of the universality of Islam.

We can cite three illustrations of the Muslim doctrine of the Compassionate nature of God. The first is the Qur'anic passage in which God states, "My Compassion embraces everything."[24] This statement of the primacy of God's Compassion is linked to its Qur'anic prescription as a Law binding upon God. In a remarkable passage that appears twice in the Qur'an[25], God is described as having "willed upon Himself the Law of Compassion" (*kataba 'ala nafsi-hir-Rahmah*). No other divine attribute or quality is described or treated in the same way. Compassion (*Rahmah*) is therefore clearly singled out as intrinsically pertaining to the divine nature.

The second example of God's Compassionate nature is the well-authenticated Hadith Qudsi, cited by both Bukhari and Muslim, in which God states, "Verily, My Compassion outstrips My Wrath."[26] As we will see later, this Hadith indicates that while the created universe manifests a variety of divine attributes, corresponding to the complementary masculine and feminine polarities described earlier, there is a quintessential quality that transcends all existential polarities and constitutes the very nature and intrinsic substance of God. The closest human approximation of this quintessential divine quality is Compassion—but it is a supreme quality of such grace and perfection, that it pertains to the Divine Essence and Spirit alone and is unknowable in any purely human sense.

The third example of God's Compassionate nature pertains to the Hadith of the Hidden Treasure, cited earlier, according to which God was impelled by "love"[27] to create the world. According to the great Muslim metaphysician, Ibn 'Arabi, Divine "love" is a form of God's

[23] *Surah Ibrahim*, 14:25, "God cites symbols for men, so that they may remember."

[24] *Surah al-Araf*, 7:156.

[25] *Surah al-An'am*, 6:12, and 6:54.

[26] *Sahih al-Bukhari*, Hadith 3194.

[27] The Arabic text of this celebrated Hadith Qudsi is "*kuntu kanzan makhfiyan fa ahbabtu an 'urafa fa-khalaqtu al-khalq likay u'rafa*". The term *ahbabtu* is derived from the root *lubb*, designating "love".

Compassion (*Rahmah*), pertaining to His innermost nature, the Divine Essence, the innermost consciousness or secret Heart (*sirr*) of Reality. Creation springs forth from and returns into the Divine Womb (*rahm*) through a projection and reintegration that is likened to the divine act of breathing. This metaphoric process is termed the Breath of Compassion (*nafas al-Rahman*): *Rahman* is God's ontological "all-embracing" and illuminating Compassion, while *Rahim* is His reintegrating Mercy. It is also noteworthy that it is precisely these two qualities of God—*Rahman* and *Rahim*—that are singled out in the Basmallah[28] that begins all Muslim prayers and commences all Surahs, except one, of the Qur'an.

Ibn 'Arabi has elaborated on the meaning of the Hadith of the Hidden Treasure to explain the concept of *wujud*. The term is usually translated as "being" or "existence", which refers to the Sole Reality or Being of God. But insofar as God is also present in His theophany, there is also a sense in which existence has *wujud*, though—because "God alone is"—this is in reality only the *wujud* of God. In this theophanic sense, the term can also mean the *mazhar* or Presence of *nur* or Light. By virtue of this metaphor, *wujud* is also Light "for it is manifest in itself and makes other things manifest."[29] According to Chittick, "Ibn 'Arabi is saying that the Hidden Treasure is both beautiful and luminous,"[30] because the divine love that impels creation is the Beauty and the Light of His *wujud*—that is, the ontological contents of His Self-disclosure within creation. Ibn 'Arabi explains, "the cause of love is Beauty"[31]—again pointing to the intrinsic Beauty or Compassion of God, which radiates like Light into the creation it thereby causes to "be" by the grace of his *wujud*.

The image of creation as illumination embeds within it the idea of diffusion, and so of universality. God is Light by His very nature, and is thereby a Self-illuminating Lamp. It is in the very nature of Light to radiate: the Good is not there to illuminate itself. Creation is the self-disclosure (*tajalli*) of God. It is the illumination of the Divine Spirit—of Goodness, Virtue, or transcendent Compassion—that radiates outwardly as Beauty. But it is only the eyes of Beauty that can perceive Beauty. The task of man is therefore "to make oneself beautiful" (*ihsan*) by prayer and by spiritual disciplines of detachment. By invoking and remembering God constantly, and by practicing detachment from contingency, one is led to the realization of one's intrinsic poverty and nothingness. This realization of emptiness (*fana*) is also a realization that our innermost self is nothing but the *wujud* of God[32]—hence, its plenitude (*baqa*). This realization constitutes the self-unveiling of the primordial nature (*fitra*)—the Heart of man. It is only from the vantage of this beatific Center that order and harmony can be "*seen*". And it is only by opening the Heart to its innate Compassion that one's participative connection with all of creation can be "*felt*." Self-realization thereby engages a cardial, sympathetic vision—the fusion of knowledge and love, of knowing and being—which is the basis of the reality of "attachment to God". This has profound ethical implications: for all relationships, though outwardly diverse and self-referential, are inwardly experienced as relationships with the Sole Subsisting Self—God.

28 "In the Name of God, the Most Compassionate, the Most Merciful."

29 William C. Chittick, *Ibn 'Arabi: Heir to the Prophets* (Oxford: Oneworld, 2005), p. 42.

30 Ibid., p. 43.

31 *Al-Futuhat al-makkiyya* (Cairo, 1911), volume II, 326.24.

32 This is one meaning of the phrase, *La ilaha illa' Llah*.

Islam teaches that the diversity within creation springs from a single Source, which is its origin and to which it will return.[33] The Qur'an states that mankind was created "from One Soul"[34]. "God gave everything its creation"[35] and "all things go back to God"[36]. This essential relationship of divine origination and return, rooted in a common spiritual paternity—among humanity, and between humanity and all creatures—is the foundation of the universal ethos of Islam. The One Soul (*Nafsin-waahidatin*) or universal Adamic spirit of humanity is the primordial nature or *fitra* of man. Thus, according to a famous Hadith: "Every child is born according to *fitra*. Thereafter its parents make it into a Christian, a Jew, or a Magian." The soul's *fitra* is its innate disposition to Goodness, its intrinsic Virtue that gives it the ability to radiate Beauty, and is also its innate disposition to Beauty that is the cause of its attraction to Beauty, both within itself and in the world. The *fitra* is the spiritual presence of God in man, his spiritual predisposition, which derives from the Compassionate Light of God. It is the source of his spiritual orientation, and is the basis of his perception of the divine theophanies. It is *fitra* that is the foundation of humanity's sympathy for the rights of others. It is this Heart-centered disposition to Goodness and Beauty that constitutes the core of human intelligence, evident in its ability to recognize the higher Self, and in its aesthetic and ethical sensibilities.

In the Qur'anic episode of the Primordial Covenant[37], God asks the pre-existential soul of man—the Adamic *fitra*—to bear witness to its divine patrimony. In doing so, the soul fulfills the primordial covenant of man to bear witness in existence to the two metaphysical truths of Reality that are encapsulated in the *shahadat*: the ontological reality of Beauty (the truth that "God alone is"—corresponding to the soul's aesthetic sensibility), and the ontological reality of Virtue ("all things are connected to God"—corresponding to its ethical sensibility)—and that together represent the universal truths of Islam. Each created thing has a "right" (*haqq*) according to its hierarchical ranking, which is discernible by the intelligence of the soul. Each "right" is owed a corresponding "courtesy" (*adab*). This is the foundation for Muslim ethics. The fiduciary responsibilities (*amanat*) of mankind are rooted in the faith (*iman*) of man—in his ability to fulfill his primordial covenant by "realizing the Real". It is by becoming mirrors of the Beautiful Light of *wujud* and by expressing its quintessential quality of Compassion, that we can be true to ourselves and fulfill our fiduciary obligations. This is the heart of the universal message of Islam.

Yet, as we stated at the outset, there lies a metaphysical tension that underlies the quest for universality. This is the tension between the need to impose outer conformity and the need to accommodate diversity. Within Islam, these needs are expressed as conservative religious

[33] The Qur'an paradoxically states in *Surah al-Hadid*, 57:3: "He is the First and the Last, the Most Present and the Most Hidden, and He has full knowledge of all things." God is therefore metaphysically transcendent and immanent, the Source and the Destination, the Most Present to the "eyes of the spirit" and the Most Obscure to the "eyes of the flesh".

[34] *Surah al-Nisa*, 4:1, "O Mankind! Be conscious of your Sustainer, who has made you from one soul, and from it created its mate, and from two spread abroad a multitude of men and women."

[35] *Surah Ta Ha*, 20:50.

[36] *Surah al-Hadad*, 57:5.

[37] *Surah al-Araf*, 7:172, "And when your Lord brought forth from the children of Adam, from their loins, their descendants, and made them bear witness concerning themselves, saying: Am I not your Lord? And they responded: Yes. We bear witness! Remember this, lest you say on the Day of Judgment: Truly, we were unaware of this."

fundamentalism, and as liberal syncretism, respectively. Both approaches are flawed from the perspective we have delineated above. What we have termed "fundamentalism"[38] expresses itself by an excessive formalism (reducing the "spirit" to the "letter" of the Law) and an exclusivism that is marked by a strong rejection of pluralism. The reasons for these tendencies are evident: they are compensations for the lack of a Center that can embrace both outer forms and inner substance, or multiple expressions of Truth. Lacking the metaphysical foundation for such a Center, universal order is therefore imposed from the outside and judged in terms of outward conformity. By contrast, what we have termed "syncretism" expresses itself in an indiscriminate embracing of diversity that minimizes all formal differences in the name of "ecumenical" tolerance. Once more, this approach is grounded in the lack of a metaphysical Center, and results in the dilution of standards and the privileging of procedural pluralism over principled pluralism, and of accommodation over substance and form.

The doctrine of *tawhid* which lies at the heart of Islam is founded on the mystery and intimacy of Reality. God is both transcendent and incomparable (*tanzih*) and immanent and the source of similarity (*tashbih*). It is therefore as misguided to emphasize only His mystery by devaluing His Manifestness (*zahir*) in the formal world, as it is to emphasize only His intimacy by devaluing His Hiddenness (*batin*) in His Essence.[39] To overvalue formalism in the name of religion (the error of "fundamentalism") is to commit *shirk* (blindness toward God) by de-spiritualizing God and His creation. Similarly, to essentialize all forms of religious expression (the error of "syncretism") is also to commit *shirk* by denying the formal significance of His theophany and of His Beauty. The Straight Path of Islam requires us to embrace Reality fully, and thereby to perceive Truth *as* Presence.

In several key passages, the Qur'an states:

> All mankind was once one single community; [then they began to differ], and God sent them Messengers[40] as bearers of good tidings and as warners, and revealed to them the Scriptures with the Truth, to judge between people with regard to their divergent views. And those to whom [the Scripture] was given, after clear proofs had come unto them, did not differ except through mutual jealousy. And God by His Grace guided the true believers unto the Truth, from whence they differed: for God guides unto the Straight Way him that wills to be guided.[41]
>
> And We never sent a messenger before you, save that We revealed to him, saying, "There is no deity but I, so worship Me."[42]
>
> And unto you [O Prophet] have We entrusted this Message, setting forth the

[38] For a fuller discussion of this term, see "Fundamentalism: A Metaphysical Perspective" by M. Ali Lakhani, published as the Editorial for *Sacred Web*, vol. 7, July 2001. The essay also appears in the anthology, *The Betrayal of Tradition*, edited by Harry Oldmeadow (Bloomington, IN: World Wisdom, 2005), p. 101.

[39] See note 33, supra.

[40] There are numerous Qur'anic references to God sending messengers for each community. See for example, *Surah Yunus*, 10:47; *Surah ar-Ra'd*, 13:38; *Surah Ibrahim*, 14:4; *Surah Anbiya'*, 21:7-9; and *Surah Ghafir*, 40:78.

[41] *Surah al-Baqarah*, 2:213.

[42] *Surah al-Anbiya'*, 21:25. See also note 40, supra.

> Truth, confirming what is true of the prior revelations, as a Guardian of it. . . . For each We have prescribed a Law and a Way. And had God willed, He could have made you one single community. But [He made you as you are] so that He might test you by means of what he has entrusted to you. So vie with each other in Virtue. Unto God you will all return, and He will clarify your understanding about your differences.[43]

The clear implication of these verses is twofold: it demonstrates, on the one hand, the falsity of a fundamentalist's rejection of pluralism (for God has willed diversity, prescribing for each community a separate "Law" and "Way"), and on the other, the falsity of the syncretist's compromise of substantive pluralism (for the "Law" is the Truth: "There is no deity but I, so worship Me"; while the "Way" is Virtue: "So vie with each other in Virtue").

While Islam rejects fundamentalism and respects the various faith traditions—each with their unique articulations of the underlying Truth—it does not extend this pluralistic embrace of other faith traditions to the level of a syncretic accommodation. Each community has its own prescribed "Law" and "Way", but only as aspects and diverse expressions of Truth and Virtue. Forms are the revelation of the Divine Essence and are metaphysically important. Further, as the Qur'an states[44]: "piety does not consist in your entering houses from the rear, [as it were,] but truly pious is he who is conscious of God. Hence, enter houses through their doors, and remain conscious of God, so that you might attain to a happy state." One interpretation of this passage is that forms, while subservient to purpose, are nevertheless important. Except by the Grace of God, in this world the Law cannot be essentialized to the point where its forms cease to matter.

The metaphysical tension between the "Rigor" of the fundamentalist and the "Mercy" of the syncretist is not resolved except by recourse to one's natural disposition or *fitra*. Islam is the final articulation to mankind of God's primordial message. That is why it is also regarded as the "primordial religion" (*din al-fitra*). It emphasizes that the disciplines of the Law and Way are to open the Heart's inner capacity for Compassion—that is, the quintessential quality of Compassion that transcends all metaphysical polarities. The Qur'an repeatedly states[45] that salvation is attained, by the Divine Grace, through "God-consciousness"[46]—which has two aspects: first, faith (*iman*) which manifests in self-surrender (*islam*) to Truth; and second, the assumption of Beauty and Virtue (*ihsan*) through piety and good works:

> If any human being, man or woman, is virtuous and has faith, that person will enter paradise and shall not be wronged by as much as the dint of a date-stone. And who could be more faithful than he who surrenders his whole being to God, and does good works, and follows the creed of Abraham?[47]

[43] *Surah al-Ma'idah*, 5:48. Yusuf Ali records this as 5:51.

[44] *Surah al-Baqarah*, 2:189.

[45] This is a constant refrain in the Qur'an. See, for example, *Surah al-Baqarah*, 2:25, 62, 82, 112, and 277.

[46] We are following Muhammad Asad in rendering *muttaqi* as "the awareness of His all-presence and the desire to mould one's existence in the light of this awareness" (*The Message of the Qur'an*, p. 3).

[47] *Surah an-Nisa'*, 4:124-125.

The elements of Truth (expressed as faith and self-surrender) and Virtue (expressed in piety and good works) are the Law and the Way of the "primordial religion." Their particular and diverse articulations in each faith tradition are revealed to each community in its own idiom[48] as a manifestation of the Compassion that has impelled the creation of the world and that sustains it in each moment. This Compassion is Beauty—the Hidden Treasure of the Heart. It is the *wujud* whose *mazhar* is the Lamp of the transcendent Heart. Man can only perceive universality to the extent that he embodies it within himself as its microcosm. He can only embrace it to the extent he transcends himself. He can only perceive its radiance to the extent he illuminates it. Its luminosity signifies the true meaning of "Revelation". Only through our self-emptying can we be filled by its radiance, and only through our stillness can its flowing be felt—the flowing of the Sacred Light whose source is "neither of the East nor of the West" and whose Center is everywhere.

Hinduism — a spiritual world
That contains everything, and shimmers in all colors;
It offers us Vedanta, the doctrine of the great Shankara:
And also gods without number,
In whose cult our heart has no interest.

Islam wants first and foremost to be Unity,
And life-wisdom. It also knows the wine
Of the heart, that turns the soul inwards.
Islam is revelation's last sanctuary.

In whichever language one honors truth:
God is Reality — the world is appearance.
*Frithjof Schuon*

[48] *Surah Ibrahim*, 14:4, "We never sent a messenger but with the language of his folk."

# Islamic Learning in Confucian Terms

*Sachiko Murata*

"Comparative Religion" is largely a modern enterprise. Muslims always had some interest in other traditions, not least because the Koran designates Islam as one religion (*dīn*) among many and describes a long line of divinely sent messengers. Serious study of other traditions, however, was rare among Muslims. India provides one of the few cases in which attempts were made, by scholars such as Prince Dārā Shukūh, to bring out the underlying unity of two different traditions. Only recently have somewhat similar attempts come to light among Chinese Muslims, who were astute readers of the Confucian tradition.

Muslims make up a sizable minority in China. Scattered all over the country, they are officially numbered at twenty million, though estimates of the real numbers range much higher. The Muslims themselves maintain that the Prophet sent an emissary to the Chinese emperor, though historians have not been able to verify this. It is known for certain, however, that a treaty was signed with a Muslim mission in the year 651, less than twenty years after the Prophet's death. Over the next two centuries, another forty missions are recorded in the Chinese annals as having arrived at the capital. The first concrete evidence of Chinese-speaking Muslim communities dates back to the ninth century.

Muslims living in China transmitted Islamic learning in their own languages, mainly Persian. Not until the seventeenth century did they begin to compose works in Chinese. The first person to do so was Wang Daiyu 王岱輿, who published the *Real Commentary on the True Teaching* (*Zhengjiao zhenquan* 正教真詮) in the year 1642. By the end of that century, several other Muslim scholars had joined him, some of them referring to themselves as Huiru 回儒, "Muslim Confucianists." In the 19th century, their books came to be called by the Chinese-Arabic hybrid word, Han Kitab, "the Chinese Books," and this expression is commonly met in the secondary literature. The Han Kitab flourished down until the end of the nineteenth century, but, with the influx of modernity, sometimes in the form of Wahhabi-style fundamentalism, it was gradually marginalized and almost completely lost.[1] Only in the past twenty years or so have Chinese Muslims made some attempt to revive the Han Kitab by re-printing the important books, producing modern editions, and writing historical studies about the texts.

One of the most striking characteristics of this school of thought is that Muslims, for the first time in history, expressed the teachings of Islam in the language of another intellectual tradition. Prior to this time, Muslims everywhere had transformed indigenous languages by using the Arabic script and importing a massive amount of Arabic vocabulary. The first example is the Persian language. What linguists call "modern Persian" bears little resemblance to the "middle Persian" of the Sassanid period, not least because it uses the Arabic script and draws at least fifty percent of its vocabulary from Arabic. In this and other languages, like Turkish and Malaysian, Muslims made relatively little attempt to reformulate their teachings in terms of native terminology. Instead, they simply imported Arabic words. This meant, among other things, that they never had to write about their religion in the languages of other great traditions. Dārā

[1] On the Huiru, see the study by Zvi Ben-Dor Benite, *The Dao of Muhammad: A Cultural History of Muslims in Late Imperial China* (Cambridge: Harvard University Asia Center, 2005).

Shukūh, for example, wrote exclusively in Persian, not Sanskrit.

Only in modern times have some Muslims attempted to reformulate Islamic teachings in terms of an alien intellectual universe, in this case the modern West. But, generally speaking, in making use of a foreign idiom, the Chinese Muslims demonstrated a great deal more originality than modern-day Muslims have done. One reason for this is that in English or French, for example, it is easy enough to transliterate Arabic words, so authors typically import a good deal of terminology. In Chinese, however, transliteration, although possible, is enormously cumbersome. Hence the authors of the Han Kitab avoided it almost totally, not least because they wanted to maintain the literary standards established by the great tradition of Confucian learning.

In other words, Chinese Muslims could not resort to the common technique of using Arabic technical terms. They could not mention words like Allah, Koran, Hadith, Shariah, *fiqh*, *tawḥīd*, *nubuwwa*, Kalam, *ṣalāt*, Ramadan, hajj, and so on. For the same reason, they rarely mentioned proper names. Because of the unique nature of the Chinese language, they were forced to express their teachings in the language current among Chinese scholars, that is, Neo-Confucianism, which is a synthesis of the so-called "Three Teachings"— Confucianism, Taoism, and Buddhism. It is precisely because they were completely comfortable doing this that they called themselves Huiru, "Muslim Confucianists."

Wang Daiyu tells us in the introduction to his *Real Commentary* that several centuries had passed since the time his ancestors had settled down in China. More recent generations of Muslims had lost their mother tongue and could not read their own literature. He was motivated to write his book because he feared that his co-religionists would gradually lose touch with their intellectual heritage and become indistinguishable from other Chinese. He also refers to the fact that some of the contemporary ulama had criticized him, saying there was no need to write in Chinese. Why should he use that language, even quoting from Confucius and Mencius, when everything was explained perfectly in Persian and Arabic? Wang responded that without writing in Chinese, it would be impossible to convey Islamic teachings to those who had gone through the standard Chinese education and had no knowledge of the Islamic languages.

The second major author of this school, Liu Zhi 劉智, was probably the best known and most widely read of the Muslim Confucianists. He was born about 1670, that is, a dozen or so years after the death of Wang Daiyu. In the introductions to some of his books, he explains his motive for writing in Chinese. He tells us that his father, with whom he studied the Islamic classics from a young age, always regretted the fact that his Chinese was not good enough to translate Islamic books. When his father died, Liu Zhi began a serious study of the Confucian classics. He isolated himself from society, and spent ten years in a mountain forest studying them along with the classics of Daoism and Buddhism. It was during this time, he says, that "I suddenly came to understand that the Islamic classics have by and large the same purport as Confucius and Mencius."[2] He concluded that, if Islam was not going to remain an isolated and provincial tradition, Muslim scholars had the duty to acquaint themselves with Chinese learning and to speak to educated Chinese—whether they be Muslims or non-Muslims—in the universal language of Chinese civilization. This is what he means when he writes,

2 Sachiko Murata, William C. Chittick, and Tu Weiming, *The Sage Learning of Liu Zhi: Islamic Thought in Confucian Terms* (Cambridge: Harvard University Asia Center, 2009), p. 94.

> Although I am indeed a scholar of Islamic Learning, I privately venture to say that unless there is an exhaustive prying into the [Chinese] Classics and the Histories and a wide inquiry into the hundred families of books, Islamic Learning will stay in a corner and not become public learning under heaven.[3]

Thus we see that Liu Zhi, like Wang Daiyu and other authors of the Han Kitab, studied the Chinese classics for the same reason that Muslims who want to write about Islam in English need to be familiar with English literature and Western thought. One large difference, however, is that the Chinese Muslims recognized that the Confucian tradition was rooted in prophetic wisdom, and they saw no basic contradiction between Neo-Confucian and Islamic learning. The same thing cannot be said about Muslims writing in the modern world, given that the fundamental viewpoints of the main streams of modern thought are intensely antagonistic toward all forms of religious thought, whether Muslim, Confucian, or Christian. For the Han Kitab, however, Confucianism was a legitimate prophetic tradition, even if, in their view, it needed to be supplemented by Islamic teachings. Indeed, an underlying theme of Liu Zhi's book is to show that the Muslim worldview, though it has "the same purport as Confucius and Mencius," is superior to it in the completeness of its metaphysical, cosmological, and spiritual vision. It is not without reason that he and other Muslim scholars, though they called Confucius "the sage" in traditional Chinese fashion, referred to the Prophet of Islam as "the utmost sage."

Liu Zhi wrote many treatises, but he is most famous for three books that can be called "The Tianfang Trilogy." Tianfang 天方, the first word in the title of all three books, means "heavenly square" or "heavenly direction." The word was commonly used to refer to Mecca, the central Muslim lands, and the Islamic tradition itself. In these books, Liu Zhi deals successively with three basic dimensions of Islamic teachings. Hence he tells us that although he wrote and published them as different books, they are in fact one book.

The title of the first book, which we have recently translated into English, is *Tianfang xingli* 天方性理. It was also one of the most important, if not the single most important, text on Islamic teachings in the Chinese language, republished many times in the eighteenth and nineteenth century. Literally, *Tianfang xingli* means "Nature and Principle in Islam." "Nature and Principle" refers to Neo-Confucianism, which is often called *xingli xue* 性理學, that is, "the learning about nature and principle," because of the central role of these two terms in Neo-Confucian thought. With this name Liu Zhi is announcing that he is presenting the intellectual roots of the Islamic tradition in terms of standard Chinese concepts. The topics of the book are precisely the underlying issues of Neo-Confucianism, that is, metaphysics, or the nature of the ultimate reality; cosmology, or the nature of the manifest reality that appears from the Ultimate Reality; and spiritual psychology, or the nature of the human soul and its final perfection, a perfection that is achieved by re-integration into the Ultimate Reality.

The second book of the Liu Zhi's Trilogy is called *Tianfang dianli* 天方典禮, "Rules and Proprieties of Islam." It addresses the basic practices of Islam, that is, the Shariah. It is not a book on jurisprudence, however, because it does not go into the nit-picking details typical of the juridical approach. Rather, it provides an overview of Islamic practices, such as the Five Pil-

[3] Ibid., p. 93.

lars, and then explains the wisdom underlying them in terms of the quest for human perfection. One of the most prominent of its many topics is the so-called "Five Relationships," which are fundamental to Confucian spiritual and social thinking and which, in Liu's understanding, are equally important in the Islamic tradition. In the first, introductory chapter, he spends a good deal of time talking about the common origins of the Islamic and Confucian traditions and the fact that they concur on the necessity of ritual action in conformity with Heaven. For example, he writes,

> What is recorded in the books of Islam is no different from what is in the Confucian canon. Observing and practicing the proprieties of Islam is like observing and practicing the teachings of the ancient sages and kings.

The third volume of Liu Zhi's Trilogy is called *Tianfang zhisheng shilu* 天方至聖實綠, "The True Record of the Utmost Sage of Islam." This is a biography of the Prophet that aims to show how he embodied the intellectual and practical teachings set down in the first two books of the Trilogy. As Liu Zhi puts it, the book explains that the Prophet in his very person was "the profound origin of both the teaching and the way." On the whole, this book is much more accessible than the first two, because it is posed in terms of narratives and tales about the Prophet's life, with an emphasis on miraculous and wondrous events.

* * *

Let me now provide a brief description of Liu Zhi's "Nature and Principle in Islam." It is divided into six main parts, the first of which is called "the Root Classic" (*benjing* 本經). This is quite short, about 1600 characters or ten pages in five brief chapters. Appended to it are ten diagrams illustrating the basic ideas discussed in the text. For example, the foundational notion of "Being" (*you* 有), which is Ultimate Reality in Itself, is represented as an empty circle.

Following the Root Classic, each of the five parts of the book elaborates on one of the Root Classic's five chapters by providing twelve more diagrams. Each diagram is supplemented by a detailed explanation of its meaning and significance. Altogether, the book has seventy diagrams, sixty of which are explained in detail.

By calling the first part of the book "the Root Classic," Liu Zhi wants to say that it is a compilation of "classic" Islamic texts in translation, and that the rest of the book is an explanation and commentary on these texts. The word *jing* or classic is used in Chinese for the great texts of Chinese civilization, such as the *Yijing* and the *Daodejing*. Muslims employed the same term to refer to the Koran and the Hadith, and they also used it to designate important books by great Muslim authorities. In this case, Liu Zhi had in mind six specific books, from which he translated the passages compiled as the Root Classic. He indicates the name of each book in marginal notes when he quotes from it. There are a total of eighty-six citations from the six classics, which means that each quotation is very brief. Many of them are as short as eight characters, and the longest is a little over one hundred.

Surprisingly, perhaps, these six Muslim classics do not include the Koran or Hadith. The bulk of the citations are from four Persian Sufi texts. Two of these were written by Kubrawī authors in the thirteenth century: *Mirṣād al-ʿibād* of Najm al-Dīn Rāzī (d. 1256) and *Maqṣad-i aqṣā* of ʿAzīz Nasafī (d. ca. 1295). Two more were written by the famous Naqshbandī teacher and poet ʿAbd al-Raḥmān Jāmī (d. 1492): *Lawāʾiḥ* and *Ashiʿat al-lamaʿāt*. All of these books have long been recognized as important and influential throughout the Persianate world. Three have been translated into English, and the fourth is a commentary on Fakhr al-Dīn ʿIrāqī's *Lamaʿāt*, which has also been translated. The least cited texts are both Arabic. One is *al-Mawāqif fī ʿilm al-kalām*, a well-known book in dogmatic theology by ʿAḍud al-Dīn al-Ījī (d. 1355), and the other the Koran commentary of al-Bayḍāwī (d. ca. 1300).

* * *

I said that the basic topics of the book are metaphysics, cosmology, and spiritual psychology. By using these terms, I am choosing English words that can easily cover the contents of the book, whether we consider it a contribution to Confucian thought, or an expression of Islamic thought, or an exercise in comparative religion. These words, however, will pose a problem for some people. They will most likely react by saying, "But this is not Islam, it is Sufism," or "It is philosophy." This would be an extremely short-sighted response. Let me say something about how one can reply to it.

If we try to find appropriate Arabic terminology for the subject matter of Liu Zhi's book, we can say that he is explicating the three basic principles of Islamic faith, upon which all Muslim theology is based. These three principles are of course *tawḥīd*, *nubuwwa*, and *maʿād*—Divine Unity, Prophecy, and the Return to God. The difference between this book and books on the same topics written in Arabic, Persian, and other languages is that none of the standard terminology is used. The three principles are not explained in the technical language of Kalam, or Islamic philosophy, or the Koranic symbolism favored by the Sufis. Instead, the principles are presented in terms of the grand edifice of Neo-Confucian thought, with its deep roots in the teachings of the ancient Chinese sages. The reason that it is possible to do so is because these principles, especially *tawḥīd*, are basic to human thought in all the great traditions, even if they are often presented in terminology unrecognizable to most Muslims.[4]

Let me finish by giving a brief description of the topics of the five chapters of the Root Classic, chapters that are elaborated upon in detail in the rest of the book. The first chapter addresses what Liu Zhi calls "the Sequence of the Ongoing Flow of the Creative Transformation in the Macrocosm." It sets down the overall scheme of what Islamic texts often call *mabdaʾ wa maʿād*, "the Origin and the Return." This, in turn, is simply an elaboration of the principle of *tawḥīd*. Given that the Ultimate Reality is one, all apparent reality must come from this Reality and return to it. However, discussion of the Origin and the Return deals not simply with the structure of the cosmos, but also with an exposition of the human role within the cosmos. Spiritual anthropology is inseparable from cosmology.

In discussing *maʿād*, or the Return to God, many Islamic texts expand on teachings found in the Koran and the Hadith concerning the end of time, the Last Day, Resurrection, Judgment, and paradise and hell. Many other texts, however, distinguish between the compulsory return, which everyone experiences by dying and being resurrected, and the voluntary return, which is the path of achieving human perfection in this life. Kalam and dogmatics look mainly at the compulsory Return. In contrast, philosophy and Sufism have been equally or more concerned

[4] For a detailed response to this objection, see Chapter 2 of the introduction to *Sage Learning*.

with the voluntary Return. In order to explicate the nature of the human soul's return to God, however, we need to understand the nature of its emergence from God, so the Origin must be discussed along with the Return. Liu Zhi stands in this tradition of Islamic thought. He has practically nothing to say about death and resurrection, but focuses instead on the becoming of the human soul and its achievement of perfection by establishing unity with God.

In Chapter 1, Liu Zhi outlines the overall scheme of Origin and Return. He concludes by saying,

> The great transformation follows a circle;
> when the end is fully realized, it returns to the beginning.
> Since only humans
> grasp uniquely the original essence,
> they are subtly united with the original Real.[5]

In other words, human beings alone have the capacity to achieve the final realization of *tawḥīd*, in which all things are seen to be re-integrated with God.

In Chapter 2, Liu Zhi addresses the nature of the human soul and the diverse types of human being in terms of their relationship with the universe as a whole. Much of the chapter is taken up with enumerating the various ranks of sages and worthies, that is, prophets and saints.

In Chapter 3, Liu Zhi explains that all human beings traverse a series of stages that parallel the development of the universe as a whole. Beginning in the womb, they gradually ascend on the path of the Return, going through mineral, plant, and animal stages, until they are born in human form. Once their external, physical make-up is established, they begin the process of developing their internal, psychological and spiritual faculties. The ultimate goal is to achieve the human perfections that became manifest in the sages.

Chapter 4 addresses the nature of the spiritual faculties inherent in human beings, especially the heart (Arabic *qalb*, Persian *dil*, Chinese *xin* 心). Liu Zhi explains that the goal of life can only be achieved by cultivating the body, the soul, and the spirit in keeping with the model established by the Utmost Sage on the three levels of Propriety (*li* 禮), the Dao 道, and the Real (*zhen* 眞). These three terms, basic to Chinese thought, translate *Sharīʿa*, *Ṭarīqa*, and *Ḥaqīqa*—the Law, the Path, and the Reality. This tripartite division of the Islamic tradition had been commonplace in later Sufism and became standard in the Han Kitab. Both Rāzī and Nasafī discuss it early on in their books.

Finally, Chapter 5 describes the ultimate human perfection, or the full realization of *tawḥīd*. Let me conclude by quoting the last few lines of the Root Classic to provide another taste of the text:

> The [three] Ones come home to the Root Suchness,
>     and heaven and humans are undifferentiatedly transformed.
>     The things and the I's come home to the Real,
>     and the Real One circles back to the Real.
>     The things are not obstructed by the guises,

[5] *Sage Learning*, p. 108.

and humans are not burdened by desire.
The subtle meaning of each is disclosed
and thereby the Root Suchness is seen.
In the beginning was the True Principle
and now is the True Guise.
When the True Being is seen as Guise,
the seed and fruit are complete.[6]

[6] Ibid., pp. 150-52.

# Images of Divine Unity and Religious Diversity: A Selection from Mīr Findiriskī's Commentary on the *Laghu-Yoga-Vāsiṣṭha*

*Shankar Nair*

## Mīr Findiriskī's Prefatory Verses

He is God most high, whose nature is exalted.

Selections from the *Yoga-Vāsiṣṭha*, which the master of the wise, Mīr Abū al-Qāsim Findiriskī (may God's mercy be upon him), has translated from the Indian language[1] into simple Persian and in the description of which he has written:

This discourse in the world is like water,
Like the Quran, pure and increasing knowledge.

Since, after[2] the Quran and Hadith,
No one has sayings of this kind,

An ignorant one who has heard these discourses
Or has seen this subtle cypress-grove,

Attaches only to its apparent form;[3]
Thus he makes a fool of himself.[4]

## Translation of a Sample Passage from the Text

The whole world is the manifestation of that Being and Reality and is found in It, which has no beginning, end, or middle, which is not born nor dies, into which change and transformation have no access. Having given space in your heart for this belief concerning It, repose at peace!

Know that all these variegated creations and determined forms which come into sight, innumerable and without limit, are all [just] occasions for the appearance of the Essence and manifestations of Absolute Being. The root of all of these

1 That is, Sanskrit.

2 "*Gudhasht*" can also have the meaning of "other than" or "besides." This reading would leave open the possibility that Findiriskī intends to affirm an absolute equality of status between the Quran/Hadith and the *Laghu-Yoga-Vāsiṣṭha*, rather than retaining the former as somehow superior (as one would more commonly expect from a Muslim author). In either case, Findiriskī's considerable appreciation for the *Laghu-Yoga-Vāsiṣṭha* is quite evident. On this and other points, I am guided by the critical edition and study of the text by Fatḥullāh Mojtabā'ī in his *Muntakhab-i Jūg Bāsasht* (Tehran: Mu'assassah-i Pizhūhishī-i Ḥikmat va Falsafah-i Īrān, 2006).

3 Literally, "does not attach [to anything] except to the apparent form in it," which effectively means "attaches only to its apparent form."

4 Literally, "he laughs at his own beard."

appearances is the one Essence of Brahman, just as with ornaments and gold-pieces, such as[5] bracelets, earrings, anklets, and rings, etc., each of which has [its own] distinct determination and form: the root of all of those ornaments is the one essence of gold, which remains the very same gold even after those forms are shattered. Or just as, upon the rising of the exalted sun, thousands upon thousands of scattering beams, radiance, and rays can be seen: [still] the root of all those limitless and endless beams and lights is the one essence of the exalted sun.

When someone attains *Brahma-jñāna* ("knowledge of Brahman") and arrives at complete knowledge of the Essence, his vision becomes effaced and he becomes annihilated in the Essence, like a drop which falls into the sea and becomes the sea.

*Shaykh ʿAṭṭār:*
The eye which is not fixed upon the source[6]—the ocean—
Is fixed upon the drop; how can [such a man] be Muslim?

So long as the drop and the ocean do not become one,
How can the stone of your unbelief become the gem of faith?

I see everything as the one sun,
But I don't know how it will shine upon you!

* * *

At some point during his extensive travels through India, the Muslim philosopher-mystic Mīr Abū al-Qāsim Findiriskī (d. 1640/41 CE)—considered to be one of the three great philosophical masters of the "School of Iṣfahān" in his day[7]—came across Niẓām al-Dīn Pānīpatī's recent Persian translation of Gauḍa Abhinanda's Hindu Sanskrit work, the *Laghu-Yoga-Vāsiṣṭha.*[8] Perhaps spurred on by the considerable interest in this Sanskrit text exhibited by numerous

[5] Literally, "of the type of." Since Findiriskī was primarily trained as a philosopher, the mention of the term "*jins*" ("type" or "genus") is probably deliberate, the idea being that the genus or "philosophical category" itself is fleeting, while the "categorized Object"—which ultimately transcends all categories—endures eternally. See, for example, ʿAbd al-Raḥmān al-Jāmī's (d. 1492) multifaceted and subtle exploration of this theme in his *Lawāʾiḥ* (*Flashes of Light*).

[6] The word is "*aṣl*," the same term that I have translated as "root" in the prose section above. The translation of *aṣl* as "root" expresses the idea of origin or source while simultaneously implying that the product is somehow continuous with, of the same essence as, and principially contained in that source, which is Findiriskī's main point here. As for the poem, however, the translation of "root" would sound somewhat odd in the context of a drop springing from the ocean, so I have opted for "source" instead.

[7] Along with Mīr Dāmād and Shaykh Bahāʾī. Findiriskī was most renowned for his knowledge and teaching of the Peripatetic (*mashshāʾī*) philosophy of Ibn Sīnā.

[8] The *Yoga-Vāsiṣṭha* takes the form of a dialogue between the Hindu epic hero Rāma and the famous Indian sage, Vasiṣṭha. In over 29,000 Sanskrit verses, Vasiṣṭha instructs Rāma, through stories and didactic discussion, on the nature of reality, realization, and enlightened life in the world. The date of composition of the *Yoga-Vāsiṣṭha*—as well as its abridged version, the *Laghu-Yoga-Vāsiṣṭha*—has been the locus of much debate among scholars, who place the text from anywhere between the sixth and fourteenth centuries CE.

members of the Mughal court,[9] Findiriskī decided to read and compose a sort of "commentary" on it: extracting and editing several prose portions from Pānīpatī's translation, Findiriskī then aligned with them various selections from the corpus of classical Persian Sufi poetry without penning a single word of his own, thus leaving his juxtapositions to speak for themselves.[10] The only words in this text—entitled *Muntakhab-i Jūg Bāsisht* or "Selections from the *Yoga-Vāsiṣṭha*"—that Findiriskī himself wrote are four prefatory verses in which, as we shall see, he affirms the esoteric concordance between Islamic and Hindu Vāsiṣṭhan[11] wisdom, despite their very real differences on the level of formal exoteric reality. Though the history, indeed the very existence, of such a text as this could shed considerable light upon the political and social conditions of pre-modern South Asia, for the purposes of this essay we shall focus on deciphering its content: what exactly is the worldview that Findiriskī expresses in this commentary, leading him to manifest such high praise for this "non-Islamic" text of the Hindus, composed by a man, Abhinanda, who has no temporal link whatsoever with the Prophet Muḥammad or to the Islamic revelation? To this end, we shall examine Findiriskī's prefatory verses, and then bring our findings to bear upon a sample juxtaposition from the main body of the *Muntakhab*.

To begin with Findiriskī's prefatory verses, since these are the only explicit words of his own that we have in the entire text, it is worthwhile to dwell on them at length and to derive from them as much information as possible. Findiriskī's praise for the *Laghu-Yoga-Vāsiṣṭha* is immediately apparent from his characterization of it as "pure" and "increasing knowledge"; the fact that he compares its purity and wisdom to the Quran, however, is particularly noteworthy. As a venerated Muslim scholar for whom the Quran is the revealed word of God and, presumably, the supreme source of spiritual knowledge, Findiriskī certainly would not declare any similarity between it and any other text unless he held that text in very high regard. But Findiriskī's praise does not end there: "after the Quran and Hadith, no one has sayings of this kind." Here the philosopher boldly asserts that, among all the words spoken in all the world, the Quran, Hadith, and *Laghu-Yoga-Vāsiṣṭha* should be grouped together in the highest category and associated with nothing else—granted, one should allow a certain leeway for poetic hyperbole, but the considerable approbation is patent nevertheless.[12] Thus, simply stated, in

[9] In this period alone, Muslim intellectuals in India had produced no fewer than ten works relating to the *Yoga-Vāsiṣṭha*. Even Prince Salīm, the soon-to-be emperor Jahāngīr, once remarked that the *Yoga-Vāsiṣṭha* "contains Sufism (*taṣawwuf*) and provides commentary on realities, diverse morals, and remarkable advice" (Carl W. Ernst, "Muslim Studies of Hinduism? A Reconsideration of Persian and Arabic Translations from Sanskrit", *Iranian Studies* 36 (2003): p. 185).

[10] Findiriskī cites, among others, Farīd al-Dīn ʿAṭṭār (d. 1220), Jalāl al-Dīn Rūmī (d. 1273), Maḥmūd Shabistarī (d. 1320), Rukn al-Dīn Awḥadī (d. 1337), Muḥammad Shams al-Dīn Ḥāfiẓ (d. 1389), Niʿmat Allāh Valī (d. 1431), and Qāsim-i Anvār (d. 1433).

[11] Though philosophically very akin to the perspective of Advaita-Vedānta, the *Yoga-Vāsiṣṭha* belongs to its own text-tradition and is thus historically distinct from the former. Nevertheless, it is clear that the two traditions were in close contact historically, exerting influence over one another at various levels.

[12] See note 2 above, and note Findiriskī's comments in another of his works, the *Risālah-i ṣanāʿīyyah*: "all the Greek philosophers before Aristotle were saying the same thing in different languages . . . if one is instructed in the secrets (*rumūz*) of *Ḥikmat*, Hindu wisdom, and the *Theology of Aristotle* (i.e., the Arabic edition of Plotinus' *Enneads*), all the different expressions will have the same meaning for him" (Seyyed Hossein Nasr "The School of Iṣpahān", *A History of Muslim Philosophy*, edited by M.M. Sharif [Wiesbaden: Otto Harrassowitz, 1966], vol. 2, p. 925).

the opinion of Mīr Findiriskī, the *Laghu-Yoga-Vāsiṣṭha* is quite special in that it reveals and permits the spiritual aspirant to plumb the profound depths of Truth as no other text can, save the revered Quran and Hadith.

In the latter half of the prefatory verses, Findiriskī sets up a distinction between exoteric and esoteric knowledge. The "ignorant one" is characterized as one who adheres only to the "apparent form," which, in this context, most immediately refers to words and ideas read at a more literal or superficial level. The "ignorant one" sees and hears the words, but, since they are "subtle," he gets caught up in their apparent meaning while missing the more essential, esoteric import that underlies these external forms. By neglecting this esoteric dimension thus, the ignorant exoterists "make fools of themselves," for they think they understand the meaning when, really, they have missed the deeper point.[13] Accordingly, when one examines the *Laghu-Yoga-Vāsiṣṭha* alongside the Quran and Hadith, the apparent differences are too numerous to mention: the images, language, formulations, teachings, injunctions, rhetoric, etc., are evidently disparate. But Findiriskī here posits a distinction between exoteric and esoteric knowledge, according to which he can assert that the Quran/Hadith and *Laghu-Yoga-Vāsiṣṭha* are similar precisely because they correspond in their esoteric dimensions, despite the fact that the apparent content is so different between them. The caveat, of course, is that the "ignorant exoterists" will not be able to discern this esoteric correspondence.[14]

We must take care to note, however, that the ignorant ones are fools not because they adhere to the external form, but rather, because they adhere *only* to the external form—that is, while ignoring the esoteric dimension. I would argue that the word "only"[15] is highly significant in this context, for its inclusion suggests that, for Findiriskī, the apparent, external form may yet have some role to play: someone may be a fool for regarding and following the external form only, but this does not mean that the wise man throws out the external form entirely. Rather, Findiriskī seems to want to say that one should take both the esoteric *and* exoteric meanings into consideration simultaneously, else he would simply have equated ignorance with adherence to external form pure and simple—without the word "only"—and thus shunned external form entirely.[16] If this interpretation is correct, then, for Findiriskī, the apparent differences

[13] No doubt included among these "ignorant fools" were the dogmatic Shīʿī jurists who, back west in Findiriskī's homeland of Ṣafavid Persia, were repressing and persecuting philosophers and mystics like himself. Such conditions may help explain why Findiriskī chose to be so allusive in this "commentary," rather than plainly expressing his views.

[14] These notions of exoteric forms manifesting or expressing the higher, universal esoteric principles to which they are ontologically connected, as well as the "fools" of limited vision who mistake those forms for the essence, are echoed in various of Findiriskī's other compositions, particularly in his famous *qaṣīdah* (translated by Nasr): "Whatever is there above has below it a form. The form below, if by the ladder of gnosis, is trodden upward, becomes the same as its principle. No outward apprehension can understand this saying . . . whatever is an accident must first have a substance. . . . Only he who is wise can discover the meaning of these mysteries. . . . In this world and the next, with the world and without it, we can say all these of Him, yet He is above all that. . . . The jewel is hidden in the mysteries of the ancient sages ... Pass beyond these words ... How good it would be if the sages before us had said everything completely, so that the opposition of those who are not complete would be removed" (Nasr, "The School of Iṣpahān", p. 923). Such assertions also recall, for example, Rūmī's rendition of the famous story of the elephant in the dark room in the *Mathnavī.*

[15] See note 3 above.

[16] Again, Findiriskī was a trained philosopher who did not use words lightly. To provide a more simple example,

between the *Laghu-Yoga-Vāsiṣṭha* and the Quran/Hadith (which, presumably, encompasses Sufi wisdom as well) are not insignificant, and, accordingly, should be taken seriously at some level. Thus, in these prefatory verses, a two-part vision emerges: Findiriskī suggests that there exist certain esoteric principles hidden amidst these divergent external forms, and that it is in the realm of these esoteric principles that the *Laghu-Yoga-Vāsiṣṭha* and the Quran/Hadith coincide; at the same time, however, we are not to ignore these apparent divergences. Rather, Findiriskī wants us to recognize these distinctions on their own formal level of reality.[17]

This notion of the simultaneous existence of exoteric forms (*ṣūrat*) and esoteric meaning (*maʿnā*) may help us to interpret Findiriskī's image of the *Laghu-Yoga-Vāsiṣṭha* being a "discourse in the world like water." According to common Persian mystical-literary convention, water is often used as a symbol for truth, reality, or essence (*haqīqat, dhāt*), which, like water, can adopt many different appearances and forms. Thus, the particular shapes that the water adopts refers to the external forms of the world, while the essentially formless water itself refers to the esoteric truth that lies hidden within those external forms.[18] Other Persian works identify the external forms of the world with the debris that covers and hides the underlying ocean (i.e., formless, esoteric reality).[19] In the same manner, it is possible that Findiriskī's phrase "in the world" might correspond to the idea of "exoteric form," while the phrase "like water" suggests the idea that these apparent forms contain hidden esoteric realities, though those esoteric realities, necessarily, must adopt particular forms in order to exist in the world. In this fashion, the water imagery of these prefatory verses may serve to emphasize Findiriskī's notion of the distinction between the exoteric and esoteric dimensions of Islamic and Vāsiṣṭhan wisdom: esoteric principles (i.e., the water) are always essentially the same, though those principles may be expressed by different words and forms in different places and contexts, just as water sometimes appears as ice, sometimes as snow, and sometimes as a river; Islamic and Vāsiṣṭhan literature will inevitably differ in language, sound, appearance, injunctions, rhetoric, and even apparent content, but there exist common esoteric realities to which such divergent elements mutually point.

we can compare the sentence "he is a fool because he eats apples" with the sentence "he is a fool because he eats only apples." In the first sentence, the very act of eating apples is deemed foolish, which implies that apples are bad. In the second sentence, in contrast, it is the act of eating *only* apples that is shunned, which does not vilify apples *per se*, but rather, simply suggests that a person should eat other things along with apples.

17 Looking back at a line from Findiriskī's aforementioned *qaṣīdah*—"the form below, if by the ladder of gnosis, is trodden upward, becomes the same as the principle"—we see that, in Findiriskī's view, the external form is necessary as the basis and starting point from which the aspirant may "climb" to gain access to the corresponding esoteric principles. Thus, even if apparent forms cannot fully describe absolute Truth, a person nevertheless needs them in order ultimately to know the Truth.

18 See, for example, the various works of Jalāl al-Dīn Rūmī (d. 1273), who, Annemarie Schimmel writes, often discusses "'the ocean of inner meaning' and the external world . . . Rūmī uses the image of the foam on the sea to express this very idea . . . [as] the ocean is hidden behind this veil of foam" (*The Triumphal Sun: A Study of the Works of Jalaloddin Rumi* [Albany: State University of New York Press, 1993], p. 77). Elsewhere, Rūmī, as well as other Sufi poets such as Ibn al-ʿArabī, speak of water which has been frozen in the form of ice or snow, requiring the warmth of the sun (i.e., the transformative grace of God) to escape from the limiting cage of its frozen form (see Schimmel, *Triumphal Sun*, pp. 80-81).

19 "[In Rūmī's poetry,] outward manifestations and all forms visible to the eyes are nothing but straw and chaff which cover the surface of this divine sea . . . the outward material forms are always conceived as something . . . which hides the fathomless depths of this ocean" (Schimmel, *Triumphal Sun*, p.77).

An example from Rūmī's *Mathnavī* may help us to illustrate this preceding theme (bearing in mind that the water-imagery employed in this poem is different from that described above):

> Consider the creatures as pure and limpid water,
> within which shine the Attributes of the Almighty.
> Their knowledge, their justice, their kindness—
> All are stars of heaven reflected in flowing water.
> Kings are a locus of manifestation for God's Kingliness,
> The learned a locus for His Knowledge. . . .
> Generation upon generation has passed, oh friend,
> But these Meanings are constant and everlasting.
> The water in the stream has changed many times,
> But the reflection of the moon and the stars remains the same.[20]

Whatever we see, for example, of generosity, mercy, or justice among the objects and events of the phenomenal world, is a limited manifestation or pale reflection of God's celestial, eternal names and attributes "the Generous" (*al-karīm*), "the Merciful" (*al-raḥīm*), and "the Just" (*al-ʿadl*). This doctrine of "names and attributes" clearly echoes the above-mentioned notion of multiple forms expressing common esoteric spiritual realities: just as a flower and a gazelle, we might say, though drastically different in appearance, are both partial manifestations of the divine name "the Beautiful" (*al-jamīl*), similarly, Findiriskī asserts, Islamic wisdom and the *Laghu-Yoga-Vāsiṣṭha*, though disparate in form and language, may possess as their content the same celestial "meanings" or spiritual realities.

The last remaining element of the prefatory verses to be discussed is Findiriskī's referring to the *Laghu-Yoga-Vāsiṣṭha* as a "cypress-grove." One use of the cypress tree in classical Persian poetry is to "praise without tongue the grace of the water which quickens them," even making of this or that water-body a symbol for the "sweet water of [the Paradisal river] *kowthar*."[21] To call the *Laghu-Yoga-Vāsiṣṭha* a cypress, then, is to affirm that it draws its life and existence from celestial waters which, as we have already seen, represent the absolute Reality that is the Essence. In this fashion, Findiriskī seems to be affirming the *Laghu-Yoga-Vāsiṣṭha* as an authentically inspired text, a product of nourishment from pure, ineffable Truth. In the world of classical Persian poetry, furthermore, "the cypress, *sarv* . . . is the generally accepted symbol for the slender, elegant stature of the beloved"[22]; in the more specific case of Sufi poetry, in turn, this cypress-beloved is effortlessly correlated with the Prophet Muḥammad, as in Rumi's verse, "[the Prophet is the] cypress of the garden of prophethood,"[23] or in Saʿdī's *Bustān*, "[t]he cypress is not as well shaped as Muḥammad."[24] With Findiriskī, in particular—working in an intellec-

[20] *Mathnavī*, VI:3172-78, quoted in William C. Chittick, *The Sufi Path of Love* (Albany: State University of New York Press, 1983), p. 43.

[21] Schimmel, *Triumphal Sun*, pp. 83, 89.

[22] Annemarie Schimmel, *A Two-Colored Brocade: The Imagery of Persian Poetry* (Chapel Hill: University of North Carolina Press, 1992), p. 164.

[23] Annemarie Schimmel, *And Muhammad is His Messenger: The Veneration of the Prophet in Islamic Piety* (Chapel Hill: University of North Carolina Press, 1985), p. 203.

[24] Annemarie Schimmel, *As Through a Veil: Mystical Poetry in Islam* (New York: Columbia University Press,

tual milieu pervaded by Sufi thinkers and Akbarī poets such as Ibn al-ʿArabī, Jāmī, Shabistarī, Niʿmat Allāh Valī, and Qāsim-i Anvār—praise for the Prophet Muḥammad is closely associated with the notion of "the Perfect Man" (*al-insān al-kāmil*). Thus, through mentioning the cypress tree, Findiriskī invokes the conception of the Prophet as, among other things, a realized sage and gnostic who has realized in his own being a synthesis of all of God's names and attributes.[25] In light of this, for him to call the *Laghu-Yoga-Vāsiṣṭha* a cypress and thus associate it with the Perfect Man, Muḥammad, is for him to declare this text a repository of total Truth. Findiriskī, however, introduces a peculiar twist into the image by describing, not a single cypress, but rather a cypress-grove, while, according to poetic convention, the cypress "is often called *āzād*, 'free,' because it stands majestically alone."[26] Usually there can only be one beloved, who must be unique, but Findiriskī, by distinguishing the one Truth from its multiple manifestations, can make of the solitary cypress a spinney of such trees; the Reality that the soul of the Prophet discloses may have equally profound and complete expression elsewhere[27]—as, for example, in the *Laghu-Yoga-Vāsiṣṭha*—without compromising the oneness of the Essence thereby.

To turn now to a sample "application" of the worldview presented in these prefatory verses within the main body of the text, we shall turn to a passage towards the end of the *Muntakhab*—translated at the beginning of this essay[28]—in which Findiriskī aligns a Vāsiṣṭhan passage with a *ghazal* from the *Dīvān* of Farīd al-Dīn ʿAṭṭār (d. 1220 CE). Our passage begins with a standard Vāsiṣṭhan description of the Absolute:

> The whole world is the manifestation of that Being and Reality and is found in It, which has no beginning, end, or middle, which is not born nor dies, into which change and transformation have no access. . . . Know that all these variegated creations and determined forms which come into sight, innumerable and without limit, are all [just] occasions for the appearance of the Essence and manifestations of Absolute Being.

1982), p. 286 (*Bustān*, p. 5). Here Saʿdī is utilizing a trope in which, when the true beloved "enters the garden, the real cypress becomes crooked and bends from envy," for it cannot compare with the real beloved, Muḥammad (Schimmel, *Two-Colored Brocade*, p. 164).

25 "Ibn al-ʿArabī makes the clearest connection between the full manifestation of *wujūd* [Being] and the human role in the cosmos in his famous doctrine of the 'perfect man' (*al-insān al-kāmil*), the complete and total human being who has actualized all the potentialities latent in the form of God. . . . They act as the Real's representatives in society, leading people to supreme happiness in the next world. In their human manifestations they are found as the prophets and the great friends of God . . . only through them does He manifest the totality of His attributes—in them alone does *wujūd* reach its full unfoldment. No creature other than a perfect human being possesses the requisite preparedness to display all God's attributes" (William C. Chittick, *Imaginal Worlds: Ibn al-ʿArabī and the Problem of Religious Diversity* [Albany: State University of New York Press, 1994], p. 23).

26 Schimmel, *Two-Colored Brocade*, p. 164.

27 In the thought of Ibn al-ʿArabī, at least, not all "perfect beings" are created equal, as some are more perfect than others in respect of being a more balanced, harmonious synthesis (see Chittick, *Imaginal Worlds*, pp. 8-9, 23). Given the paucity of Findiriskī's words in the *Muntakhab*, however, we simply cannot be certain whether he perceives a hierarchy, or rather a stricter equality, between Islamic and Vāsiṣṭhan wisdom.

28 This Persian passage corresponds to a section about halfway through the *Nirvāṇa-prakaraṇa* ("Book of Extinction"), the sixth and final book of the original Sanskrit *Laghu-Yoga-Vāsiṣṭha* (see Gauḍa Abhinanda, *Laghu-Yoga-Vāsiṣṭha* [Bombay: Nirnaya Sagar Press, 1937]). It is unfortunately beyond the scope of this essay to discuss the nature and quality of the Persian translation from the original Sanskrit.

Ultimate Reality, in short, is beyond all description and transcends all conceptual categories, mysteriously abiding completely and immutably unchanged even through the process of the manifestation of Itself as the phenomenal world. Here we immediately see an echo of the pervasive Sufi conception of creation as God's self-disclosure of His divine names and attributes, though God's Essence remains transcendent and entirely unchanged for all eternity. We have already encountered such notions in our discussion of Findiriskī's prefatory verses, wherein the formless, transcendent, single Absolute appears in the world in multiple limited forms—forms which simultaneously reveal the Absolute but also veil It, since no temporal, formal entity can ever express the ineffable Truth in anything more than a partial, fragmentary manner.

The Vāsiṣṭhan passage continues, introducing the image of golden ornaments to help explain the doctrine:

> The root of all of these appearances is the one Essence of Brahman, just as with ornaments and gold-pieces, such as bracelets, earrings, anklets, and rings, etc., each of which has [its own] distinct determination and form: the root of all of those ornaments is the one essence of gold, which remains the very same gold even after those forms are shattered.

The analogy in this passage emphasizes the fact that the gold of which any given ornament is made is far more enduring than the particular form which the gold adopts in order to appear and exist as that given ornament: insofar as the fact of being, e.g., a "bracelet," refers merely to the physical form of the object, a little heat or hammering could alter the bracelet's shape and thus destroy it; the gold, however, still remains gold throughout the whole process, no matter whether it is made into shattered shards, melted into liquid, recast as an earring or anklet, or whatever else may occur. In the same way, no matter which forms the Absolute may assume in order to be manifest in the phenomenal world, and whatever may be the fate of those myriad transient forms—whether they be produced, altered, or destroyed—the single Absolute in Itself will remain transcendent and wholly unaffected. Accordingly, while any given phenomenal entity in the world is transient and ultimately unreal insofar as it is just a fleeting external form, that entity is also essentially identified with the Absolute insofar as its basic being and substance derive from the immutable, imperishable Absolute Being.[29]

The Vāsiṣṭhan passage then continues through invoking another analogy, that of the sun and its rays:

> Or just as, upon the rising of the exalted sun, thousands upon thousands of scat-

[29] As is stated elsewhere in the larger Sanskrit *Yoga-Vāsiṣṭha* (III, 61: 3-5): "only the infinite consciousness or Brahman exists. Just as there is no division between a bracelet and gold . . . [so] there is no division between the universe and the infinite consciousness. The latter alone is the universe; the universe as such is not the infinite consciousness, just as the bracelet is made of gold but gold is not made of bracelet" (quoted in Swami Venkatesananda (tr.), *Vasiṣṭha's Yoga* [Albany: State University of New York Press, 1993], p. 87) [more literally: "just as the quality of being a bracelet is not distinct from the gold (itself) . . . in the same way, the universe is not distinct from God. God is the universe, though the universe is not (inherent) in God; the gold is the bracelet-state, though the bracelet-state is not (inherent) in the gold"]. The Absolute is the only reality; It alone exists. Therefore, the universe, insofar as it actually exists, *is* Brahman and, insofar as it merely consists of fleeting forms, is transient and unreal.

> tering beams, radiance, and rays can be seen: [still] the root of all those limitless and endless beams and lights is the one essence of the exalted sun.

As with the image of the golden ornaments, this analogy expresses the doctrine of the essential identification of the phenomenal universe with absolute Reality. If the innumerable rays of the sun be likened to the countless entities of the phenomenal world, one can see that, as was the case with the golden ornaments, the essential substance and reality of each fleeting individual ray of light (the phenomenal object) is really no different from the sun itself (Absolute Being). No matter what may happen to a given ray during the course of its trajectory—it may be reflected off of a lake, assume the color of a stained-glass window, etc.—the sun, the source of that ray, stands aloof in the sky, detached and transcendent, completely unaltered by any apparent transformations. In the same way, the Essence is the source of the whole manifest order, though It never suffers any modification Itself;[30] still, the Absolute and Its manifestations are ultimately not distinct, just as every beam of sunlight is essentially no different from the sun.

The Vāsiṣṭhan passage then continues with the third analogy of the drop and the ocean: when one attains this realization of the Essence, "his vision becomes effaced and he becomes annihilated in the Essence, like a drop which falls into the sea and becomes the sea." How this analogy expresses the same philosophical doctrine as the preceding two is apparent enough: the ocean represents the Absolute, while the drop—a sort of individuation of the ocean—represents the myriad forms of the phenomenal world. The appearance or disappearance of a drop inflicts (virtually) no modification upon the ocean as the whole—analogically referring to the immutability of the Absolute despite Its self-disclosures—while the drop, being inescapably made of the same water as the ocean, is essentially non-different from it, despite its fleeting apparent existence in the transient form of a drop—just as any phenomenal form is identified with the Absolute in its essential reality.[31] The unique contribution of this analogy, however, is that, more so than the previous two, it emphasizes the *subjective* condition of the realized individual, rather than merely the objective metaphysical state of things. The realized spiritual aspirant is thus himself annihilated in the Absolute Being, having attained true knowledge of the Essence. No doubt Findiriskī had in mind at this point of the passage the aforementioned Sufi notion of *al-insān al-kāmil.* We shall see why this is significant as we now turn to the Sufi

[30] The wider Indian intellectual tradition makes frequent use of this image to illustrate this point. Śaṅkarācārya, for example, writing in the Advaita-Vedānta tradition, asserts that "Brahman [the Absolute], like the sun, appears to be affected when the nature of the reflecting medium changes—when, for example, it becomes dirty and the light becomes pallid—but neither Brahman nor the sun are really affected" (Potter's paraphrase of Śaṅkara's *Brahmasūtrabhāṣya*, III.2.11 21, in Karl H. Potter (ed.), *Encyclopedia of Indian Philosophies: Advaita Vedānta up to Śaṃkara and His Pupils* [Princeton: Princeton University Press, 1981], vol. 3, p. 85). The following line from Findiriskī's *qaṣīdah* is also interesting in this regard: "The sun is itself light and shines upon all things while keeping its unity" (Nasr, "The School of Iṣpahān", p. 923).

[31] This notion directly echoes the "in the world like water" imagery of Findiriskī's prefatory verses. B. L. Atreya summarizes the cumulative message of the analogies in this passage of the *Laghu-Yoga-Vāsiṣṭha*: "One form may be separate from another form as such, but they can never be separate and distinct from the Reality of which it is a form. An ornament of gold is never separate from gold with which it is ever one and identical. Bubbles, ripples, waves, etc., are never different from water of which they are forms, and abstracted from which they will cease to be anything at all. Everything, in the same way, in this universe . . . is *identical* with the Reality. . . . Everything in this universe, thus, *is* Brahman" (*Yogavasistha and Its Philosophy* [Moradabad: Darshana Printers, 1966], p. 45).

poem that Findiriskī chose to align with this Vāsiṣṭhan passage.

The *ghazal* from the *Dīvān-i ʿAṭṭār* that Findiriskī inserts as his commentary upon this passage is as follows[32]:

> The eye which is not fixed upon the source—the ocean—
> Is fixed upon the drop; how can [such a man] be Muslim?
>
> So long as the drop and the ocean do not become one,
> How can the stone of your unbelief become the gem of faith?
>
> I see everything as the one sun,
> But I don't know how it will shine upon you!

These verses from ʿAṭṭār utilize several of the same images as the Vāsiṣṭhan passage—namely, the sun and the ocean—which provides the most immediate justification for Findiriskī's inserting it here. To begin with the ocean and the drop, the questionable Muslim of uncertain faith regards them as separate entities, which is, of course, the incorrect view; the man of true understanding, on the other hand, sees the ocean and the drop as identified, being one and the same entity. Some of ʿAṭṭār's other writings corroborate this message of non-duality as expressed by these images:

> The man of God here sees nothing besides God. . . . He at no time sees anyone other than Him . . . the whole world is the Worshipped One (God).[33]
>
> Everything is God! . . . See this world and the other world in such a way that they are He! Nothing exists besides Him, and if something does exist, then it too is He.[34]

Hellmut Ritter explains how ʿAṭṭār uses the image of the drop and the ocean specifically to describe the non-dual vision of Reality, in which the transient, unreal aspect of worldly objects disappears as they become indistinguishable from the Absolute: "In ʿAṭṭār there is also found a cosmic extinction which consists of all things except God disappearing in God . . . [as] the world . . . disappears like a drop in the ocean."[35] We can also find numerous expressions of this doctrine elsewhere in the Sufi tradition. Annemarie Schimmel lists a few of them:

> The poets . . . like to speak of the ocean, the billows, the foam, and the drop, which in each instance look different and yet are the same water. Niffarī seems

[32] This poem is part of a larger *ghazal* entitled *Har gadā'ī mard-i sulṭān kay shavad.*

[33] *Manṭiq al-ṭayr* (*The Conference of the Birds*), p. 147, verses 3690-93, quoted in Hellmut Ritter, *The Ocean of the Soul: Man, the World and God in the Stories of Farīd al-Dīn ʿAṭṭār*, translated by John O'Kane, edited by Bernd Radtke (Boston: Brill, 2003), p. 591.

[34] *Manṭiq al-ṭayr*, p. 3, verses 52-54, quoted in Ritter, *Ocean of the Soul*, p. 625.

[35] Ritter, *Ocean of the Soul*, p. 631.

> to have been the first to use the symbolism of the divine ocean. Ibn ʿArabī had visualized the divine essence as a large green ocean out of which the fleeting forms emerge like waves, to fall again and disappear in the fathomless depths. Rūmī emulated him in many of his poems, which speak of the ocean and God. But the image is found much earlier: everyone who meditated upon the similarities and differences between God and the world and wanted to illustrate their basic unity and temporal differentiation, would use the image of the ocean.[36]

Thus, according to ʿAṭṭār (and all of these Sufi authors), the phenomenal universe essentially is God, the absolute Reality; the transient drop essentially is the abiding ocean. This image of the drop and the ocean in ʿAṭṭār's poem, then, expresses the same doctrine that we observed in the Vāsiṣṭhan passage. Similarly, when ʿAṭṭār speaks in this poem of seeing everything as the "one sun," he again echoes this notion: when the poet looks upon anything in the universe, he only sees the sun (i.e., God, the Absolute). Once again, his true vision perceives that the phenomenal world essentially is the absolute Reality.

A notable difference emerges, however, with the image of the stone and the gem, which is absent in the Vāsiṣṭhan material but present in ʿAṭṭār's *ghazal*. In the *ghazal*, disbelief—a state in which one mistakenly views the drop and the ocean as distinct—is likened to a stone, while correct faith—a state in which the drop and the ocean are seen as one—is likened to a gem. Schimmel writes that many Sufi authors, influenced by "an old Oriental belief that stones can be changed by the light of the sun into rubies,"[37] depict in their poetry a process in which a "ruby is created from coarse rock by the transforming rays of the sun, as the heart . . . after much suffering and patience, may be transformed . . . into a valuable and beautiful material."[38] The sunlight, of course, represents the "the activity of the Beloved," the transformative grace and power of God that remolds the spiritual seeker.[39] Thus, in ʿAṭṭār's poem, the "one sun" shines upon the stone and changes it into a gem, i.e., God extends His grace to the aspirant and transforms his heart for the better, in this case, teaching him to see the universe as it truly is.

Thus, with the inclusion of this theme of the transformation of the heart toward faith, ʿAṭṭār expresses a theme that can only vaguely be seen in this Vāsiṣṭhan passage through the notion of *Brahma-jñāna* ("knowledge of Brahman/the Absolute"). The difference only becomes sharper with the explicit mentioning of the word "Muslim," which, of course, has more universal meanings even in the Quran—various pre-Muḥammadan prophets, for example, are called "Muslims"—but inevitably carries along with it, at the very least, overtones of the more usual definitions, e.g., one who prays the canonical prayers (*ṣalāh*), pays the alms-tax (*zakāh*), believes Muḥammad is the messenger of God, etc. In the context of this poem especially, where the word "Muslim" is associated with he who has a correct recognition of the divine unity that pervades the universe, one immediately thinks of the distinctive, characteristic Islamic notion of *tawḥīd* (oneness of God) and the condemnation of *shirk* (association of partners with God).[40]

36 Annemarie Schimmel, *Mystical Dimensions of Islam* (Chapel Hill: Univ. of North Carolina Press, 1975) p. 284.

37 Schimmel, *Triumphal Sun*, p. 74.

38 Schimmel, *As Through a Veil*, p. 77

39 Schimmel, *As Through a Veil*, p. 77.

40 According to Ibn al-ʿArabī, "to believe in any order of reality as autonomous apart from the Absolute Reality is

We have already seen above, however, that Findiriskī does not mean to shy away from religious particularity: to his mind, *tawḥīd* and the Vāsiṣṭhan perspective are fully reconcilable in the transcendent realm of esoteric principles, despite their undeniably disparate articulations and formulations in the here-below. The mere fact that the *Laghu-Yoga-Vāsiṣṭha* does not mention "stone," "gem," and "Muslim" does not at all compromise Findiriskī's vision; what is significant is that, to his mind, these disparate forms all point to common esoteric realities.

It is possible, furthermore, that the image of the stone and the gem may be a reference to the Prophet Muḥammad, who, in much of Islamic literature, is said to be like a gem among the stones that are regular human beings.[41] If ʿAṭṭār did intend this reference, then this poem takes on another level of meaning: to be transformed and attain to the gem of faith is to emulate the particular soul of Muḥammad, the Prophet of the *Islamic* faith. Such an interpretation provides an even stronger connection between this Sufi selection and the religion of Islam specifically, as opposed to the "Hindu" or "Vāsiṣṭhan" tradition of which the *Laghu-Yoga-Vāsiṣṭha* is a part. While there is evidently much in the person of Muḥammad that would seem, apparently, foreign to the Vāsiṣṭhan universe, we have already seen Findiriskī's assertion in his preface—by way of the cypress-grove—that *al-insān al-kāmil*, being a single principial reality, can take multiple manifestations which, at the level of the here-below, will surely appear disparate in numerous respects. Once again, I would argue, Findiriskī's metaphysical vision allows him to embrace religious particularity in this world in light of correspondence and unity in the realm of transcendent, esoteric principles. Even though the Prophet Muḥammad and the *Laghu-Yoga-Vāsiṣṭha* are two "beings" with more disparate characteristics and qualities than could ever be listed, it is nevertheless fully possible that they may both be sound repositories for the total Truth.

While a more "foolish" or "exoteric" individual might demand that Findiriskī, to demonstrate his point, should find a Sufi passage to line up with every single sentence and image of the *Laghu-Yoga-Vāsiṣṭha*, Findiriskī is not interested in convincing such individuals. Rather, he is content to indicate the universal esoteric principles to which, in his mind, all of these images and expressions mutually point. Findiriskī seems to believe, furthermore, that a person of esoteric insight too would be satisfied with just that much.

to fall into the cardinal sin of Islam, namely, polytheism (*shirk*) . . . ultimately there is no reality other than Absolute Reality. . . . [For] the world and the things in it . . . their reality is none other than His [Reality]; otherwise they would be completely independent realities, which is the same as considering them to be deities along with Allah" (Seyyed Hossein Nasr, *Three Muslim Sages: Avicenna, Suhrawardī, Ibn ʿArabī* [Cambridge: Harvard University Press, 1964], pp. 106-107). Only the person mired in illusion will take the drop to be an enduring entity that exists in its own right; ʿAṭṭār, in contrast, affirms that the drop owes whatever reality there is in it to God. Thus, the drop is completely dependent upon God for its existence; to view it as an independently existing entity is to violate the central tenet of Islam (*tawḥīd*) and therefore to be a questionable Muslim. ʿAṭṭār expresses his disdain for polytheism in this manner in several of his other works. See, for example, the *Ilāhīnāmah* 12/10, quoted in Ritter, *Ocean of the Soul*, p. 616.

41 "[Muḥammad] said 'I am a human being like you' (*anā basharun mithlukum*), to which Muslim sages over the ages have added, yes, but like a precious gem among stones (*ka al-yaqūtu bayna al-ḥajar*)," the idea here being that the Prophet, who is so much closer to God than the rest of humankind, has a soul that is somehow more transparent to God's light (Seyyed Hossein Nasr, *Ideals and Realities of Islam* [Boston: George Allen & Unwin, 1975], p. 88).

# Universality in Islam[1]

## *Abdul Hadi*

### Introduction

In the year 1869 two great Sufis were born who, in parallel ways, played pivotal roles in the introduction of Sufism to the West. One of them was the initiator of Frithjof Schuon, the Algerian Sufi Shaykh Ahmad al-'Alawī, and the other, the initiator of René Guénon, the Swedish wandering dervish Shaykh 'Abd al-Hadi al-Maghrebi.

Perhaps one of the most peculiar characters in the history of Western Sufism, Abdul Hadi was born John Gustaf Agelii on May 29, 1869 in Sala, Sweden. His father, the town veterinarian, stemmed from a family of prosperous farmers, while his mother was a distant relative of the 18th century Swedish metaphysician and aristocrat Emanuel Swedenborg.[2] Growing up on the family farm, Abdul Hadi soon showed a great passion for painting, and to salvage his academic future his father sent him away to private educational institutions, first on the island of Gotland and then in the capital of Stockholm.

It was while living in Stockholm that Abdul Hadi came to study the teachings of his kin Swedenborg, and it was most probably through him that he came to learn of Islam and the Prophet Muhammad. Influenced by the writings of Dostoyevsky and Baudelaire, he soon began to refer to himself by the Russian word for John and the French spelling of his surname, which was how John Agelii became Ivan Aguéli.

By the year 1890, the young painter had moved to Paris to seek his luck as an artist. Settling in the Quartier Latin, Abdul Hadi became the student of the French Symbolist painter Émile Bernard, who introduced him to the works of his friend Paul Gauguin, and also to Loge Ananta, the French branch of the Theosophical Society.[3]

In 1891 Abdul Hadi traveled back to Stockholm where he continued his studies in Islam.[4] It was then that he began to openly display Oriental character traits. At one well-known occasion, having been invited to the elegant Café du Nord, he suddenly rose up from the table and seated himself on the floor, cross-legged in the fashion of a Turk. Inviting his friends to join him, they all came to settle down in a wide circle, much to the annoyance of the waiters.[5]

By 1892 Abdul Hadi had returned to Paris, where, as an aspiring anarchist, he took part in street battles with French police. Mixing in radical circles, he became acquainted with Marie Huot, the eccentric leader of the French Anti-Vivisection League[6] and the anarchists Alexander

1 Editor's Note: First published in *La Gnose*, No. 4, April, 1911. The Introduction and English translation are by Farid Nur ad-Din.

2 Erik Hellerström, *Släkt och Hävd*, edited by Genealogiska Föreningen (Stockholm: Alfa Boktryckeri, 1964), no. 1, p. 18.

3 Axel Gauffin, *Ivan Aguéli: Människan, Mystikern, Målaren* (Stockholm: Sveriges Allmänna Konstförening, 1940-1941), vol. 1, p. 61.

4 Ibid., vol. 1, p. 73.

5 Ibid., vol. 1, pp. 75-76.

6 Ibid., vol. 1, p. 123.

Cohen and Felix Fénéon, the latter the future art-critic and editor of *La Revue Blanche.*[7]

It was while living in Paris, sometime in 1893, that Abdul Hadi came to have a dream-vision in which he beheld the Sufi Shaykh Muhyiddin Ibn 'Arabī, dressed in the traditional garb of Muslims of old.[8] Although the true identity of the man was not revealed to him until much later, the vision came to play a crucial role in Abdul Hadi's attraction to Islam.

In the Spring of 1894 Abdul Hadi and Fénéon, together with twenty eight other anarchists, were arrested and put on trial in what would become known as "La Process de Trente"—"The Trial of the Thirty". Although accused of being the intellectual elite of French Anarchism, Abdul Hadi and Fénéon managed to defend their cause successfully and were released without charges in August of 1894. His three months of incarceration at the Mazas prison were used by Abdul Hadi to deepen his study of esoterism and to improve his mastery of Arabic and Hebrew. Thus, at his release, it was a well-prepared youth who stepped unto a boat bound for the Orient.

His one year in Egypt kindled a great love for the beauty of traditional Islam and, when returning to Paris in 1895 he enrolled at the École Spéciale des Langues Orientales Vivantes and at the École Pratique des Hautes Études, where he studied both classical Arabic and Sanskrit.[9]

It was also in Paris, sometime in 1898, that the young Swede officially converted to Islam and took the name Abdul Hadi (*'abd al-Hadi* = "servant of the Guide").[10] In 1899 he set out on a voyage to Ceylon, where he settled amongst the Muslim Malays of Colombo. The same year Abdul Hadi also made a brief journey to South India, but due to monetary constraints he was finally forced to return to France.

In the summer of 1900 while protesting with Marie Huot against a bullfight in a Parisian suburb, he drew a revolver and fired two shots at a carriage of passing bullfighters. Wounding a Spanish toreador, an unapologetic Abdul Hadi was again put on trial, but with the backing of nearly the entire French public he was handed only a suspended sentence and a nominal fine.[11]

It was in the Dreyfusard circles of Paris that Abdul Hadi came to know the Italian doctor and journalist Enrico Insabato. They traveled together to Cairo, where Abdul Hadi became a student at Al-Azhar University and a confidant of the Egyptian Sufi Shaykh 'Abd al-Rahman Ilaysh al-Kabir, who in 1902 initiated him into the *Shadhiliyah-'Arabiyyah Tariqah.*[12]

In 1904, with the blessing of Shaykh Ilaysh, Abdul Hadi and Insabato founded a periodical published in Italian and Arabic under the name of *Il Convito.* It promoted Sufism and anti-Modernism and argued for a dialogue conducted through the Italian civilization, as it was the only one of the European powers not tainted by colonialism. But it did not take long before Italy's own ambitions in Libya were brought to light, and taking the side of the Italians, Insabato returned to Rome, leaving a aggrieved Abdul Hadi to face the mounting hostility of Muslim modernists and British officials.

By the end of 1909, still reeling from the betrayal of Insabato, Abdul Hadi received instruc-

[7] Ibid., vol. 1, p. 103.

[8] Ibid., vol. 2, p. 143.

[9] Ibid., vol. 2, pp. 19-20.

[10] Kurt Almqvist (ed.), *I Tjänst hos det Enda: ur René Guénons Verk* (Stockholm: Natur och Kultur, 1977), p. 18.

[11] Gauffin, *Ivan Aguéli*, vol. 2, p. 94.

[12] Almqvist, *I Tjänst hos det Enda*, pp. 18-19.

tions from Shaykh Ilaysh to return to Europe as his *muqaddam* and spread Islam through the Sufi teachings of Ibn 'Arabī. Thus, after spending some time in Geneva, Switzerland, Abdul Hadi returned to Paris where, in 1910, he made the acquaintance of a young editor of *La Gnose*, an esoteric periodical.[13] Agreeing to provide Abdul Hadi with a platform for his discourse on Islam and Sufism, René Guénon thus became his loyal student and confidant. Abdul Hadi then proceeded to found a secret Sufi society which he called Al-Akbariyyah.[14] Presiding over its first gathering in Paris on the 22nd of June 1911,[15] Abdul Hadi initiated Guénon ('Abd al-Wahid) into the *Shadhiliyah-'Arabiyyah Tariqah.*[16]

In the Summer of 1911 Abdul Hadi traveled back to Sweden where he stayed until 1913. Returning then to Paris, he became an art-critic and, though somewhat reclusive, was sometimes seen in artist circles where he made the acquaintance of van Dongen and Apollinaire. After only a few months, however, his love for the Orient lead him back to Egypt, arriving there by the end of 1913.

In order to escape the crowds of Cairo, Abdul Hadi settled in the countryside, where he suffered greatly from chronic deafness and bouts of malaria. While painting the Egyptian landscape he was constantly harassed by certain fanatical villagers who accused him of being a sorcerer. After having been robbed and badly beaten by a gang of village brutes, Abdul Hadi again took to the road and finally found refuge at the farm of a Jewish family who, despite his evident poverty, gave him a room on his word of honor. It was during this period of his life that Abdul Hadi came to paint some of his greatest works of art.[17] Eventually he returned to Cairo, where his Islamic faith, Beduin clothing, and Arab friends soon made the British suspect him of harboring pro-Ottoman sympathies,[18] and thus in 1916, they ordered his deportation to Spain.

Lacking the funds needed to return to Sweden, Abdul Hadi was then stranded in Barcelona. He pleaded for money from friends and family, who, however, were either unable or unwilling to come to his aid. To make matters worse, he soon found himself caught in the midst of a political uprising in which his reclusive habits made him the target of revolutionary mobs who thought him to be a foreign spy.[19] Finally, Prince Eugén Bernadotte, having heard of Abdul Hadi's plight, sent the necessary 1,000 pesetas to the Swedish Consulate in Spain on the 2nd of October, 1917. But it was too late. On October 1st, 1917, Abdul Hadi wandered out in the early morning hours to paint the mist-shrouded landscape in the village of L'Hospitalet, near Barcelona. He attempted to cross a rail track, but, being almost fully deaf, he failed to hear the sound of the approaching train which thus hit him at full speed.[20] The ever wandering dervish Shaykh

13 Paul Chacornac, *The Simple Life of René Guénon* (Hillsdale, NY: Sophia Perennis, 2004), p. 34.

14 Gauffin, *Ivan Aguéli*, vol. 2, p. 189.

15 Viveca Wessel, *Ivan Aguéli: Porträtt av en Rymd* (Stockholm: Författarförlaget, 1988), p. 80. In *The Simple Life of René Guénon*, p. 35, Paul Chacornac mistakenly states that the year 1429 AH, given by Guénon in his Introduction to *The Symbolism of the Cross*, corresponds to the 1912 AD; whereas, as Wessel points out, 1429 AH corresponds to 1911 AD. This was also noted G. Rocca in his Foreword to *Écrits pour La Gnose*, (Milan: Arché, 1988), p. xix, n. 13.

16 Almqvist, *I Tjänst hos det Enda*, p. 18, n. 1.

17 Gauffin, *Ivan Aguéli*, vol. 2, p. 250.

18 Ibid., vol. 2, p. 255.

19 Ibid., vol, 2, p. 287.

20 Ibid., vol. 2, p. 288.

'Abd al-Hadi al-Maghrebi departed from this world a mere forty eight years after he entered it.

When the news of his tragic death reached Sweden, Prince Eugén ordered that the money he had sent be given to Abdul Hadi's impoverished mother, who had given up her wealth to support her son's countless escapades. The Prince also oversaw the repatriation and preservation of Abdul Hadi's belongings, and in 1920 arranged an exhibition of some two hundred of Abdul Hadi's works from his time in Sweden, Spain, and Egypt. Winning critical acclaim, he thus came to be known as one of his country's greatest artists in addition to being one of the first Muslims to introduce Sufism to the West.

In 1981, Abdul Hadi's remains were brought back to Sweden and buried in Sala, the town of his birth. Since then, a street, a park, and a museum have been named after him and dedicated to his memory.

## Translation

Our intention has been to develop, in the form of a solar transfiguration of the exotic landscape, the doctrine of reality in accordance with the "Supreme Identity".[21] In spite of absolute unity, we have seen that from the human point of view, particularly or disjunctively, there are two realities: the collective and the personal. The former is acquired (imposed or adopted), historical, hereditary, temporal, and hence, so to say, Adamic. The latter is original, innate, extra-temporal, and dominical. It is perhaps more or less obscured or curtailed, but it exists nonetheless. It cannot be renounced, nor can it be destroyed; it is fated, for it is everyone's reason for being, that is to say his destiny, to which all spiritual and cosmic striving is but a returning motion.[22] The first is reality as seen by ordinary men, that is to say by the perceptions of the five senses and their combinations according to mathematical laws and elementary logic. The second reality is the "sense of eternity".[23] In the concrete world, one corresponds to quantity and the other to quality. The collective reality is often called Universal Will, but I prefer to refer to it as *Need*, and reserve the term *Will* to indicate, as far as possible, the personal reality. The *Will* and the *Need* could correspond to *Science* and *Being*. These terms are not only familiar to European thought since Wronski,[24] but also to a prominent school of Muslim esoterism currently present in India.[25] Science and Being is literally "*Al-Ilmu wal-Wujūd*", the

[21] Translator's Note: Abdul Hadi is referring to his previously published article "Pages Dedicated to the Sun".

[22] See the *Yi-King*, as interpreted by Philastre (vol. 1, p.138; the 6th Koua; Song § 150): "The word destiny signifies the very reason for being of things; to neglect the precise reason for being of things constitutes what one calls 'contravening ones destiny'; also submission to destiny is considered a return. To contravene is not to conform with submission." (The traditional commentary of the Tsheng) "Destiny or the celestial mandate, is the true and accurate reason for being of each thing." (The commentary entitled "Primitive sense.")

I further add that in Chinese, Muslims are called "Hweï-Hweï", those who return, obeyingly, to their destiny. Muslim tradition states that Allah calls unto Him all things in order that they may come, willingly or unwillingly. Nothing can ignore this call. This is why all things in general are considered to be Muslim. Those beings who go unto Him willingly are called Muslims in the true sense of the word. Those who do not go unto Him—that is to say those who do not follow their destiny but are forced, despite themselves—are the infidels.

[23] See *La Gnose*, 2nd year, No. 2, p.65. [Translator's Note: Abdul Hadi is referring to his article "Pages Dedicated to the Sun."]

[24] According to Warrain, *La Synthèse concrètet*, p. 169.

[25] Translator's Note: Abdul Hadi is most likely referring to the *Akbariyah Tariqah*, which he may have encountered on his journey into South India in 1899. See G. Rocca's Foreword to *Écrits pour La Gnose*, p. xxiii.

two primordial aspects of Divinity. It need hardly be repeated that it is the Will alone that truly exists in a positive sense, while the Need has only a relative and illusory existence. On this point, all the different religions and philosophies agree; and this is why aristocratic natures are to be found everywhere. Thus, as the Muslims say, "*At-Tawhīdu wāhidun*", which means literally, according to the commentary: "The doctrine of the Supreme Identity is, in essence, everywhere the same", or even "The theory of the Supreme Identity is always the same". But here I would wish to insist on a distinguishing feature of Islam, on the crucial concept of the Prophet Muhammad. The *Will* can attain perfection only through the *Need*: through having, on the one hand, a need of the celestial, and through striving, on the other hand, to respond to the legitimate need of the collective reality. Thus it is that *Need* is indispensable to salutary striving, as a means of developing the latent faculties of the *Will.* The negative inertia of the former is no less indispensable than the positive energy of the latter. The one has as great a need of receiving as the other has a need of bestowing. They are hence interdependent, the one unto the other. In those rare cases where they function as intended, it is difficult to determine which of them is the most important.

On the plane of humanist and romantic psychology, the personal reality corresponds to Don Quixotesque elements, while the collective reality corresponds to those of Sancho Panza. The immortal masterpiece of Cervantes must be considered as a confession of the impotence of Christianity(at least of the forms with which we are familiar today). Has this religion ever been both Catholic (that is to say esoteric, Oriental) and Roman (exoteric, Occidental)? It has never been able to be the one without forsaking the other. What of those Christians who have no allegiance to Rome, are they truly Christian? I do not know. When a religion declares with all seriousness that its rituals and dogmas have neither a sense of mystery nor of the inward, it makes a public profession of superstition and deserves no less than to be sent to a museum of antiquities.

Europe has made several attempts to merge Don Quixote and Sancho Panza into a single personage. They have all failed, since those few who did succeeded parted from Christianity by founding free-thinking. I shall mention only two extremes of these failed attempts, the satanic and the grotesque: The Jesuit and Tartarin de Tarascon.[26] There is but one Occidental who managed to resolve this problem: Saint Rabelais.[27] But since he was an initiate, he most probably knew that throughout the centuries the solution lay with the *Malāmatiyah.* In order to illustrate our analysis we can contrast the *Malāmati* with Tartarin. The former shows his Sancho Panza while hiding his Don Quixote in his inner depth, as a kind of thought at the back of his mind which always haunts him but is never pronounced. The hero of Daudet, on the

[26] Editor's Note: Tartarin is a character from the 1872 novel of the same name by Alphonse Daudet. It tells the burlesque adventures of Tartarin, a local hero of the town of Tarascon in southern France, whose imaginary heroism and bravery as a hunter lead him to travel to Algiers in search of lions. The word *tartarinade* has been forged in French to refer to burlesque boastfulness. The attribution of "satanism" to the Jesuit is no doubt to be taken as a "shocking" hyperbole, in conformity with aspects of the *malāmatiyyah* spirit extolled by Aguéli. It may allude to the increased worldliness of too many representatives of the Society of Jesus in Western history, i.e. a "satanic" inversion of Jesuit ideals.

[27] Translator's Note: Abdul Hadi was a keen reader of the bawdy French Renaissance writer François Rabelais, and at one point attempted to translate his works into Arabic. See Gauffin, *Ivan Aguéli*, vol. 2, p.119. [Editor's Note: Aguéli's expression "Saint Rabelais" can be taken as a profound allusion in the form of a joke.]

other hand, exposes his Don Quixote in the far-off exploits of Tartarin, while his Sancho Panza, who is Tartarin in private, is dissimulated unto all except for his servant.

The personal and collective realities, the Will and Need, the exterior and interior, the unity and plurality, the One and the All, merge into a third reality which Islam alone among religions knows, recognizes, and professes. This reality is the Muhammadan or Prophetic reality. Our Prophet was not only a *nabī*, or a man eloquently inspired, but also a *rasūl*, or legislating envoy. He touched the (intellectual) aristocracy by *An-nubūwah*, or inspired eloquence, and he prevented the total decadence of the common people and the weak by *Ar-risālah*, or Divine Law. A fusion of the elite and the common, the Islamic aristo-democracy, can be realized without need of violence or excessive familiarity because of the peculiarly Islamic institution of a conventional type of humanity, which for lack of a better term I shall call the "average man", or "human normality".[28] Some Anglo-Saxon philosophers do indeed speak of the "average man" or the "man of mediocrity," but I am not sufficiently familiar with their theories to hazard an opinion in this regard. Such a man is always fictitious, never real. He serves as a neutral and impersonal insulator which facilitates certain perceived and expected relations by ruling out any irregular interactions between people who wish to maintain a social separation. Being everybody and nobody, lacking any concrete reality, always being the rule and never the exception, he serves but as a universal standard of measurement for all social, moral, and religious rights and obligations. This very formalism or this just equilibrium of interests (material, spirito-material, or religio-material) encompasses fully all such outward circumstances as may arise in the course of social and religious life, and it becomes thereby the foremost means of promoting Islam. It is thanks to him that the social norms of the Arabo-Semitic tribe—those of ideal justice, unity, co-operation, and solidarity—can spread throughout the universe.

The perfection of certain truly primitive societies has been noted by several sociologists, ethnographers, and poets. But the virtues of the "man of the wild" never pass beyond the narrow confines of the tribe itself. It remains, therefore, a lyrical ideal only. Its antitheses, present-day civilized man, can hardly excel him as regards human wholeness. With the latter we have quantity, which counts for something, this is true, but their quality is far from being laudable. Formalism, the institution of the average man, allows primitive men to attain universality without forsaking those precious characteristics which connect them to primordial and quasi-paradisic Adamism.

It is precisely this "average man" who is the object of the *Shari'ah*, or sacred Law of Islam.[29] It is very simple when there is no great outward difference between the elite and the common. The literal rule then suffices. But with the course of social progress, the complications of life and the shifting of exterior conditions, the direct application of the letter would have contradicted the spirit of the law. As the average man had different varieties, so the texts were given commentaries, and thus the understanding of the legislators progressed with the passage of

28 Translator's Note: This sentence was quoted by Frithjof Schuon in his *Sufism: Veil and Quintessence* (Bloomington, IN: World Wisdom, 2006), p. 88, n. 26. [Editor's Note: It bears adding that Schuon's quoting of Abdul Hadi does not amount to an endorsement of Abdul Hadi's entire perspective or all of the ideas presented by the Swedish Sufi. Abdul Hadi's references to Buddhists in a latter part of this article is, among other examples, a clear indication of this, when compared with Schuon's profound recognition of the spiritual truths of Buddhism.]

29 Translator's Note: This sentence is quoted on two occasions by Schuon, once in *The Transcendent Unity of Religions* (Wheaton, IL: Quest Books, 1984), p. 157, and once in *Sufism: Veil and Quintessence*, p. 88.

life; though the difference between text and commentary is only an appearance. This evolution is natural and logical, whatever may be said by the Orientalists of barracks or sacristies.[30]

Certain *Shariate* prescriptions may appear absurd to Europeans eyes. They have, nonetheless, their own reason for being. A universal religion must take account of all the various moral and intellectual degrees. The simplicity, weaknesses, and particularities of others do, to a certain degree, have a right to consideration. But intellectual culture has its rights and requirements as well. The average man establishes around each person a kind of neutrality, which guarantees all individualities while obliging them to work for humanity as a whole.[31] History knows of no other practical form of human integrality. Experience bears irrefutable witness in favor of Islamic universality. Thanks to the Arabic formulas there is a mean of perfect understanding amongst all the human races found between the Pacific and the Atlantic. It is hardly possible to find ethnic differences greater than those that exist between, for example, a Sudanese and a Persian, a Turk and an Arab, a Chinese and an Albanian, an Indo-Aryan and a Berber. No other religion or civilization has ever managed to accomplish such a feat. One can state, therefore, that Islam is the foremost means of spiritual communication that exists. Europe can establish the international only on the material level. It is something, but it is not everything. Furthermore, it is not Christianity which achieves this feat, but Occidental positivism, not to mention free-thinking.

This is why we consider the prophetic chain as concluded, *sealed*, since he is its apogee, with Muhammad, the Prophet of both Arabs and non-Arabs. The Prophetic Spirit is the doctrine of the "Supreme Identity", the One-and-All in Metaphysics, Universal Man in psychology, and integral Humanity in social organization. It began with Adam and was completed by Muhammad.

* * *

The word Islam is an infinitive of the causative verb *Aslama*, to give, to deliver, to hand over. There is an implied ellipsis: *Lillāhi* (to God). "*Al-islāmu lillāhi*" thus signifies: to deliver oneself to God, that is to say to follow docilely and consciously one's fate. Now, as man is a microcosm, composed of all the elements of the Universe, it follows that his fate is to be universal. He does not follow his fate when his higher faculties are dominated by inertia. Islam, as a religion, is the way of unity and totality. Its fundamental dogma is called *At-Tawhīd*, that is to say, unity or the act of unification. As a universal religion, it admits of degrees, but each of these degrees is truly Islam in the sense that each and every aspect of Islam reveals the same principles. Its formulas are extremely simple, but the number of its forms incalculable. The more numerous the forms, the more the law is perfect. One is a Muslim when one follows one's destiny, that is to say one's *raison d'être.* As each one carries his destiny within himself, it is evident that all discussions of predetermination or free-will are foolish. Islam, be it exoteric, is beyond this

[30] Translator's Note: Abdul Hadi harbored a great dislike of Western Orientalists. He was one of the first to comment upon their misapprehension of Ibn 'Arabī, Islam, and Sufism, stating, for example, in 1917: "Our Orientalists do not know Muhyiddin's true place in Sufism, nor Sufism's place in Islam" (quoted in Gauffin, *Ivan Aguéli*, vol. 2, p. 282).

[31] Translator's Note: These sentences were quoted by Frithjof Schuon in his *Sufism: Veil and Quintessence*, p. 88, n. 26.

question. This is why the greatest scholars have never wished to express their opinion on the matter. One cannot explain to the ordinary man how God accomplishes all things, how He is everywhere present, and how we all carry Him within ourselves. All this is clear to the man "who knows his soul" (*man yaraf nafsahu*), that is to say himself, and who knows that all is in vain except the "sensation of eternity". The *ex cathedra* utterance of the *mufti* must be clear and comprehensible to all, even to an illiterate black man. He has no right to make any pronouncement on any matter other than the commonplaces of practical life, and in fact never does so, since he can avoid questions which do not lie within his area of competence. It is this clear delimitation, known unto all, between Sufic and Shariate questions which allows Islam to be at once esoteric and exoteric without ever contradicting itself. This is why there is never a serious conflict between science and faith amongst those Muslims who understand their religion.

Now, the formula of *At-Tawhīd*, or monotheism, is a *Shariate* commonplace. The scope that you give this formula is your own personal affair, since it depends on your Sufism. All deductions that you possibly can make from this formula will to a greater or lesser extent be good, on condition that they in no manner abolish the literal meaning; since then you would be destroying the unity of Islam, that is to say, its universality, the faculty by which it is adaptable and suitable to all mentalities, circumstances, and epochs. Formalism is indispensable; it is not a superstition, but a universal language.[32] Since universality is the principle and the reason for the existence of Islam, and since, on the other hand, language is the means of communication between beings endowed with reason, it follows that exoteric formulas are as important to the religious organism as are arteries to the animal body.[33] I have allowed myself to express the analogy above in order to show that *intelligence* (*inter+legere*; *Al-'Aqlu*), I mean *universal intelligence*, resides in the heart, the center of the circulation of blood.[34] Sentimentality does not belong there, since its place is in the mucus of the intestines, when, that is, it occupies the place it should in the physiological economy.

Intelligence and discernment are the two principal aspects of human reason. One conceives of unity, the other conceives of plurality. Sound reason possesses these two faculties developed to their utmost limits and thus can conceive of the One-and-All Being; but this Being is not the Absolute, which is beyond any intellectual operation. One has reached the outer confines, not only of science, but also of the *scibile*,[35] when one knows that one cannot reach any further. The acknowledgement of the impossibility of knowing is the knowledge of the Infinite (*Al-ajzu an al-idrāki idrākun*). This is the only knowledge, it is true, but one would touch upon the divulgence of secrets by affirming that it is neither a paradox nor a manner of speech, but

[32] Translator's Note: Abdul Hadi's fascination with Islam was its very universality, and its ability as a spiritual language to form bonds between different nations and peoples. Indeed the concept of a universal language was what he had been seeking from his earliest youth. In a letter from the Mazas Prison in 1894, the young seeker wrote the following line to a friend: "You, on your part seek a religion. I, a language" (Gauffin, *Ivan Aguéli*, vol. 1, p. 151).

[33] Translator's Note: Frithjof Schuon quotes this and parts of the paragraph above and below in his *The Transcendent Unity*, pp. 157-158, n. 1.

[34] Translator's Note: René Guénon would be inspired by this last sentence in the fourth chapter of his *Man and his Becoming According to the Vedanta* (London: Luzac & Co, 1945), p. 39.

[35] Editor's Note: Literally "that which can be known", the "knowable."

a science that is real, fertile, and, after all, sufficient. All that is only exoteric ends inevitably in skepticism. Now, skepticism is the point of departure for the elect. Beyond the limits of the *scibile*, there is, however, a "scientific progress", but now the knowledge becomes negative, which makes it all the more fertile, since it comes to reveal our "poverty" (*Al-faqru*), that is to say our, need of Heaven. Conscious of our need, we will know how to make our petitions. I say petitions and not prayers since we must shun anything which resembles in any way whatsoever a clergy. It is not important to know how to make a petition, since, in this case, Heaven is like nature, which always answers truthfully when one pleads well—but only then. A physical or chemical experience produces a revelation. However, if done badly, it will lead to error. Heaven always awards something good when one petitions as one must petition. But it awards nothing, or even something bad, when one petitions in a bad manner. This is an effect of the divine mutuality, or the law of universal catadioptrics.[36]

Sentimental moralists, Christians, Buddhists, and others, have glorified humility. Very well, but to be humble means nothing, since we are all naught.[37] They have turned humility into a virtue, a goal, while it is nothing but a means, an exercise, a training. It is nothing but a brief stop along the way, one at which one halts in accordance with one's needs on the journey. Vanity is a stupidity. Misplaced humility can be so too.[38]

We have previously seen[39] how the Muslims' credo commences with a negation, which is then followed by an affirmation. That which I deny and that which I affirm both carry the same name, A L H; but, in the first case, it is indeterminate (36); and, in the second, it is determinate (66). I am stating that the vague is non-existent, but that the distinction is real. By considering only the shape of the letters, it represents a transformation of infinitude represented by the straight line (vertical) (A), into the indefinite, represented by the circle (H), crossed through by the angle (L). For the sake of affirming the distinction, the angle (L) is repeated twice.

The greatest part of practical esoterism concerns destiny, the identity of the I and the non-I, and the art of giving, based on *faqirism*. The requirement is to follow *docilely and consciously* one's destiny, which is *to live*, to *live one's whole life*, which is that of all lives, that is to say, that of all beings.[40]

36 Translator's Note: An optical system that involves both the reflecting and refracting of light, in order to reduce aberration. Life is ordered in accordance with *lex talionis*, according to a *hadīth*.

37 Editor's Note: In typically "provocative" fashion, Aguéli clearly points to the limits of individualistic and sentimental "humility," while alluding to the real "metaphysical" humility based on the consciousness of our "naught-iness."

38 Translator's Note: Although a great admirer of the arts and cultures of China and Japan, Abdul Hadi had a problematic relationship with the Buddhism he encountered on Ceylon. Having originally intended to travel to Tibet and visit a Buddhist monastery, it was during his stay in Ceylon in 1899 that he was drawn into the rivalry between the Buddhist Singhalese majority and the Muslim and Hindu minorities. As a Muslim, he was often harassed by his Buddhist neighbors, whose wild dog on numerous occasions broke into his home, defiling his sacred texts and attacking his favorite cat Mabruka (see note 45 below). Although René Guénon's early antipathy towards Buddhism was mostly rooted in his Hindu sympathies, his initial uncompromising stance may also have been influenced by Abdul Hadi's biases.

39 *La Gnose*, 2nd Year, No. 2, p.64, and No.3 p.111. [Translator's Note: "Pages Dedicated to the Sun".]

40 Here I am not addressing the Ibsenian concept of "living one's life". Those who do not dare, who do not restrain their pleasures, are all too unprepared to be addressed with an esoteric concept. Ibsen, Tolstoy, Nietzsche etc. are very respectable as individuals, I do not dispute that, but they are of no traditional value whatsoever. They are

Life is not at all divisible; what makes it appear as such is its proneness to gradation. The more the life of the "I" identifies with the life of the "non-I", the more intensely one shall live.[41] The transfusion of the I into the non-I is accomplished by a more or less ritual, conscious, or voluntary gift. It will easily be understood that the art of giving is the main arcanum of the Great Work. The secret of this art lies in absolute disinterestedness, in the perfect purity of the act's spirit—that is to say, the intention—and in the complete absence of any hope of any return or repayment, even in the next world. Your act must in no way be perceived as an exchange for profit. Consequently, it is more perfect, more pure, to give to those who appear to be inferior or weak, rather than to those who appear to be equal or stronger.[42] From an esoteric perspective, it is far better to give to a type of person who is distant from one's own type, than to those who are like oneself. This is why an attraction to the Antipodes, a taste for the exotic, a love for animals, or a passion for nature, are all indicators of an esoteric disposition. The famous poet, *Abu-Alā Al Moarrī*, while considered by some to be a heretic, a materialist, and a free-thinker, occupied in fact a highly elevated rank in the spiritual hierarchy of Muslim esoterism. To stop oneself at the level of humanitarianism is, therefore, a socio-sentimental error.[43] An initial training (or taming) of animic egotism will suffice for one to be considered by others as socially flawless, since all civic virtues are nothing more or less than politics, that is to say, advantageous. It is impossible, in fact, to do good for humanity without having ulterior utilitarian motives. Charity to those who are like oneself is either a duty, an act of precaution, or an act of foresight. It will thus be difficult for it to comprise anything performed "uniquely for God". Sentimentalism gives an egotistic touch to anything done in one's own name, and transforms it into nothing other than a way of attributing grand motives to the simplest of deeds.[44] The *Malāmatiyah* always give themselves a number of bad reasons for carrying out any good deed they have been called upon to perform.

The good that one does to an animal brings us closer to God, since there egotism is taken less account of, at least in ordinary cases. As the mental displacement becomes greater, the conquest within the universal soul becomes further-reaching. When you are attached to other humans, they attach themselves to you for all kinds of practical reasons. The attachment between an animal and a human is thus of a higher order. Moreover, it is exceedingly instructive, for according to the following formula: x will stand in relation to you, as you stand in relation to your cat; by this example, one can discover the greatest secrets of destiny.[45] It is true that gestures of

moralists with a local influence and hence they fail to gain our interest, as they are like small provincial prophets.

41 Translator's Note: This is quoted by Ananda K.Coomaraswamy in his *The Living Thoughts of Gotama the Buddha* (London: Cassell, 1948), p. 36.

42 Translator's Note: Here one can perhaps make out Abdul Hadi's reasoning for having shot the matador.

43 Translator's Note: Compare to Mevlana Rumi in his *Divani Shamsi Tabriz*: "If thou art Love's lover and seekest Love, take a keen poniard and cut the throat of bashfulness. Know that reputation is a great hinderance in the path." Translated by Reynold Nicholson, *Selected Poems from the Divani Shamsi Tabriz* (Richmond, Surrey: Curzon Press, 1999), p. 3.

44 Translator's Note: Abdul Hadi, whose original Swedish name was John Gustaf Agelii, nearly always wrote articles under pseudonym. This was not only to guard his anonymity, but also to keep his pride in check.

45 Translator's Note: While living in Colombo in 1899, Abdul Hadi found a starving, one-eyed, toothless, and pregnant street-cat which he adopted and named Mabruka ("the blessed one"). Becoming his constant companion, he took her with him on his journeys to South India, where he readily adapted his travel plans to suit her

loving-kindness towards animal are of great use from a sidereal perspective; but, in order to comprehend this usefulness, one's egotism must have been developed toward the transcendent. The man who realizes that the Great Powers shall judge him as he judges weaknesses will no longer need a spiritual guide. He is definitely on the right path, on the way to becoming himself the universal Law as an incarnation of destiny itself. He may have need of technical instruction in order to progress faster, but as he knows how to give without barter, he already has his heaven to himself. One would hardly, therefore, be in a position to label as egotistic those who cultivate loving-kindness towards animals in view of an astral goal, for example, by warding off what is called "a bad destiny"; or to reinstate, where possible, the state of primitive Adamism.[46] These are people who know something, and who use their knowledge to attain a terrestrial happiness which is considered by Tradition as licit.

I cannot insist enough on the fact that the art of giving is the act of the Great Arcanum. The purest and most selfless gift is the sensation of nothingness in the practice of realization. This crystallized perception is a touchstone—the foremost one—to control Existence in the Absolute. This precious tool for investigating the beyond may appear quite simple, rustic, or even coarse, but it is instantaneously spoiled by a single atom's weight of sentimentality. One could again say "Saint Rabelais," but one can never be too wary regarding theories that are Christian (in an ordinary sense) or Buddhist.

The reader who has been willing to follow me up to this point without weariness or irritation can easily see that humanitarian giving is but the right understanding of our material advantages and disadvantages. Everyone understands, of course, that it is useful for us to be in possession of that which is indispensable for us to live in a human way. True charity only commences with animals, which is then continued by plants, but then it requires the sciences of the initiates. These sciences will lead to Alchemy, which is the charity of man in relation to stones and metals, that is to say, in relation to inorganic nature. The height of this charity is the gift of the Self to primary numbers, for then one sustains the Universe by one's rhythmic breathing. I hereby allow myself to emphasize that Cosmic Charity presents an inverse line of progression when compared to material evolution, as it is commonly called.[47]

Thanks to the perfect harmony that Islam establishes between the esoteric and the exoteric, one can speak of it on different levels, which is to say that it supports proselytism even as regards esoterism, at least to some extent. Proselytism fortifies it, in the sense that it enriches it from a purely intellectual point of view. It is true that numerous branches of Islamic science were only developed after several non-Arab peoples joined Islam. Many Orientalists, having

requirements. When leaving Colombo, Abdul Hadi refused to abandon her, and instead took her with him to Paris. At almost every stage of Abdul Hadi's life, be it in Paris or Cairo, he nearly always had a number of street-cats in his care.

[46] Islamic tradition states that wild animals did not begin avoiding mankind until after Cain's fratricide. Before this event, they sought man's nearness in order to be comforted and protected by the great peace that emanated from him.

[47] Translator's Note: Compare to Mevlana Rumi in his *Mathnawi* III: 3901: "I died to the inorganic state and became endowed with growth, and (then) I died to (vegetable) growth and attained to the animal. I died from animality and became Adam (man): why, then should I fear? When I have become less by dying? At the next remove I shall die to man, that I may soar and lift up my head amongst the angels. And I must escape even from (the state of) the angel: everything is perishing except His Face." Translated by Reynold Nicholson, *The Mathnawi of Jalauddin Rumi* (London: Gibb Memorial Trust, 1990), vol. 3, p. 219.

observed this phenomenon, have attributed it to a juxtaposition of the Aryan or Turanian spirit with the Arabo-Semitic mentality. This is an error.

The seeds of these sciences were to be found already in primitive Islam. Since it admits rationalism and freedom of thought, it was obliged to explain itself to newcomers, to put on a form which would suit their mentality. This development occurred by the collaboration between students and teachers. Questions provoked responses. The outward need of explaining its subconsciousnesses nourished the rational and scholastic sciences of Islam. The Arabs took nothing new from the foreigners. They did nothing but, so to say, transform some of their gold into coins, their only goal being to facilitate the connection between different peoples.

I invite students of Kabbalah[48] to take note of the fact that, from a purely scientific point of view, one instructs oneself by teaching others; the inward will be enriched by the outward work; Heaven gives unto you in the same measure as you distribute amongst the creatures the little you already possess. But this one must know how to do.

Let it be said straightaway that *altruism* is an empty word; it should be banished from metaphysical discourse, because "another" does not exist. There is no difference between you and the others. You *are* the others, all other people, and all the other things. All other people and things are you. We do nothing but reflect one another. Life is unique, and individualities are nothing other than the inference of destiny shining through the crystal of creation. The identity of the I and the non-I is the Great Truth, as the realization of this identity is the Great Work. If, with regard to a theft, you cannot grasp that you are both the thief and the victim; that in a murder, you are both the murderer and the murdered; if you do not know to blush with shame and guilt on account of monstrous crimes, novel ones, inconceivable ones, that you would never in your entire life have dreamed of committing; if you do not feel that you are somehow responsible, if only in a small measure, for the earthquake in Turkestan or the plague in Manchuria, then you are better off not to study esoterism, for you would only be wasting your time.

It is always the criminal collectivity that demonstrates that the isolated act almost does not exist, and that it is difficult to distinguish one man from another. I do not claim that all men are the same, but I am claiming that they are "of the same". Observe, for example, the following chain of actions. Have you noticed that a general suspicion, although unjust, gives rise to the sufficient evidence of the guilt of the presumed culprit? This happens all the more quickly when he is innocent to the point of not knowing how the crime was perpetrated. If he is guilty, but intelligent, he can create around his person a negative, willful aura that diverts the collective aura which wants to overflow it. It is easy to see how the moral aura of a collective gradually amasses around certain nerve-centers in a society, which then are condensed and take on a human form, most often that of the author of a crime. But this criminal is only the hand that strikes. The true origin of the act is to be found in the collectivity. It has done nothing, to be sure, but it makes it happen, which in the end is the same. This is why there are no innocents.[49]

When I declare everyone to be guilty, I am not pleading for the criminal's acquittal. Even less am I calling for the chastisement of all. Esoterism has nothing to do with the code of law,

[48] Translator's Note: A term used by Abdul Hadi, not to indicate Jewish Kabbalah in particular, but rather esoterism as a whole.

[49] All impersonal and anonymous crimes are, *a priori*, collective crimes.

which is a natural product, with all the defects, of a society's history. Man cannot exercise human justice in its totality. Divine justice will always remain an enigma to him. To seek to emulate this justice is, from our perspective, among the gravest crimes a man could commit. I permit myself to quote a number of examples. Theft and murder are crimes, at least in principle; hence, the thief and the murderer must be punished in accordance with present social conventions, but that is all. You are free to avoid them or to refuse giving them the hand of your daughter, etc., but if you say that the man is bad, that he deserves hellfire etc., in that case you are worse indeed than he is, for you wish to seat yourself upon God's throne. You seek to pass judgment in a matter of which man has no knowledge.

Another example: you condemn prostitution, and you are not wrong to do so. However, you can condemn the prostitute only when she commits indecent exposure in public. But her crime is only one of reflex. On the plane of current society, the man is the interior, the cause, and the woman is the exterior, the effect. The woman sells her body because the man has sold his soul. You can apprehend the one, but the other, the true culprit, escapes altogether because he is anonymous and legion. One should restrict oneself to judging facts only. But to judge a conscience is impossible.

One final example: the scandalous acquittals of crimes of passion. Some have wanted to see in them a sign of amorality. This is not at all the case. They are only as many declarations of incompetence by the tribunal. The scrupulous judge avoids making decisions in cases whereof God alone can know.

The universal conscience becomes increasingly fatalist. There is an old saying, "nations only have the governments they deserve". A good government cannot reign a nation of rascals; it will be obliged to be corrupt if it wishes to stay in power. Day by day, one understands more of the great truth by the mere logic of events: that man is always judged in accordance with his own laws, that is to say, the laws that he imposes on beings that belong to his vital influence. There are subtle bonds between the torturer and the victim, for they are two aspects of the same event.[50] Everyone realizes that it is because of the rich that there are paupers; that it is because of the wise that there are fools; that there are vicious men because the men of virtue leave much to be desired. Several saints of Islam complained of having been given the gift of secondary sight. They have seen too many extraordinary things in the minor occurrences of everyday life. The naive ones are those who seek super-human faculties outside of the given order. When these sorcerer's apprentices do not fall into intellectual or moral deviation, it means God has been merciful to them.

* * *

The law of universal poverty (*Al-faqru*) is indeed an Islamic principle. Each one of us is a pauper (*faqīr*). We are all paupers (*fuqarā*), because we all have a need for the Creator or the creation, most often for them both. As one must give in order to receive, it follows that the greatest

[50] Translator's Note: Here Abdul Hadi is possibly inspired by one of his favorite poets, Charles Baudelaire. See Poem 51 of *Les Fleurs du Mal*: "Je suis la plaie et le couteau! Je suis le soufflet et la joue! Je suis les membres et la roue, et la victime et le bourreau!" ("I am the wound and the knife! I am the blow and the cheek! I am the limbs and the wheel, and the victim and the torturer!"). Translation by Carol Clark, *Charles Baudelaire: Selected Poems* (London: Penguin Books, 2004).

misfortune lies in not being able to do any good, in having lost the right to exercise charity. When one gives, one must give more modestly than the pauper who receives the alms from one's hand.

It is above all through its conception of the collective reality that Islam stands apart from other religions, civilizations, and philosophies. All enlightened ones know that the collective reality is a fiction. The enlightened Muslims know this just as well, if not better. Therefore, aiming to follow the Prophet, one does not retire into the desert, but one pretends that one takes the world seriously. A *hadīth* states that we must work for this life as if we were to live for a thousand years, and for the next world as if we were to die tomorrow. The doctrine of identity and unity is developed further in Islam than anywhere else. Its most precious quality of esotero-exoterism provides above all its concept of the collective reality as an indispensable means by which it can transform the personal reality into the Universal humanity or the Prophetic reality. Christianity and Buddhism reject the collective reality with horror or disdain in order to make the universal Man exist in a minute quietude. Hence, they differ from Islam in a way that is both qualitative and psychological. Islam differs quantitatively from esoteric Brahmanism, as it is more vast. Brahmanism is only a local phenomenon, at least from a practical point of view, while Islam is universal. It differs from anti-doctrinal positivism on the point of formalism and metaphysics. It stands in direct opposition to German philosophy, which, through its confusion of feudalism with aristocracy, has totally distorted the idea of government. Everywhere except for Germany, responsibility is a measure of nobility: the more one is noble, the more responsible, and *vice-versa.* According to the *Sharī'ah* the crimes of the free or the noble are judged more severely than those of the slaves or the ignorant. Unfortunately, feudalism is everywhere turned into a system that assures impunity; but everywhere it is kept apart from nobility, while in Germany feudalism is the sole condition for aristocracy. The strongest has no obligation in regards to the one whose unhappy fate has placed him in an inferior situation.

In contrast, Islam has points of comparison and contact with most forms of beliefs and social structures. It is, however, neither a religious mixture nor a novelty. The Prophet expressly stated that he had invented nothing new relating to dogmas or laws. He merely restored the primitive and ancient faith. This is why there is much resemblance between Taoism and Islam. I am not the one who dares to make such an assertion of similarity, but it has been made by celebrated authors on Islam in China. Taoism differs from Islam only by the fact that it is exclusively esoteric, while Islam is esotero-exoteric. This is why the one can promote its doctrines, while the other cannot. Islam knows both neophyteness and adeptness, while Taoism recognizes only the latter of these two forms of expansion.

*Translated by Farid Nur ad-Din*

# BOOK REVIEWS

# The Other in the Light of the One: The Universality of the Qur'ān and Interfaith Dialogue

BY REZA SHAH-KAZEMI

Cambridge, UK: Islamic Texts Society, 2006

The purpose of this beautifully inspiring and timely book is, in the author's own terms, to present "an exposition of the universality of the Qur'ānic message of *tawhid* . . . and the implications of this universality for dialogue". In his cogent and rigorously developed argument, Reza Shah-Kazemi sets out to articulate and substantiate a few fundamental theses that may pave the ground for a genuinely renewed religious dialogue in the wake of the post-September 11 era. This book is intended for a general readership with an interest in religious and Islamic studies, but it clearly addresses two kinds of audience—not necessarily exclusive of one another, the first being more attuned to inter-religious dialogue, the second more involved in intra-religious debates within the Muslim community. In other words, the inclusiveness that the perspective of the book fosters is from the outset defined both with a view to universality and in compliance with a religious commitment to identity. Although the richness of the argumentation and the wealth of illustrations called to buttress it defy an exhaustive treatment of the whole book, what follows is an attempt at summarizing some of the main articulations of the hermeneutic theses that are instrumental in bringing out the fundamental inclusiveness in respect of the confessional differences that the author has set as his goal.

First of all, Shah-Kazemi argues that the healthy state of a religious universe is proportional to the presence of a profound spirituality within its fold. Such a vital presence is moreover inversely proportional to the advent of ideology in religious life and discourse. In the absence of a strong spiritual consciousness within the community the "revealed text becomes an ideological pretext; morally reforming oneself gives way to violently rectifying the Other; spiritual contemplation is scorned in favor of political machination; the subtleties of revelation become submerged by the exigencies of revolution" (p. ix). The spiritual sap of Islam is particularly apt to bring fruits within the domain of Qur'ānic exegesis. The methodological thrust of this entire book lies precisely in a reading of the Qur'ān from the standpoint of spiritual hermeneutics, as exemplified in the Sufi tradition of such as Ibn 'Arabī, Kāshānī, Rūmī, and Haydar Āmulī. In this hermeneutic tradition "religion . . . is divine dis-closure, not human 'closure', openings to higher truths and deeper realities, not simply exclusive affirmations of simple dogmas combined with perceptions limited to surface phenomena" (p. xvii). Now this very "dis-closure" is a fundamental way to opening oneself to the universal horizon of the revealed text, and such an opening is the main objective of this book. Its four chapters are devoted to laying out the principles and illustrations conducive to this objective.

In a first chapter, Shah-Kazemi clears the methodological way for his approach to the Qur'ān by contrasting the Sufi hermeneutics for which he has opted with modern and postmodern theories of interpretation. He brings to the attention of his readers the fact that Sufism, in its earlier phases, can be viewed as a response to two tendencies of the Islamic society, that is, worldliness and formalism. Although Shah-Kazemi does not explicitly make the point in this historical context he certainly implies that these two negative tendencies are not without relation to the modernist and fundamentalist faces of contemporary Islam. The thrust of his methodological emphasis on Sufi hermeneutics lies precisely in that this type of hermeneutics is the only effective answer to the concerns for universality and integrity that are central respectively in modernist Islam and in fundamentalist Islam. Sufi hermeneutics provides Shah-Kazemi with the tools to formulate a radical critique of these two contemporary movements while satisfying the concerns that they harbor, i.e. respectively the aspiration toward universality and the need for religious identity.

A second part of this initial chapter engages the reader in a condensed and cogent critique of postmodern types of hermeneutics by highlighting both the ground that they share with the Sufi perspective, but also and above all the point where they clearly part with the latter. Shah-Kazemi fully acknowledges that the traditional Sufi perspective is not to be equated with a blind imitation of traditional authorities nor "a funeral cortège or a register of conformist opinions" (Henry Corbin) (p. 27); in addition, he underlines that Sufi hermeneutics is given to highlight the relativity of forms as well as the limitations of reason and language. Capitalizing on these dimensions of Sufi hermeneutics, some contemporary commentators have been tempted to draw parallels between mystical perspectives and postmodern approaches. As a response to these attempts, the author stresses the assumptions and contradictions of the various forms of "hermeneutics of suspicion"—through a discussion of such influential figures as Paul Ricoeur, Mohammed Arkoun, Jacques Derrida, Hans-Georg Gadamer, and Ian Almond—while unveiling the radical chasm that separates the mystical emphasis on "points of view and aspects" (to use Schuon's phrase) and the postmodern "suspension" of belief (Arkoun), concessions to the epistemological criteria of contemporary social sciences and ideologies (Ricoeur's critical hermeneutics), and deconstructionist self-contradiction and anti-metaphysical obsession with language and unending *différance* (Derrida.) Shah-Kazemi shows that Ibn 'Arabī's "stability in variegation" is to be understood as a kind of spiritual method—aimed at preventing a rational "freezing" of spiritual insights—that does not preclude the position of the Absolute beyond all determinations, aspects, and perspectives; quite to the contrary since it is precisely predicated on an understanding of the infinite Essence as free from conceptual and linguistic determinations.

Chapter II is focused on answering the question that may be raised from a defective comprehension of *wahdāt al-wujūd*, i.e. "if nothing but God is real, and there is no 'otherness', in reality, what is the meaning of dialogue with the Other?" (p. 75). The fundamental answer to this question lies in an understanding of existence as a kind of "dialogue" between archetypical possibilities. The key is to grasp that divine unity and existential multiplicity are not exclusive of one another but that they are in fact the two "faces" of the same Reality. Relying primarily on Kāshānī's commentary on the *Surat al-Ikhlās*, Shah-Kazemi highlights the "resolution of the outward multiplicity of phenomena within the single reality of God by means of the relationships constituted by the divine Names" (p. 86). These Names constitute as it were the "multiplicity within unity". Multiplicity, then, is viewed from the standpoint of essential unity, as expressing this unity through particularity—which is a manifestation of unity on the plane of relativity—so that the divine unity of *tawhīd* is understood as perfectly compatible with metaphysical "polytheism"—but not of course with theological polytheism as commonly understood—since metaphysically "plurality is viewed in its principial aspect, as expressing the unique principle, and (is therefore) re-endowed with the reality that was veiled by the appearance of crude, empirical multiplicity, or of ontological plurality" (p. 91). Thus understood the One is both the principle of the manifestation of multiplicity and, in addition, its principle of integration. This perspective is to be applied to the question of religious diversity in order to reach a full grasp of the nature and function of differences and dialogue in that realm. It is a key to the integration of universality—by virtue of the transcendent principiality of the One—and identity—by virtue of the integration of diversity within unity. Bringing in Haydar Āmulī's theosophy—and its stress on the constant renewal of reality in each manifestation without any room for mere repetition (a kind of Sufi commentary on Heraclitus' *panta rhei*)—the author asserts the paradox of a "uniqueness which manifests infinite diversity, and a diversity which reproduces uniqueness" (p. 106). The Qur'ānic expression of this double relationship appears in a series of verses that highlight the spiritual significance of differences and "otherness" in creation. On the basis of such verses as 30:22, 5:48, 2:62, 4:124, 2:136, and 29:46 Shah-Kazemi shows how the Qur'ān invites "the sensitive reader to contemplate divine 'signs' in the other, thus to learn more about the divine reality—and about themselves—through the other. . ." (p. 115).

The recognition of "otherness" that is inscribed in the Qur'ānic injunction must moreover be situated within the context of an integral understanding of the *shahādah* that prevents any form of association or *shirk*, whether on the individual level (the ego) or in the collective realm (the group, the nation, the religion as a collective psyche). When penetrated in its deeper metaphysical implications, *Tawhīd* is therefore the best protection against idolatry, narrow exclusivism, and fanaticism. To the sensible objection that such heights of metaphysical understanding and spiritual recognition are not likely to be of much help when dealing with a general religious audience which is predetermined by unexamined reflexes and biases, mental laziness and collective passions, the author expresses the conviction that the Qur'ānic emphasis on human "nothingness" and the ephemerality of all that is not His Face can be an effective theme of meditation for exoteric believers by preventing them from absolutizing the forms of their faith. Whatever one may think concerning the concrete "horizon" of this possibility—which may be deemed by some to underestimate the "gravity" of the fallen state of mankind including its "believing" segments—there is little doubt that a willingness and a capacity to enter the mold of such a meditation could and would constitute a fundamental criterion of religious understanding and sincerity on the part of believers. In fact, a recognition of this kind would amount to reaching the mystical sap of faith through "the relationship between extinction and contemplation: between knowledge of one's nothingness and truly witnessing the divine 'Face' in the other, and in Itself" (p. 117).

In the third chapter of his book, Shah-Kazemi delves into the question of the universalism of the Qur'ān in the light of Sufi exegesis. The thrust of his argument lies in a clear recognition that the Qur'ānic term *muslim* must be understood in two different senses that are not contradictory but complementary. In the first sense, which touches upon the universalist chord of the Qur'ān, the term *muslim* refers to those who surrender themselves to God and to one of His revelations, the latter being only a means toward the former. In a second, more restrictive sense, the terms *muslim* and *islam* refer specifically to the community following the Prophet Muhammad. It is clear that for Sufis such as Ibn 'Arabī and Kāshānī these two meanings of *muslim/islam* point to two different ontological and epistemological levels. That distinction is encapsulated by Kāshānī's assertion, quoted by Shah-Kazemi, that "the right religion (*al-dīn al-qayyim*) is tied to that which is immutable within knowledge and action; while the revealed Law is tied to that which alters in respect of rules and conditions" (p. 148). The "right religion" can in fact be equated with the *fitra*, or an ontological and epistemological stratum that is deeper than any confessional affiliation. Shah-Kazemi lucidly acknowledges that this point of view should not blind one to the fact that, for Sufis like Kāshānī and Ibn 'Arabī, Islam as a confession "would be seen as resonating most harmoniously with this inner substance" (p. 157). In one sense, "Islam" is "religion as such", in another sense it is "such or such a religion" (Schuon). Shah-Kazemi's goal is to show that both visions of Islam must be upheld in order to preserve a truly universalist and inclusivist perspective. In fact, the differentiation that is at the source of confessional exclusiveness is not to be interpreted, according to the author, in terms of a deplorable insufficiency, so to speak, but rather as a metaphysical necessity, a reflection of the infinity of the Divine nature. On that point, some readers might be tempted to argue that such a differentiation is still on a certain level the result of an ontological and epistemological fragmentation which, albeit "necessary" on the highest plane, is nonetheless manifested by a defectiveness on the human level, as illustrated in a sense by the exile of Adam and Eve from the Garden and the episode of the Tower of Babel. In the words of Ramana Maharshi: "It is a great wonder that to teach such a simple truth a number of religions should be necessary, and so many disputes should go on between them as to which is the God-ordained teaching. What a pity!"[1] This consideration is not without relation to the discussion of Ibn 'Arabī's "bringing together of opposites" with respect to nondelimitation (the point of view of God's omnipresence, "wherever ye turn, there is the face of God") and delimitation (the confessional "orientation", the *qiblah*): "Nondelimitation is not contradicted by delimitation; if nondelimitation were devoid of delimitation it would be delimited: by the absence of delimitation" (p. 166). On the one hand this echoes on the highest plane the "need" within the Infinite for finite manifestation; on the other hand—and when considered simply on the human level—one may fail to see why nondelimitation would be "delimited" by the absence of delimitation, or at least why it should necessarily be so by absence of confessional "limitations", not to mention the question of the extent, abuse, or legitimacy of such limitations.

A parallel question may be raised with respect to Sufi hermeneutics as a whole: such an hermeneutics is based on the *'ilm min ladunnā*, i.e. the Intellect as embodied by al-Khidr in the famous passage of the *Surat al-Kahf* in the sense that the very selection and understanding of Qur'ānic verses that Sufis bring to the fore to foster their universalist perspective cannot but be informed *a priori* by an intellective grasp that has precedence over the revealed text in its literality. The status of this immanent "universal consciousness" that is akin to the dimension of sanctity is undoubtedly higher, as confirmed by Kāshānī, to that of prophethood, in the sense that the latter pertains to the law-giving, outer dimension of a particular message. However, that Ibn 'Arabī and most Sufis in fact subordinate sanctity to prophethood on the grounds that the latter "is the source of the sanctity of the saint" proves that their gnostic perspective is mitigated by a confessional outlook that sees, for all practical purposes, intellection necessarily and universally dependent upon revelation, or that the question of the consequences of the superiority of the *wilāyat* over the *nubuwwat* remains at least shrouded, in their perspective, in a halo of ambiguities that are the ransom of their more or less unavoidable confessional solidarity. This is confirmed by the principle, enunciated by Ibn 'Arabī, according to which the criterion of truth in religious matters is revelation, this criterion being defined in terms of "felicity", or eschatological opportuneness, and not in terms of truth pure and simple: "The road to felicity is that set down by revealed religion, nothing else." Arguably, the questions that have just

[1] *The Essential Teachings of Ramana Maharshi: A Visual Journey* (Inner Directions, 2001), p. 48.

been raised may have an incidence on our understanding of esoterism but they are not directly relevant to the main matter at stake and to the specific objectives of Shah-Kazemi's book, that is, the unveiling of the universal dimension of the Qur'ān in full respect of the Islamic "right" to exclusiveness. The most important task is, in this respect, to highlight the transcendence of God over any form that points to Him and the primordiality of immanent knowledge of Him and the *fitra*. In this respect the main lesson of this chapter lies perhaps in the author's very penetrating remarks concerning the fact that an exclusivist confessional restriction of the Divine is not only a confinement of objective truth but it is also, and perhaps more importantly on the level of the argument of the book, a "diminishing receptivity to the mercy that *encompasseth all things*".

The final chapter of this book is an application of the principles of Sufi hermeneutics to the intra-Islamic dialogue concerning the compatibility, or lack thereof, between the call of universality and the demands of religious preaching, or "invitation". In this part of his work, Shah-Kazemi presents the thesis, championed by Seyyed Hossein Nasr, of the need for a third way between liberal pluralism and conservatism exclusivism, the latter being insensitive to the universal horizon of Islam, the former being oblivious of the rights of Muslim particularism. In this context, Sufi universalism may paradoxically be conceived as one of the best tools of *da'wa* or "invitation" to Islam, as it may both satisfy the need for an opening to the Other while preserving the attachment to the "normativity" of Islam. The main thrust of Shah-Kazemi's thesis is expressed in the Sufi paradox of "both a greater degree of 'rootedness' in one's own religion . . . and a greater degree of detachment from it" (p. 257). A quote from Martin Lings illuminates this paradox: "as each mystical path approaches its End, it is nearer to the other mysticisms than it was at the beginning. But there is a complementary and almost paradoxical truth . . . : increase of nearness does not mean decrease of distinctness, for the nearer the center, the greater the concentration, the stronger the 'dose'" (p. 257). The general context of the book, informed by a "distinction between confessional formalism and spiritual essentiality" (p. 180) leads the reader to understand that this "rootedness" and this "dose" are best understood as referring to "archetypal Islam" than to "formal Islam": however, if this higher and deeper concentration is to be grasped as referring to the quintessential archetype of the religion, then the question remains of the relationship between this archetypal Islam and the integration of the complex network of forms that defines Islam as a religious world. Such a question has no absolute answer since the connection between archetype and formal system offers a spectrum of stages and intermediaries that defy absolute separations or distinctions. It is safe to say, however that to the extent that Islam is considered "from the archetype" its distinctiveness will be all the more transparent to universal gnosis. Schuon's distinction between an "essential *Sunnah*" and a "formal *Sunnah*" or his differentiation between an "Islamic esoterism" and an "esoteric Islam", not to mention his contradistinction between a "quintessential esoterism of Islam" and a Muslim "exo-esoterism" suggests the subtleties arising when trying to define degrees of "confessional distinctness" and their relationship to the essence. In this connection, Reza Shah-Kazemi's final pages may well suggest a sort of resolution, or at least relativization, of such challenges and ambiguities through an emphasis on the dimensions on Beauty and Presence. William Chittick and Sachiko Murata had also emphasized, in their *Vision of Islam*, the conspicuous absence of *ihsān* and a sense of beauty from most of contemporary Islam. Beauty—inner and outer—and Presence—the source of Love—opens onto universality by virtue of the non-conceptual and non-dogmatic character of their language. And not the least of the lessons of Shah-Kazemi's very rich and nuanced book is that in order to be fully understood and realized, Islam and the Qur'ān, as any other authentic tradition, need to be lived through a sense of the sacred and a beautiful wisdom, *ihsān*, that make our presence in the world both a way of witnessing and a mode of blessing. That is no doubt the most precious and most effective form of "dialogue", the spiritual foundation of which consists in cultivating a sense of objectivity, as well as a discipline of attentive silence.

*Reviewed by Patrick Laude*

## L'islam sera spirituel ou ne sera plus

BY ÉRIC GEOFFROY

**Paris: Éditions du Seuil, 2009**

The author, Éric Geoffroy, is an Islamicist, an expert of Sufism and Islamic sainthood, and a professor in the Department of Arab and Islamic Studies at the Université Marc Bloch in Strasbourg, France. Among his works are *Initiation au soufisme* (Fayard, 2003), recently published by World Wisdom as *Introduction to Sufism: The Inner Path of Islam* (2010), *Une voie soufie dans le monde: la Shādhiliyya* (Maisonneuve & Larose, 2005), and *Le Soufisme, voie intérieure de l'islam* (Éditions du Seuil, 2009).

The title of the book under review, translated from French into English, is *Islam will be spiritual or will no longer be.* Encompassing aspects of socio-cultural, juridical, political, ideological, and spiritual dimensions of Islam, the book's scope is quite broad. The author's method is well-balanced, as it consists in both relatively objective presentations of historical facts and relatively personal observations and interpretations, supported by an admirable, in-depth knowledge of the Qur'an, commentary and scholarship concerning it, Sufi writings and spiritual practice, as well as an extensive erudition regarding not only Islam, but also Western philosophical, socio-political, and scientific developments throughout history. As the book takes its place within the general context of writings on the theme of Islam and the spiritual crisis of the modern world, it is related to the works of authors such as René Guénon, Frithjof Schuon, Seyyed Hossein Nasr, William Chittick, and others.

Geoffroy's thesis is that fundamental Islamic principles have been inverted, leading to various crises and aberrations, but that these principles may be actualized anew through a spiritual reinvigoration of their meaning; furthermore, postmodern conditions may, seemingly paradoxically, offer certain advantages for undertaking this task, which, if accomplished, may in turn result in a more qualitative world. The book is therefore, in a way, about the "death" of Islam and its hoped-for "renaissance." In this work, the author explores the following topics: the process of the inversion of values in Islam; a possible "revolution of meaning," and a possible, resultant spiritual "reformation" of Islam; postmodernity in the context of its being either an obstacle or a providential condition; and what is at stake for Sufi brotherhoods.

Through an examination of the inversion of principal Islamic values, the author shows the mechanism that led to the present-day condition. Examples of this process include the following reversals: the virtue of modesty, which has turned into an obsession with sin; the principle of freedom and responsibility, having now become a tendency toward fatalism; a retreat into the ethnic dimension as opposed to the opening of Islam to the universal; the current consideration of Islam as a monolithic whole, instead of the sense of the internal pluralism of opinions; the confusion between universality as a principle and conformity as a contradictory, actual condition, i.e., a sense of the integral character of Islamic ethics, neither totalitarian thinking nor the standardization of behaviors; the respect for all forms of life, and Islam's place within universal morality, not a deviant "jihadism"; and the principle of spiritual soberness and simplicity, as over and against the cultural impoverishment of some contemporary Muslim societies. According to Geoffroy's point of view, the reason for the slow degeneration of Islamic culture during the later periods is to be found in the dominant influence of Asharite dogmatism in the Sunni world, which produces the *a posteriori* illusion of a homogeneous credo throughout history. Despite the fact that pluralism has always characterized Islamic civilization, and is moreover an integral part of its nature, many have launched ideological slogans of unification because they consider that religious and cultural pluralism is a weakness to be eradicated, and since they want to see Muslim life as something monolithic, as insensitive to the variations of mentalities, as well as to the permutations of history. In this way, confusion has been created between *unity* and *uniformity*, the former pertaining to things spiritual, the latter to things material; through such a reification of Islam, its vital essence is being depleted.

Thus Geoffroy claims that Islam is currently in an advanced state of exoteric fossilization, and is therefore devoid of the tolerant pluralism that is one of its fundaments. He furthermore postulates that if it were to remain in this condition, Islam would likely become a globalized, monolithic hegemony, hardly better than American-style worldwide homogenization. The counter-hegemonic thrust of the developing argument places considerable importance on certain aspects of postmodern circumstances, which could, according to the author, facilitate a hoped-for spiritual reinvigoration of Islam. Suggesting that this religious crisis will be resolved by a spirituality in which transcendence and immanence coincide harmoniously, the author believes that the Sufis are the forerunners of such a resolution, which would see humanity move out of a first phase associated with religion, and into an ultimate phase consisting in a spiritual assumption of the individual. Accordingly, Sufism can play a vital role in this transformation because of its universal quality, its ideal of spiritual "verticality" thanks to which the Sufi transcends terrestrial conditions, and because of Sufism's power to awaken the latent spirituality of the individual.

We are convinced that many will agree with the author's insightful analysis concerning the inversion of Islamic principles, which, in our opinion, provides an accurate and factual summation of the prevailing circumstances within Islam. Moreover, this summation constitutes a very sound premise for the author's ensuing arguments. These arguments are nonetheless of a more theoretical order, and concern, for instance, ways in which the current condition might be improved. Since these arguments are more speculative, and thus less factual, one may take exception to some of the author's suggestions.

We foresee reservations that are both general and particular in nature. In general, the author's opinion of, and attitude toward, the postmodern world sometimes gives the impression of being overly favorable. More particularly, certain modalities of a "new paradigm," which the author considers to be a necessary basis for a spiritual reinvigoration, impress us as being unlikely. Perhaps one could say that the book paints a hopeful future for Islam if one is convinced that adherents of the religion are likely to accomplish, both individually and socially, the kind of transformation of which the author speaks: a transformation based, in some of the author's reflections, for example, on a convergent assimilation of knowledge stemming from certain scientific and technological revolutions, on the one hand, and, on the other hand, from esoteric spiritual knowledge and practice; a transformation thereby paving the way for the beginning of the next cosmological cycle by transforming our relationship with the world. In close connection, however, the author also states that the traditional cosmological doctrines of the Four Ages, as expressed in Hinduism, for instance, "are not only obsolete, but also harmful for the safeguard of humanity and of the planet," and that, furthermore, "it is necessary to seek the most serious premises of the new paradigm in the quantum revolution that was experienced in physics in the 1920s" (literal translation from page 89). It may be difficult for some to see how a traditional doctrine, which, according to their understanding, is by definition true, could be obsolete and harmful. Since, in one form or another, all the revealed religious traditions, including Islam, provide cosmological doctrines that specify a general decline in spirituality over the course of the human cycle—and especially inasmuch as this same downward slope is corroborated by the author's own convincing analysis of the current exoteric hardening within Islam—some may tend not to be as optimistic concerning the future possibility of an emerging spirituality that would be sufficiently pervasive as to reverse current conditions. Moreover, some may fail to comprehend how a traditional doctrine could ever be obsolete, since truth is for all time, not just for some moments in time; and some may be of the opinion that these doctrines cannot possibly do harm, for they are providentially intended to enlighten humanity by means of their expression of the truth, precisely, and must therefore be helpful. Needless to say, such a perspective could hardly be accused of fatalism, and both optimism and pessimism are, from this vantage point, equally irrelevant in the final analysis.

The hoped-for spiritual reinvigoration could perhaps be envisaged as an occasional upward surge of limited scope and duration with respect to the predominant downward movement to which we have just referred. In this case, we would agree wholeheartedly with the author in saying that certain modern and postmodern developments could furnish a basis for a small and discrete reversal. Nevertheless, we cannot concur when the author speculates, for instance, that the scientific revolution operated by quantum mechanics, which may have led certain elite scientists to see through phenomena to their metaphysical origin, could produce such an effect on the general public, even if various vulgarized interpretations within a philosophical holism are disseminated widely by unprecedented means, such as the Internet. While it is certainly true that, for some, the pervasive availability of esoteric knowledge regarding the physical and the spiritual can be a limited heavenly compensation for the overall declivity of the human cycle, it is not at all clear that it could be anything more than that. In other words, whereas one can no doubt predict such a possibility in some relatively rare cases, it is difficult to believe that this could have a far-reaching, durable impact. However, one has no trouble understanding that a ruse of *Māyā* could perhaps convince certain individuals or groups that they may constitute a bridge between the end of the current cycle and the beginning of the next cycle. Be that as it may, such considerations must surely lie in the domain of the imponderable.

In conclusion, notwithstanding a few reservations, we heartily recommend this very well-written, informative, insightful, thought-provoking, and engaging book to prospective readers who are interested in the history of Islam, Islam in the modern and postmodern eras, Sufism, and, more generally, to anyone who feels that the world in which we live is sorely in need of a spiritual infusion.

*Reviewed by Patrick Meadows*

## What Do the Religions Say About Each Other? Christian Attitudes towards Islam, Islamic Attitudes towards Christianity

COMPILED BY WILLIAM STODDART

**San Rafael, CA: Sophia Perennis, 2008**

In this slim but precious volume, William Stoddart provides his readers with a treasury of texts written by Muslims about Christians and Christianity, and vice versa. This collection spans centuries, countries, and cultures. It is a delight, and sometimes a surprise, to read statements that exceed mere tolerance to reach spiritual insight and communion. One thinks, for example, of Pope Pius XI telling his apostolic delegate to Libya in 1934: "Do not think you are going among infidels. Muslims attain to salvation. The ways of Providence are infinite" (p. 12).

This anthology is a clear argument against the prejudice that exclusively sees the past as a stage for religious intolerance and fanaticism. In fact one of the lessons that contemporary readers may draw from this inspiring book is that something has gone seriously wrong between the two communities in recent times. The ideologization of religion that has resulted from the loss or neglect of the spiritual Center and the science of inner and outer beauty is clearly responsible for this sad state of affairs. As the Emir 'Abd al-Qādir remarks, "When we think how few men of real religion there are, how small the number of defenders and champions of truth—when one sees ignorant persons imagining that the principles of Islam are hardness, severity, extravagance, and barbarity—it is time to repeat these words: 'Patience is beautiful, and God is the source of all succor'" (p. 78).

One must be grateful to William Stoddart for having compiled this set of beautiful testimonies to the inner convergence of true faiths. One wonders what effects this volume may have should it become required reading in Christian schools and Muslim *madrasāt* the world over. It is encouraging to hear that the book has already been translated into German, Bosnian, and French, with a Portuguese edition slated for the near future.

*Reviewed by Patrick Laude*

# Notes on the Contributors

**'Abd al-Qādir al-Jazā'irī** (1808-1893) was an Algerian metaphysician and mystic, as well as a political and military leader who led the Algerian resistance against the French in the mid-nineteenth century. The Emir was a major commentator and continuator of Ibn 'Arabī. He is considered by the Algerians as a national hero, and his remains were brought back from Damascus to Algeria in 1962.

**Ivan Aguéli** ('Abd al-Hadi Aqhili) (1869-1917) was a Swedish painter and author. He was the initiator of René Guénon into Sufism and an early Western expositor of the metaphysics of Ibn 'Arabī. Aside from his reputation as a creative post-Impressionist painter and as a somewhat eccentric traveler in the tradition of the *Malāmatiyah*, he is credited with expounding similarities between Sufi and Swedenborgian metaphysics.

**Amadou Hampaté Bâ** (c. 1900-1991) was a well-known Malian diplomat and author of the last half of the twentieth century. His fiction and non-fiction books in French are widely respected as sources of information and insight on West African history, religion, literature, and culture. From the time of his youth, Bâ was a student and disciple of an extraordinary Malian Sufi master, Tierno Bokar. He left a testimonial of his teacher, *Vie et enseignement de Tierno Bokar: Le sage de Bandiagara*, which has been translated into English and published by World Wisdom as *A Spirit of Tolerance: The Inspiring Life of Tierno Bokar.*

**Titus Burckhardt** (1908-1984) was one of the leading Perennialist writers of the twentieth century. His writings showed remarkable scope, covering topics on metaphysics, on tradition and modern science, on sacred art, on history and political science, and on various other aspects of traditional civilizations. Burckhardt was also a translator (from Arabic into French), an editor and publisher, and a respected consultant on restoring traditional cities to their former beautiful states. His main books include *Sacred Art in East and West* and *Introduction to Sufism.*

**William C. Chittick** is one of the most important contemporary translators and interpreters of Islamic mystical texts and poetry. He is a professor in the Department of Comparative Studies at the State University of New York, Stony Brook. Among his publications are *The Sufi Path of Love: The Spiritual Teachings of Rumi*, *The Psalms of Islam*, *The Self-Disclosure of God: Principles of Ibn al-'Arabī's Cosmology*, *Sufism: A Short Introduction*, and *The Heart of Islamic Philosophy: The Quest for Self-Knowledge in the Teachings of Afdal al-Dīn Kāshānī.*

**Tayeb Chouiref** is a French scholar, translator, and teacher. He is the author of *The Spiritual Teachings of the Prophet*, an annotated collection of authoritative Prophetic traditions commented upon by masters of Islamic spirituality. He is also the translator of several works of al-Ghazzālī.

**Michael Oren Fitzgerald** is an author, editor, and publisher of books on world religions, sacred art, tradition, culture, and philosophy. He has written and edited many publications on American Indian spirituality, including *Yellowtail: Crow Medicine Man and Sun Dance Chief*, and was adopted into Yellowtail's tribe and family. Fitzgerald has also taught university classes on religious traditions of North American Indians and lectured widely.

**Éric Geoffroy** is an expert on Islam and Professor in Islamic Studies in the Department of Arabic and Islamic studies at the University of Strasbourg. He also teaches at the Open University of Catalonia, at the Catholic University of Louvain (Belgium), and at the International Institute of Islamic Thought (Paris). He is a specialist in the study of Sufism and sanctity in Islam. Among others, his research also extends to comparative Sufism, mysticism, and to issues of spirituality in the contemporary world (spirituality and globalization; spirituality and ecology, etc.). He is the author of *Initiation au Soufisme*—translated into English and published by World Wisdom as *Introduction to Sufism: The Inner Path of Islam*—and *L'islam sera spirituel ou ne sera pas.*

**René Guénon** (1886-1951) was a French metaphysician, writer, and editor who was largely responsible for laying the metaphysical groundwork for the Perennialist or Traditionalist school of thought in the early twentieth century. Guénon remains influential today for his writings on the intellectual and spiritual bankruptcy of the modern world, on symbolism, on spiritual esoterism and initiation, and on the universal truths that manifest themselves in various forms in the world's religious traditions.

**M. Ali Lakhani** graduated from Cambridge University before moving to Vancouver, where he has practiced as a trial lawyer for 25 years. In 1998, he founded the Traditionalist journal, *Sacred Web*, with the aim of identifying the first principles of traditional metaphysics and promoting their application to the contingent circumstances of modernity. The bi-annual journal has included contributions by many leading Traditionalists. In the words of Professor Nasr, "Along with *Sophia*, *Sacred Web* is the most important journal in the English language devoted to the study of tradition."

**Martin Lings** (1909-2005) was a leading member of the Perennialist or Traditionalist school and an acclaimed author, editor, translator, scholar, Arabist, and poet whose work centers on the relationship between God and man through religious doctrine, scripture, symbolism, literature, and art. He was an accomplished metaphysician and essayist who often turned to the world's great spiritual traditions for examples, though he is probably best known for his writings on Islam and its esoteric tradition, Sufism. World Wisdom is planning to publish an anthology of his work called *The Essential Martin Lings.*

**Patrick Meadows** is professor of French at the Georgetown University School of Foreign Service in Qatar. After a brief, early career in music, he earned a B.A. in both French Literature and in English Literature from the University of California, Santa Cruz, as well as an M.A. and a Ph.D. in Romance Languages and Literatures from Princeton University. His publications include *Francis Ponge and the Nature of Things: From Ancient Atomism to a Modern Poetics*, while he is one of the authors of *Littératures de la péninsule indochinoise.*

**Sachiko Murata** is a professor of religion and Asian studies at the State University of New York at Stony Brook. She received her B.A. from Chiba University in Chiba, Japan, and later attended Iran's Tehran University where she was the first woman ever to study Islamic jurisprudence, and where she received her Ph.D. in Persian literarure. Murata teaches Islam, Confucianism, Taoism, and Buddhism. She is the author of several books including *The Tao of Islam*, *Chinese Gleams of Sufi Light*, *The Vision of Islam* (which she co-authored with William Chittick) and *Temporary Marriage in Islamic Law.*

**Shankar Nair** is a Ph.D. candidate in the Study of Religion at Harvard University. His academic interests include Hindu and Islamic philosophy, Sufism, and Indian religions. His research focuses on Hindu-Muslim intellectual interaction and the exchange between Arabo-Persian and Sanskrit textual traditions in South Asia.

**Seyyed Hossein Nasr** is University Professor of Islamic Studies at George Washington University. The author of over fifty books and five hundred articles, he is one of the world's most respected writers and speakers on Islam, its arts and sciences, and its traditional mystical path, Sufism.

**Farid Nur ad-Din** is a Swedish scholar. He is a student of Perennialism and Sufism who is currently working on a biography of Ivan Aguéli.

**Frithjof Schuon** (1907-1998) is best known as the foremost spokesman of the Perennialist or Traditionalist school and as a philosopher in the metaphysical current of Shankara and Plato. He wrote more than two dozen books on metaphysical, spiritual, artistic, and ethnic themes and was a regular contributor to journals on comparative religion in both Europe and America. Schuon's writings have been consistently featured and reviewed in a wide range of scholarly and philosophical publications around the world, respected by both scholars and spiritual authorities. Besides his prose writings, Schuon was also a prolific poet and a gifted painter of images that always portrayed the beauty and power of the divine, and the nobility and virtue of primordial humanity.

**Reza Shah-Kazemi** is a Research Associate at the Institute of Ismaili Studies in London. Dr. Shah-Kazemi writes on a range of topics from metaphysics and doctrine to contemplation and prayer. He is the author of *The Other in the Light of the One: The Universality of the Qur'ān and Interfaith Dialogue*, *Paths to Transcendence: According to Shankara, Ibn Arabi, and Meister Eckhart*, a look at how three sages—a Hindu, a Muslim, and a Christian—approached the transcendent Absolute, and *Common Ground Between Islam and Buddhism.*

# Note on the Editor

**Patrick Laude** teaches theology at the Georgetown University School of Foreign Service in Qatar. His interests lie in contemplative and mystical traditions, particularly in their relationship with poetry, as well as in Western representations and interpretations of Islam and Asian religions. He is the author of ten books, including *Pray without Ceasing: The Way of the Invocation in World Religion*, *Divine Play, Sacred Laughter, and Spiritual Understanding*, *Singing the Way: Insights in Poetry and Spiritual Transformation*, and *Frithjof Schuon: Life and Teachings*. His latest book is *Pathways to an Inner Islam: Massignon, Corbin, Guénon, and Schuon.*